C4313

'20

AF412356

GRAINCOLLECTION

GRAINCOLLECTION

Humans' Natural Ecological Niche

Sergio Treviño

Translated by Rebeca San Martín–Feeney

VANTAGE PRESS
New York

Contents

Preface

Throughout history, it has often been noted that many technical or scientific problems have been solved by the good fortune of researchers—amateurs or laymen—who serendipitously make a discovery that opens their eyes.

I think I had that stroke of good luck just over eighteen years ago. I will now describe how I came upon my discovery:

One day in 1972, while my friend Augusto Corona and I were horseback riding through the fields that are suburbs of Mexico City, we passed by some oatfields when he remarked: "Have you noticed that the gramineous plants that are most often sowed, and that are the main human nourishment, grow their seeds at the height of the human hand?" I thought that indeed this was true, but I remained a bit confused since corn, the main crop in Mexico, does not produce its cobs at hand height. It soon came to my mind that America is the homeland of corn, and it was here that man domesticated it; but the cereals native to the Old World—whether wild or domestic—do have that character: wheat, barley, oats, rye, rice, etc. At the time, I attached no particular importance to that thought.

One day in 1974, while reading a textbook on anthropology, and looking at photographs of the stone tools of our early hominid ancestors—Oldowans and Acheulians—I noticed that they mainly consisted of small stones fashioned into extremely crude scrapers and flakes. The thought occurred to me that no one could slaughter animals using these tools, much less hunt them. I wondered how they could have been used, and for what purpose.

Suddenly, like an electric shock, the answers became clear: The wheat, indigenous to the Old World; humans, also native to the Old World; cereals, the main food for human consumption, provide their seeds at hand level. Could this be a human evolutionary adaptation to them or just a coincidence? I imagined the protohominids, with a small stone in one hand, scraping oat seeds directly from the stem, threshing them by rubbing them with their fingers against the stone and, still with some of the husk, bringing them to their mouth with the other hand. While doing all this they were also trying to maintain themselves in an upright position to facilitate their task. Many other things came to my mind. I was so excited I could hardly sleep that night. I couldn't wait for the next morning to go to the wheat and oat fields to practice *graincollection*, using the *grainthreshers*, as I later called, respectively, the operation and some small Paleolithic tools.

I wanted to find out whether it was easy to scrape and thresh oat seeds or spikes of wheat with a very small flake-shaped stone in one hand; or alternatively, scrape or cut oat seeds or spikes of wheat with that small flake-shaped stone in one hand, and thresh them by rubbing them against both hands, with the stone and some seeds or spikes between them.

The next morning in the field, my excitement increased when I realized that all I had imagined relating to the use of the small stone tools to serve as grainthreshers was not only possible, but easy as well. It was almost impossible, and very painful, to perform that task without a small stone in hand. Using the bare hand, it was only possible to collect seeds one by one. *Protecting* the hand with a small *natural* stone in the shape of a scraper or flake, however, made it a fast and efficient task since, with only one action, a fistful of seeds could be removed and threshed. The origin of bipedalism, the origin of tool use, and many other hominid characteristics then became clear to me.

I kept investigating and studying the subject for many years. At present, I feel confident in my hypothesis, and believe that I am able to support my arguments with facts. My purpose in writing this book has been to interest the scientific community in this theory, since investigating our origin and knowing it are very important for all human beings.

My arguments have all the scientific support I have been able to find, but the subjects are so wide and diverse that a life span would be inadequate to study in depth all of them. I have, therefore, tried to see the whole from a distance—not just a small part at close range.

Long before I knew I would write this book, Dona, my wife, had already inculcated in me her goals and objectives which, little by little, I later assimilated, so that they are now also mine. The basic concepts developed in Part Two of this book were contributed, over the years, by Dona. She has instilled in me the belief that all the virtues and human values that we presently possess have their origin in our animality, and not in our culture, civilization, or "superior intelligence." Her ideas are the result of her goal: to stop the suffering of so many people, children, animals—in short—the innocent beings of the whole world. Through Part Two, she wants to accomplish her goal— that, as humans, we take from nature only the share that belongs to us, according to our animal essence, according to the natural and universal laws, as all other living beings do.

To the Reader:

At the end of the book, from page 253 on, I've included a glossary. The terms and definitions in it were selected to aid the nonspecialist reader in understanding some terms presented in this book.

I recommend that the nonspecialist reader go through this glossary before starting to read this book, so that, on the one hand, you will familiarize yourself with the special vocabulary used, and on the other, you will know what is included, and can go back to it if necessary while reading the book.

I have chosen for this glossary those definitions I deem most suitable for the nonspecialist reader. However, if the reader prefers to consult definitions more widely accepted within the scientific community, he must turn to specialized dictionaries from the various scientific fields covered in this book.

Color Plates

Facing Page

Acknowledgments

I am very grateful to Juan Manuel Hallivis for the support and encouragement he has given me throughout the development of this work, for his ideas and suggestions and, above all, for his contagious enthusiasm. I am also grateful to Rebeca San Martín-Feeney, Robert A. Feeney, Dr. Alberto Folch, Dr. A. Oriol Anguera, Dr. Fernando Ortega López, and Dr. Juan García Calva, for their enthusiasm, ideas, and suggestions. The mistakes that remain in the book are totally my responsibility.

The original paintings reproduced on the dust jacket and throughout the book were done by Angel Martín; I thank him for his enthusiastic help. I very much admire his artistic capabilities.

I am very grateful to Rebecca Pieken and the editors at Vantage Press for their kind assistance. I find their editing work outstanding and feel I have received the necessary help which has greatly improved my book.

I am especially grateful to Augusto Corona. His perspicacious observations originated in me thoughts which became the bases of this work.

During the development of this work, Dona, my wife, has offered me her advice, encouragement, and support. I would not have been able to write this book without her help and her ideas.

To all of them: Thank you very much.

GRAINCOLLECTION

Introduction and Presentation of the Two Basic Hypotheses

Since the 1871 publication *The Descent of Man* by Charles Darwin, many areas of controversy about the origin of hominids have appeared. At present there is no accepted explanation of their origin that would make all the hominoid fossil remains discovered, as well as all the findings from current research, form a unique, harmonious, and congruent panorama. This lack of harmony, despite the many studies done in the past, the latest scientific advances, and the studies of recently discovered fossil remains, strongly indicates that the facts are misinterpreted, and that this misinterpretation most probably has only one source: we are missing a key fact, with the aid of which all other facts and studies will form a general, harmonious, logical, and congruent panorama.

A few years ago, the controversy between those paleoanthropologists supporting the late divergence hypothesis (occurring about 4 million years ago) and those supporting the early divergence hypothesis (occurring about 25 million years ago) between apes and humans, continued unresolved. Simons (1961) identified *Ramapithecus* as the first hominid because of a robustly built jaw, and " . . . because of reduced canines, reduced anterior dentition, and thick tooth enamel." (Simons, 1989: 1343) Many paleontologists and paleoanthropologists, based on Simons (1961), have come to accept the early divergence hypothesis. Other researchers, based on biochemical research, such as immunological and molecular (Goodman, 1963; Sarich and Wilson, 1967), place the gorilla and chimpanzee as close genetic relatives to humans, and believe their respective lineages split from that of humans between 3 and 5 million years ago. This has influenced Simons and many other researchers to change their opinion and consider the late divergence as more probable, and therefore look for other alternatives.

Many researchers accepted, since its publication, Jolly's model (1970) called "The Seed-Eaters: A New Model of Hominid Differentiation Based on a Baboon Analogy." The analogy to anatomical and behavioral characters was made with *Theropithecus gelada*, and his examples were Villafranchian (Middle Pliocene–Lower Pleistocene) hominids. He suggests that the populations of *Ramapithecus* relied on grass-seed feeding, with their consequent adaptations to it and to life in the grassland savannas. Years later, Jolly's model lost the support of those researchers and scientists *due to its opposition to the late divergence hypothesis*, and also for the following reasons:

Wolpoff (1983: 656) says: " . . . it was the application of this model for interpreting *Ramapithecus* that carried the seeds of its destruction." As Wolpoff (1983) suggests, this occurred, firstly, because the widespread occurrence of the powerful masticatory complex is also seen in many other primates, and beyond them, and they do not necessarily feed on small objects; secondly, because "Jolly's hypothesis has always been weak in its explanation of how other basal hominid features might have followed from small-object feeding" (Wolpoff, 1983: 657); and thirdly, because rigorous studies have shown that the dental/gnathic complex of *Ramapithecus* was similar or identical to other Asian hominoids (Frayer, 1976, 1978; Greenfield, 1974, 1975, 1977, 1979; mentioned by Wolpoff [1983]).

Despite the fact that Jolly's model has recently lost support, I consider *Phase 1* of his model to be scientifically sound for interpreting *Ramapithecus*. It also has the added attraction that it explains many facts in a simple and probable way. That is why it was widely accepted when first published. I have taken the hypothesis of *Phase 1* of Jolly's model (1970) as the basis of the theory that I propose:

We will now examine the feeding behavior of the *Theropithecus gelada* because, as mentioned, the analogy made by Jolly involves them.

The food intake of the *Theropithecus gelada* of Sankaber and Bole, in Ethiopia, consists almost exclusively of grass blades certain times of the year, which they remove with both hands (Dunbar and Dunbar, 1974, 1975; Iwamoto, 1979). The food for the geladas of Sankaber is 93% grass blades during the month of July, and 45.5% as a yearly average; however, 69.7% of the nourishment of these geladas of Sankaber during November *consists of only gramineous seeds* (Dunbar and Dunbar, 1975). Therefore, the seasonal changes in feeding for the geladas are very noticeable. Based on these facts, it can be assumed that the same could have happened in the feeding behavior of *Ramapithecus*.

In *Phase 1* of his model, Jolly hypothesizes the following: As seed eaters, *Ramapithecus* had already adaptively acquired an incipient upright posture similar to what the gelada baboons presently have; that is, not full-time. They had acquired the development of thumb opposability, and with that, certain manual dexterity; they had also already acquired the canine reduction, the dental/gnathic complex, and many other characters present in the living gelada baboons.

While placing my hypothesis following Jolly's hypothesis of Phase 1 of his model, my own scenario would be as follows:

At a time of plentiful grasses and their seeds, a troop of *Ramapithecus*, including pregnant or nursing females that for several months had been feeding exclusively on seeds and some grass blades, found that their hands were hurt and sore from removing them. *To protect her hands*, a nursing female thinks of taking in her skillful hands a small stone in the shape of a flake or scraper, of a size that fits perfectly in the palm of her hand and allows her almost to make a fist with the stone in it. She then places the stone in her right hand, and presses, between the small stone and the ball of the thumb (thenar eminence), the top part of the stem she intends to scrape the seeds from (in this case, the raceme, panicle, etc., of the grasses) and slides the tool over this top part of the stem. With just that one action her fist is filled with seeds, and she has achieved an additional and unanticipated advantage, since she had only been trying to protect her hurt hand with that small stone.

This speculation is not based on extraordinary assumptions, since there are several animals that habitually use *natural* tools to obtain food, such as sea otters, woodpecker finches, and Egyptian vultures; with all the more reason we can accept that primates can develop abilities to use natural stone tools to obtain food, since they have enhanced manual aptitudes.

I have performed these actions and movements (see Illustrations 1 and 2) with a small, natural stone tool in one hand, and also with my bare hands; I have removed spikes of wheat, scraped oat seeds, etc. Doing it with the stone tool is faster and more efficient, and the hands are not hurt. So, probably that *Ramapithecus* female never again

Illustration 1

Illustration 2

Illustration 3

Illustration 4

removed gramineous seeds or cut blades, stems, etc., without a small natural stone tool in hand.

In times of great abundance of seeds, the tool was very useful since, in just one action, with just one movement, she was able to remove many seeds, rather than one at a time with her fingers as she used to do before. In addition, and this is almost as important as the preceding, she could *thresh* them in that same action; that is, she could remove the awns, the rachis, and maybe some glumes (hull), as she rubbed with her fingers the fistful of seeds against the same stone in her one hand. She would then take the seeds, already sufficiently free of hull, with her opposite hand and put them in her mouth.

(A natural stone, chosen in the shape of a small flake or scraper, and the ball of the thumb, in humans, forms a very effective device for cutting or scraping seeds from grasses, or cutting the stems, since it is similar to the natural dental system of some ruminants who cut the stem of grasses by pressing them with the lower incisors against their hardened upper gum, and then making a quick and short head movement forward.)

Still more important is the fact that that tool would now allow easier access to grains with spikes and hard awns, such as wheat and barley (see Illustrations 3 and 4), since previously, it had been very difficult to cut those spikes with the bare hands, or to remove seeds individually with only the fingers.

It may be assumed that subsequently, through imitation, all the members of the troop learned to use the *grainthresher*, and in this way the troop now sustained itself exclusively through *graincollection*, since their niche had widened considerably and had been modified by use of natural stone tools. They could now depend almost exclusively on seeds for their nourishment by being able to feed more effectively from different types of grains; in this way, they obtained more nutritious food, although not as high in fiber. Possibly, the threshing of the seeds didn't coincide with the use of the stone when it was first used to scrape the stems—but, being such a simple, effective, and useful action, this added benefit must have occurred shortly thereafter when the rest of the troop had learned to use the grainthresher.

With this hypothesis, one of the greatest objections presented by many authorities to Phase 1 of Jolly's model (1970) is overcome. To quote the objection: "Jolly's intriguing reconstruction is not accepted by many authorities who, among other things, doubt that a primate as large as the earliest hominid would have a diet based mainly on small objects like seeds." (Swartz and Jordan, 1976: 266.)

The following objections, presented by Kay (1981) to Jolly's model, are also overcome.

In his first objection, Kay suggests that even though Jolly's model (1970) can be valid to explain the massive jaws of the ramapithecinae, it cannot account for the molar pattern, since grass-eating mammals, including the *Theropithecus*, have flat molar crowns which allow them to effectively grind thin shelled grass grains and shear grass blades. "By contrast, as Jolly recognized, ramapithecines and australopithecines have flat, relatively featureless molars on which shearing is deemphasized . . . unlike mammalian grass-seed eaters. To account for this difference, Jolly argued that . . . early hominids must have eaten grass seeds but not grass blades." (Kay, 1981: 142) Kay indicates that this argument is difficult to accept since it is very unlikely that the early hominids were capable of separating successfully grass seeds from fibrous grass stems and leaves; and even if this was possible, they would have required a mechanical procedure to separate the thin-shelled grass hulls. Kay adds that these grass hulls are also abrasive like the blades.

It is my contention that this objection is overcome assuming the users of the grainthreshers were able to scrape or cut only the seeds, and leave the stems and blades and, by the movement of their fingers against the grainthresher and the fistful of seeds between them, were able to remove a good part of those abrasive hulls.

To quote from Kay's second objection, "Species that eat grain ordinarily incorporate grit, seed hulls, and grass blades in their diet as well." (Kay, 1981: 142) This second objection, I contend, is partly overcome by what was already said against the first one, and additionally: When threshing the seeds, rubbing them with the fingers against the grainthresher, a great part of the grit is expelled together with the hulls.

Kay's third objection is similar to the one already mentioned made by Swartz and Jordan (1976), except that Kay refers to the *Gigantopithecus bilaspurensis*, since he doubts that such a large ramapithecine, similar to the gorilla, would be able to find enough grass seeds the year round to survive with this type of diet. To overcome this objection we may assume that *Gigantopithecus*, with a tool in hand, was able to cut not only the seeds, but at the same time a *small* portion of the stems of grasses, which he would eat without threshing them. (As we will see in Chapter I, section 4, it is probable that by having this diet, similar to that of the equines, *Gigantopithecus* adaptively acquired its huge size.)

In his fourth objection, Kay suggests (1981: 142):

Finally, Kinzey (1974) has demonstrated that a number of the features identified by Jolly as grain-feeding adaptations are seen in arboreal primates such as *Callicebus* and *Cebus apella*, which eat hard seeds and nuts, but not grain. Thus the similarities between the *Theropithecus* and early hominids were probably not due to both being grain eaters.

This objection may be refuted with the same argument as the previous objections: by eliminating the abrasive part of the grasses with the help of the grainthresher, and eating only the hard seeds, the similarity of a small hard gramineous seeds diet with the " . . . hard seeds and nuts . . . " diet supports graincollection, which is complementary to Phase 1 of Jolly's model. There is a very low probability that our early hominid ancestors had acquired the morphological and physiological characters that we humans possess at present, by climbing or by living in the trees; our characters are those of terrestrial, not arboreal primates. Therefore, it is more probable that our ancestors acquired those characters mentioned by Jolly (1970) by their terrestrial habits, just as Jolly assumes. It is not valid to assume a " . . . hard seeds and nuts, but not grain . . . " diet for a primate if we do not assume also that he has to climb trees to collect them; and it is valid, given its probability, to assume that a primate *with terrestrial habits* would eat grass seeds, just as *Theropithecus gelada* does nowadays. In brief: our human characters, on their own, stand against Kay's fourth objection.

We can assume that the feeding success of *Ramapithecus*, when using the small stone tool as grainthresher, was great and sudden. This inevitably brought about behavioral changes that allowed them to suddenly enter a new adaptive zone. They previously stayed all year round in the same narrow geographical area, but only at certain times of the year did they have an abundance of seeds to feed themselves, while at other times they fed mainly upon blades and rhizomes, as done by the gelada baboons of Sankaber and Bole (Dunbar and Dunbar, 1975). Now, however, because of their efficiency as tool-users, they were able, and in fact forced, to look for only seeds; and, due to this, to live like the migrant ungulates in the medium- and long-grass open plains during the wet season, and in the woodlands in the dry season. I base this statement on the possible similarities with the feeding strategies of the migrant ungulates of Serengeti studied by Jarman and Sinclair (1979) and by Maddock (1979). Furthermore, in these migrations *Ramapithecus* would most probably have gone ahead of the generalist grazers' successions, always searching for new grasses (good quality food). I assume this, firstly, because they would look for and eat the most nutritious part of the grasses; and secondly, because searching all year round for seeds as their main source of nourishment forced them to become full-time migratory bipeds.

By entering this new adaptive zone they probably had to partially enter the niche of *Hipparion* (three-toed mammals related to the ancestors of the horse), migrating ahead of them at the front of the grazers' successions. To support this, I also take as my basis the probable similarities with the migrations and grazing successions of the ungulates of Serengeti (Maddock, 1979; Jarman and Sinclair, 1979), and because the greatest part of the discoveries of *Ramapithecus* have been made in extremely rich *Hipparion* faunas (Simons, 1976; Prasad, 1982).

There is a suggestion and a fact, proposed and found by Prasad (1982), that until now have not been taken into account since they oppose the late divergence hypothesis; therefore, paleoanthropologists would accept them cautiously. From the point of view of graincollection that suggestion and fact don't oppose the late divergence hypothesis; instead, they support it. Prasad (1982: 101, 102) states:

> The possibility of *Ramapithecus* from the Siwaliks of India as an *ad hoc* tool-user was postulated by Prasad (1969) and Simons & Pilbeam (1965). From previous studies, deduction based on dentition alone was not considered sufficient, without supporting evidence of implements. The present discovery of a proto-hand-axe pebble tool from below the cuesta scarp at *Haritalyangar*, where most of the *Ramapithecus* remains have been recovered, is therefore of considerable significance.

Prasad believes that this crude pebble tool recovered *in situ* from Middle Miocene deposits is one of the oldest implements made by a hominid. Furthermore, Prasad finds some important mammal fossils in those same deposits, and among them, the *Hipparion theobaldi*. All of

EVOLUTIONARY SCHEME

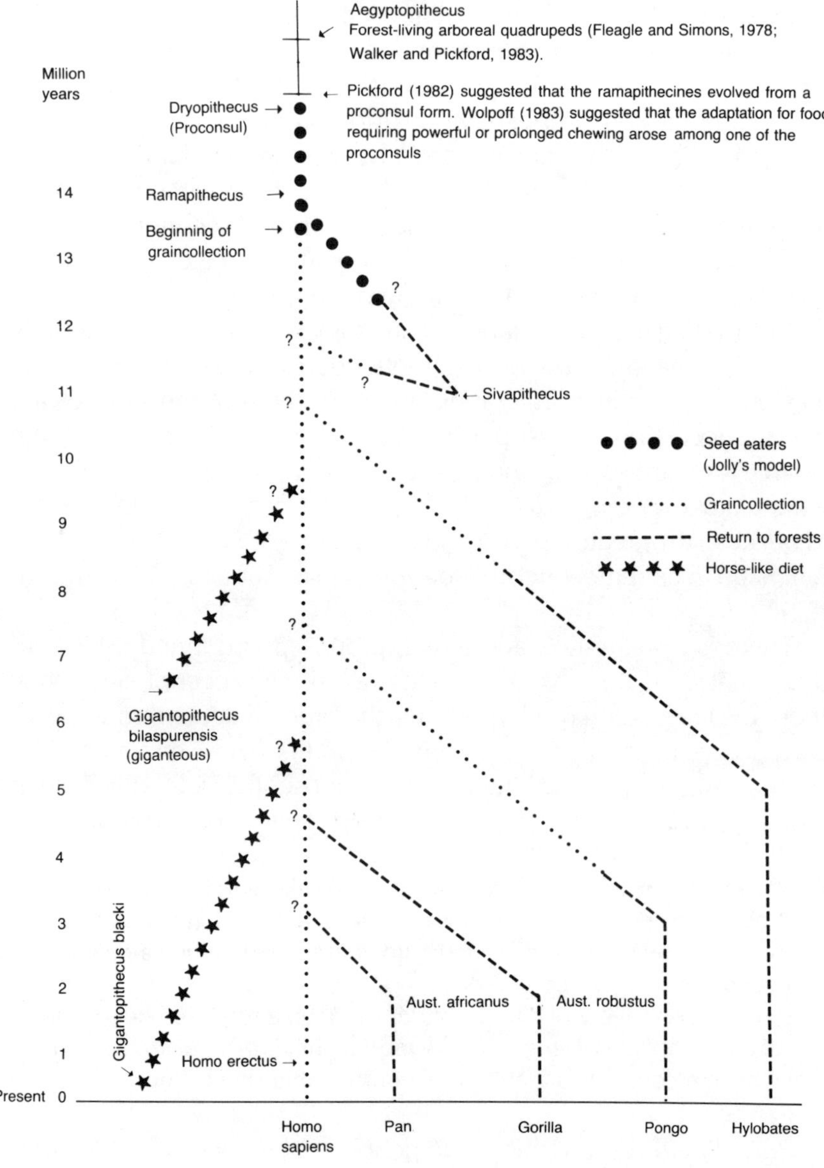

Chart 1

this makes my assumption regarding the change of adaptive zone undergone by that population of *Ramapithecus*, and in general, my assumption regarding the whole theory of graincollection, more acceptable, since this theory reconciles the facts with the late divergence hypothesis.

Graincollection was the selective pressure that made *Ramapithecus* acquire many more hominid characters, which we will analyze later throughout this book. Furthermore, we will see that during the 14 million years of evolution of the *Ramapithecus* lineage (hominid lineage), which gave origin to the human lineage, several lines split through speciation that gave origin to all lineages of the other living hominoids.

Regarding the abovementioned, I will present an evolutionary scheme that shows the phylogenies of the living hominoids based in the theory of graincollection. At first glance it will appear speculative and not very parsimonious; however, I will present throughout this book the bases I have to support my arguments and theory. Now, I will advance a brief explanation of this scheme so the reader will know where my arguments are heading in the presentation of this theory. Such theory, as already mentioned, is based on two complementary hypotheses: first, *Phase 1* of Jolly's model that assumes protohominids were part-time seed eaters; and second, my model, which assumes that the stone tools of the early hominids were grainthreshers, and that, due to their use, hominids remained full-time seed-eating graincollectors during 14 million years, that is, from the Middle Miocene until the start of Würm's Glaciation 50 thousand years ago more or less.

It Is evident in this scheme (see Chart 1) that the hylobatids and all the living pongids descend from bipedal tool-users. For this to be possible, evolutionary reversals and parallelisms would have had to occur in their respective lineages. At first glance, this comes as a shock; firstly, since we have always been told, from elementary school up until college, that we descend from beings similar to the living apes, and to assume that the living apes descend from beings similar to us seems unorthodox; secondly, because "evolution is not reversible" (Dollo's Law) has always been insisted upon. It has only been considered by very few students that adaptive evolution towards the reacquisition of recent ancestral characters, not completely lost, and towards the reacquisition of primitive ancestral characters, not completely lost and deeply fixed in the genoma, is possible; and that these evolutionary reversions can include even complete anatomical areas.

Darwin asserted that the place of origin of humankind is Africa. It has been in Africa that the greatest part of fossil remains attributed to *Australopithecus* have been found, from which studies have concluded that they walked in more of an upright position than that of the living African pongids. It has been accepted that they are intermediate links between beings like the African pongids and the *Homo sapiens*, and not intermediate links between beings like us and the living African pongids, which is also possible. Kleindienst (1975) had already suggested the possibility that the ancestors of the African pongids must be from among the australopithecines.

Campbell and Bernor (1976: 452) state:

[the] Reduction of the forest was more drastic in Asia than in sub-Saharan Africa and in many areas only forms adapted to grasslands could survive. *Ramapithecus* and *Gigantopithecus* are at present considered to represent such adaptations. . . . At the present time, we believe with von Koenigswald that it is slightly more probable that the first hominid adaptations took place in Asia, in that great land mass which lies between the forests of the African apes to the southwest and the forests of the Asian apes which lie to the southeast.

Simons (1989: 1343) states:

A second hypothesis, with which I have been associated, was that the shift from trees to savanna was brought about through a dietary change in the Miocene that evoked the great thickening of cheek tooth enamel which characterizes *Sivapithecus* and *Ramapithecus*.

Wolpoff (1983: 665, 666) states:

I would suggest that an adaptation for foods requiring powerful or prolonged chewing arose among one of the proconsuls, and that because this provided the basis for utilizing a much wider range of dietary resources, a very successful adaptive radiation of hominoids resulted. . . . Genetic evidence relating *Pan* and *Homo*, and the morphological relations of *Pan* and *A. afarensis* indicate that during the late Miocene, one of the African ramapithecine lineages further split into lines leading to the adaptively specialized African apes, and a hominid line.

Assuming that early hominids were graincollectors, the possibility arises that all those fossil remains of australopithecines discovered in Africa originated from individuals who were descendants of hominids of several different migrations of graincollectors coming from the grasslands of Europe and Asia. These, throughout the Upper Miocene and Pliocene, were heading south during droughts or prolonged cold weather, and sometime later during the great glaciations of the Pleistocene, were looking for better weather and conditions. The abrupt change in habitat forced them to survive on the food they found; that is, from gathering and not from graincollecting. Generally, the forests would provide their last shelter. Therefore, the possibility exists that those fossil remains do not belong to our ancestors, but to the African pongids' ancestors.

Because the cereals are aboriginal of Europe–Asia, I believe that the whole evolution of the graincollector hominid lineage took place in Europe–Asia, and not in Africa.

Since the fossil remains of the australopithecines found in Africa might belong to those mentioned individuals from various different migrations of graincollectors coming from Europe–Asia, *and each migration could have evolved separately or could have interbred with the previous ones*, they seem to present a picture of total disharmony and incongruency when we want to take them as representing different stages in the evolution of only one or two lineages.

When trying to explain the origin of all living Hominoidea, I believe that the two basic hypotheses, and the whole theory of graincollection are, as I will try to demonstrate throughout this book, logical, harmonious, and congruent with all the facts; therefore, the reconstruction of the hominoid phylogenies based on them and suggested in Chart 1 is parsimonious. Farris (1984: 701) states:

> . . . phylogenetic analysis is most certainly empirical, for in applying the parsimony criterion, it chooses among alternative hypotheses of relationship *on the basis of nothing other than their explanatory power.* (Italics mine)

PART ONE

Chapter I
Mistakes in Basic Anthropological Concepts. Speculation without Support. Omissions.

Mann (1981: 10, 11) states:

> One of the most important activities engaged in by an animal is the search for and consumption of food. . . . It is evident that many of the most important morphological changes in human evolution, such as reduction in the size of the teeth and development of bipedalism, must be directly related to the ways in which these complexes were used in obtaining and preparing food. Thus our attempts to understand fully the evolutionary development of these changes will be limited if we do not know how they made hominids more successful in getting food.

1. Unskilled (Beginner) and Skilled (Expert) Tool-Using

To date, extensive research has been done and many books and articles have been published regarding the use of tools by pongids in captivity, and about their learning abilities, curiosity, and inventiveness. The explicit or implicit conclusion in these investigations is that it is *surprising* for us that pongids do not use more tools in the wild, given the great ability and aptitudes they show in captivity. However, the tool use of the chimpanzee in the wild (as limited as it is), and in general the manual dexterity of all the living pongids, are *not* taken into consideration in our reasoning despite it being so surprising; we do not recognize in it any merit; on the contrary, we judge the pongids as unskilled (beginner) tool-users. This is due to the fact that we are truly skilled (expert) tool-users, and we judge according to our capabilities. It is a judgment similar to the following: Rather than say that a foreigner speaks our own language poorly or with difficulty, we would say that he is clumsy, "since speaking our language is very easy."

In books and articles regarding this subject, statements like the following can be found: "Chimpanzees are the most accomplished users of tools among the nonhuman primates and therefore provide a reasonable model for an examination of tool use among early hominids." I am sure that, at present, this statement seems correct to many scientists; however, none of those scientists would think of taking as a model for the first spoken language of our ancestors the deficient use of our own language by the foreigner mentioned previously. This poorly spoken language is in itself a language; furthermore, the foreigner has all the cerebro-muscular connections as well as the intelligence *grammatically and syntactically* to speak any language, not only ours; that is, he is a true expert of the spoken language. Something similar can be said of the tool-using capabilities of the chimpanzee, and in general of all the living pongids.

Pongids have to learn to use tools, just as we humans have to learn how to use them; but there is something surprising: Their learning ability is similar to ours, and like ours, it is not fixed or executed by conditioned reflexes, since they use the tools in *novel* situations chosen by them, and with "*syntax*"; that is, with the needed planning, preparation, coordination, and association to carry out a *foreseen and novel* task. This shows that living pongids, as well as humans, have a very developed cerebro-muscular organization and intelligence, capable of foreseeing a result, and capable of using *various* types of tools *in very different situations and in very different contexts*. That is to say, they are complete experts in tool-using, maybe a bit forgotten, but not, as we'll see immediately, unskilled (beginner) tool-users.

Let's take a look at how some living *unskilled* (beginner) tool-user animals utilize their tools. We'll first examine the description of the woodpecker finch, which is convincing in showing it to be an accomplished tool-user:

Curio (1973) speaks of the woodpecker and the mangrove finch of the Albemonte and Norborough Islands, and indicates that both species eat fruit and mangrove leaves, but they also hunt insects; he indicates that the arthropods are captured by the mangrove finch in the manner of woodpeckers, and adds something very important:

They hack off pieces of rotten wood, detach bark from tree trunks, break off thin twigs and then probe the insects out of their hiding places. However, they accomplish the latter not with their beaks but by using a cactus thorn or a small stick. . . . The woodpecker finch breaks off its tool, spine, small piece of stick, or a fork of a twig, and then probes with it in tree holes or among cactus shoots which are in contact. Beforehand, it checks visually and possibly also by ear whether the hole is occupied; it may also feel along the passage with its thorn and finally it levers out its prey. Woodpecker finches kept in a cage by Bowman and Millikan never tried to spike a mealworm which has kept hidden in wood, with a thorn. A male kept by Eibl-Eibesfeldt hid unwanted mealworms in clefts and later fetched them out again; it thus created the probing situation itself. Woodpecker finches usually only go to fetch a thorn when they have spotted prey. *There are indications that this behavior is not simply inherited but also has to be learned*, but how this happens has not been studied. Such an investigation would be well worth-while for so few other animals use tools; other examples are certain bower birds (Chapter 19), the Egyptian vulture among the raptors (Vol. VII) the sea otter (Vol. XII) and a number of species of monkeys (Vols. X and XI). (Curio, 1973: Vol. 9, pp. 364, 365; italics mine)

Fischer (1972) indicates that the Egyptian vulture eats dates, palm nuts, and other plant food; and adds the following which is also very important:

British investigators Jane van Lawick-Goodall and Hugo van Lawick observed that this agile vulture has a tendency to use tools. "When a grass fire in the East African steppe had driven ostriches from their nests, their eggs remained behind undamaged. White-headed and lappet-faced vultures tried in vain to open these eggs with blows of their beaks. Then two Egyptian vultures arrived. *At first they too tried to open the eggs with their beaks.* When this was in vain, they searched out stones in the vicinity weighing 100 to 300 grams, took them in their beaks, raised themselves up before the egg, and flung the stones at the egg. After four to twelve blows the egg cracked and the meal could start. At the end, a third vulture which was lowest in the peck order tossed stones at the remaining egg shells." (Fischer, 1972: Vol. 7, p. 400; italics mine)

In regard to the use of tools by the sea otters and their ability with their forefeet, Herter (1975) quotes part of a report made by Georg Wilhelm Steller during the winter of 1741–42 on the Commander

Islands, and published posthumously in 1751. Herter (1975: Vol. 12, pp. 86, 88) states:

"Females carry the young in their mouth, but in the sea the mother lies on her back and holds the baby between her fore feet just like a human mother holds a baby in her arms. The mother otter plays with her baby, tossing it in the air and catching it like a ball, putting it in the water so it learns to swim, and taking it back when it is tired and kissing it in a very human way." . . . . Sea otters are the only mammals that feed principally on echinoderms. The sea otter picks up sea urchins (sometimes several at once) from depths of 5 to 10 m, *lies on the surface of the water on its back, and beats the sea urchin against its chest.* Since the fur is quite loose, it forms depressions or pockets along the side of the sea otter when it lies on its back, and these pockets are used to hold the sea urchin. The sea urchin is turned about with the front paws, breaking off the spines and pressing in the lower part of the armored covering. The sea otter bites through the sea urchin shell along the bottom edge and licks up the contents of the upper shell or empties the upper shell contents with a fore paw. After it licks up the shell contents in that half, the shell is thrown away and the sea otter begins on the next sea urchin.

Molluscan prey includes mussels, cephalopods, and snails. *The shells are shattered on rocks; the rock, however, is first put on the sea otter's chest and then the shell is pounded against the rock.* This is one of the most intriguing examples of tool-using. If the shell is too hard for the sea otter to break, it will put out the original occupant or the resident hermit crab. (Italics mine)

Bonner (1980: 10, 11) states:

By culture [in animals] I mean the transfer of information by behavioral means, most particularly by the process of teaching and learning. It is used in a sense that contrasts with the transmission of genetic information passed by the direct inheritance of genes from one generation to the next. . . . Culture, as I have defined it, is a property achieved by living organisms. Therefore in this sense it is as biological as any other function of an organism, for instance, respiration or locomotion. Since I am stressing the way information is transmitted, we would call one *cultural evolution* and the other *genetical evolution* with the understanding that they are both biological in the sense they both involve living organisms. (Emphasis author's)

The meaning I am giving to the word *culture* throughout this book is the preceding one by Bonner.

Jay (1968: 499) states:

> In summary, the outstanding difference between nonhuman and human manufacture and use of tools is *skill* (Oakley 1954), and the biology that makes skill possible. Many primates use tools, usually in the context of feeding, whereas only a few species use tools or objects in agonistic displays and these are limited almost exclusively to apes and men. *Tool use per se does not indicate intelligence,* as evidenced by man's history when for a long time his ancestors had small brains and yet used tools as part of their way of life. (Italics mine)

After seeing the behavior of some unskilled tool-user animals who use tools to obtain food and not to attract females (as done by the bowerbirds), or with some other goal, I believe we can conclude the following:

First: Their tool-using is partially inherited and partially learned; that is, they inherit the aptitude (physical dexterity) but it has to be culturally learned (Bonner, 1980; Curio, 1973; Eibl-Eibesfeldt, 1974). Living pongids and humans are in this same category; in other words, skilled (expert) tool-users also inherit the aptitudes, but they have to culturally learn to use tools.

Second: They use only one absolutely natural tool to obtain only one kind of food, in only one situation and in only one context; that is, in the same or very similar place of their natural habitat and with a combination of circumstances, of the individual as well as of the environment, which are always the same or very similar (Bonner, 1980; Curio, 1973; Eibl-Eibesfeldt, 1974; Fischer, 1972; Herter, 1975); and they have the ability to learn and teach this activity, imitating and allowing other individuals of the same species to imitate them, but they do not have the ability to learn or teach the use of the same or other type of tool in other situations, in the same or in different contexts. Their tool-using has all the appearance of being a self-fixed conditioned reflex (Curio, 1973; Bonner, 1980). *This second conclusion is the reason why I have called them "unskilled (beginner)" tool-users;* and it is the principal difference they have with the "skilled (expert)" tool-using of the living pongids and humans.

Third: There is an immediate reward. If reward in unskilled tool-users wouldn't be immediate, the action would tend to operate inappropriately since the conditioned reflex wouldn't be completed and therefore tool using would tend to be forgotten.

Fourth: *Success* allows them to depend on the tool to obtain a good percentage of their total nourishment. This makes the use of such tool *continuous.* If by using the tool they didn't achieve great success, its use wouldn't be continuous and it could also be forgotten; furthermore, it would probably not be learned by those individuals that still don't know how to use the tool. In this case tool-using would also tend to be forgotten.

Fifth: There is an obvious *common* pattern present in *all* unskilled tool-users: *All of them use a tool to facilitate the obtention of food which they already obtained before using such tool*, but with greater difficulty. Now, using a tool, food is obtained much more efficiently. The tool only reinforced their ability to obtain it, but did not give them new or unknown food. They were improving their efficiency over what it was previously.

The woodpecker finch already ate those mealworms before using tools, and presently obtains some without using tools; but, with the tool, it has access to many more, and can depend to a greater degree on that type of nourishment.

The Egyptian vulture would first try to break the eggshell with its beak; if not successful, it would throw stone after stone until broken. Thus, we can state that before using tools, the Egyptian vulture could break some eggshells with its beak. With a tool, its efficiency and dependency to that type of food increases. The sea otter successfully beats the sea urchins against its bare chest. Probably, at the beginning, before using tools, it would beat abalone and other molluscs against its bare chest, but its success was less than that achieved with the sea urchins. Perhaps it would be limited to " . . . put out the original occupant [of the shell] or the resident hermit crab." (Herter, 1975: 88) It wasn't until it placed the stone on its chest that it was able to break the shell easier and was therefore more successful. In this way it could depend more on this type of food.

If at present that happens to some of the studied unskilled tool-user animals, *when they already have the tool-using culture by imitation, and the genetically inherited aptitudes to use such tools*, then with all the more reason we can assume that the *first* individual (ancestor of any of these studied species) and also the whole population to which he belonged, when beginning to use a natural tool to obtain food, *already obtained that same kind of food before learning to use that tool,* but obtained it less efficiently.

Teleki (1974: 576) states:

> Although Primates in general tend to apply their technical skills mainly in contexts other than subsistence (Hall, 1963; Kortlandt & Kooij, 1963), the meager records of technical performance among baboons are in fact restricted to this one context. Marais (1969) observed chacma baboons break open hard fruits with stones; Kortlandt & Kooij (1963) reported accounts of baboons using objects to crush a scorpion before eating it, to widen the entrances of ant and termite nests and to stir up insects under rocks; and van Lawick-Goodall, van Lawick & Packer (1973) observed a baboon wipe her lips with a small stone after feeding on sticky pods . . . when considering the many thousands of field observation hours spent with the baboons during the past decade or so, this list is seen to contain a mere sprinkling of incidental cases which fall rather short of establishing baboons as technologically adept Primates.

Here, Teleki is referring to the incidental, not cultural, use of tools by baboons; and, as we can see, it is a common behavior among them. This type of behavior is common in other animals, mainly among other primates, due to their more developed manual abilities. The incidental use of tools (that which is not transmitted and fixed culturally in the population), so common in baboons, demonstrates the following: if an already present feeding habit does not become more efficient with the use of a tool, it will be improbable, or even impossible, that the use of that tool can be retained, disseminated, and culturally fixed in a population, since it would be very improbable to observe the coincidence, at the same time, of the initial use of a tool by one individual, who would later be imitated by all the members of that population, and the acquisition of a new feeding habit by all those members of that population. Of little help has been up to now the natural manual aptitudes and higher intelligence of the primates, except in the Hominoidea, to even turn some other species, families, etc., into unskilled tool-users, since in order for the use of tools to appear culturally in the feeding context of a population, the primary use of that tool must improve an already present feeding habit in that population; this is so, even though the probability of the appearance of tool-using (first unskilled and then skilled tool-using) among the members of that order are greater than among other animals who don't have those manual abilities.

If an animal population is living within its natural ecological niche, and one individual of this population starts using a tool as a new intelligent action in order to obtain food, and this action disseminates throughout the whole population, it is most probable that the use of such a tool will *improve the efficiency in obtaining the same food they used to eat before*, since they wouldn't need to obtain a different type of food if everything in their habitat and ecosystem is normal. But if that population is living out of their natural ecological niche as a result of some abnormal cause, and if an individual of that same population starts to use a tool for the first time to obtain food, and this action disseminates throughout the whole population, it is most probable that such a tool would be used to obtain food which all the members of the population *were not used to eating* since, under those abnormal circumstances, *they would have the need to obtain any kind of food*. But in this latter case it is more probable that the use of such a tool would be forgotten once they return to their natural niche; or, if they do not return to their natural niche, most probably that population would become extinct. Therefore, it is most probable that the use of a tool would emerge and be culturally kept in an animal population, if that population is living within their natural ecological niche, in a calm, stable, and normal environment; as well, it is also probable that the use of that tool would force the population to enter a new adaptive zone *very similar* to the original one they lived in when they didn't use such tool.

In Chapter IV, Section 1, we will see that if many members of an animal population, pushed by an abnormal cause which disturbs their normal life within their natural ecological niche, resort to the execution of an intelligent action such that they start consuming nutrient resources that *naturally do not belong to them, but to other animal species of the same ecosystem*, that action will disturb even more the biological balance of the whole ecosystem, thus damaging all the members of that ecosystem as well as all the members of that population; in this way, the net effect inverts and hurts the executors of that action. Many reasons exist, therefore, that compel us to think that the initial intelligent use of a tool for the purpose of obtaining food, and the dissemination and cultural permanence of that action in an animal population, *can only happen if that intelligent action increases the efficiency of an already present feeding habit in that population*, such that, in this way, this action does not harm any organism and does not damage or disturb the biological balance of the whole ecosystem.

The causes above mentioned are not the only causes that make tool using in animals difficult to emerge; we also have to take under consideration that cultural transmission by imitation of the use of a tool among the individuals of a population can be difficult, and can even disappear when in that population its use is forgotten due to a seasonal lack of the food formerly acquired by the use of that tool, or, as above mentioned, due to abnormal periods of extended cold weather or drought, etc., which disturb the way of life of that population. This oblivion must be another of the main reasons so few animals use tools. We may therefore assume that when *Ramapithecus* learned to use the grainthresher, they fed *continuously*, all year round, on gramineous seeds, because if they had used this tool seasonally, it is unlikely that they would have acquired their tool-using culture. Also, this gives us a basis to assume that the *Ramapithecus* population in which tool-using first appeared then became migratory grazers.

At present we can state the following:

(a) The skilled tool-using capability, like that of the living pongids, is very uncommon (it could be said that together with that of humans, is unique) in all the animal kingdom.

(b) The living pongids and humans descend from a common distant ancestor that, at some time in their evolution, was an unskilled tool-user who, for million of years, successfully used only one kind of tool to obtain only one type of food, in only one situation and in only one context. At the beginning, its use must have worked as a self-fixed conditional reflex with immediate reward; since that has to be the start of *all* animal tool-using for subsistence activities; and because in order for the pongids to attain skillful use of tools, their ancestors must have developed, step by step, by cumulative selection, their aptitudes of using, first, the same tool and much later other types of tools in different situations and in different contexts, despite the fact that before starting to use tools as beginners they surely already had manual abilities similar to those of the living gelada baboons.

(c) Apes in captivity use several types of tools because they can see some humans using such tools and they imitate them. If the pongids do not use one or several tools in the wild, it is because the transmission of that culture among them no longer exists; in other words, *it is because nobody has taught them their use, rather than from lack of genetic aptitude to use them.* And, if they haven't been taught how to use tools, it's because they don't need them in their current niche and habitat, or because the tools they knew how to use, and maybe even manufacture, have no application in their new niche.

Schaller and Emlen (1974: 98) explain:

The forest is for these powerful vegetarians an evolutionary dead-end road in that there is no selective advantage for improvement of manipulative skills or mental activity along the lines which characterized human evolution. There is no reason to carry a tool if vegetable food is abundant everywhere, and no preparation of the food is required beyond stripping or shredding with the teeth and fingers. There is, it would seem, little selective pressure to try anything new or to improve on the old.

Hannah and McGrew (1987: 32) state:

This paper reports the spread of stone tool-use to crack open palm nuts in a group of 16 semi-captive chimpanzees living on a natural island in Liberia in a release program of the New York Blood Center (Prince et al., in press). Apes were released onto an island from June 7 to August 13, 1985. Nut-cracking was first observed on July 20, when a female released on that day exhibited the behavior. Nut-cracking was then acquired by others, including six juveniles who had already been on the island for six weeks and two adolescents who had been on the island for four weeks. These eight individuals had shown no interest in palm nuts or signs of tool-use before the release of the innovative female. Later, all acquired this skill, suggesting that they had learned the technique from her. Another adult female released on July 20 and three adolescent males released later also acquired the technique of nut-cracking, so that in the eventual group of 16, 13 were successful nut-crackers.

Van Lawick (1986: 207) states:

In addition chimpanzees will use weapons: they often throw large stones or rocks and will use sticks as clubs. This makes them tool users. More importantly they are also tool makers. The difference between the two is that a tool user may merely use an object at hand in its unchanged form while a tool maker changes the object first. Chimpanzees, finding water in a hole in a tree and unable to reach it with their lips, will crumple some leaves in their mouth and use them as an efficient sponge. They will also fashion a tool by stripping leaves off a twig or breaking a piece of grass to the required length and poking the made tool into one of the small holes in a termite mound. The termites in defence of their nest bite on to the twig or grass and so the chimpanzee can extract them and eat them.

Kortlandt (1974: 445) states:

Every zookeeper and circus man knows, however, that it is relatively easy to keep most beasts of prey at bay by means of a broom because they will bite the wood and thus take the invulnerability of the man for granted. Apes, on the other hand, will snatch away the broom and bite the keeper *because they are themselves weapon-users by nature* and understand the trick. (Italics mine)

If we compare what Kortlandt says with what was previously said by Schaller and Emlen, with Hannah and McGrew, and with Van Lawick, a great contradiction is noticed: How can it be admitted that the pongids are tool-users, tool-makers, and weapon-users by nature, and that they do not have any real and genuine selective pressure to use tools in their wild life? How can we explain the easy spread of the use of stone tools among captive chimpanzees? How can we explain that chimpanzees can even change and fashion a tool before using it, the better to adapt it to the type of work they will do with it? These matters can only be reconciled if we assume that all living pongids descend from skilled tool-users and that, little by little, in the last 2 or 3 million years of evolution of their respective lineages, they have been losing that character due to a lack of selective pressure to maintain it.

In light of the above, it is not valid to state that if living pongids do not use tools in their wild life, they are not skilled (expert) tool-users.

The genetic capability for learning to use different kinds of tools in different situations and in different contexts demonstrates that humans and apes have a long evolutionary history, first, of being unskilled tool-users for many millions of years, and later, *before their respective lineages diverged, of being skilled tool-users.*

(d) If all the studied unskilled (beginner) tool-user animals, when they began to use a natural tool to obtain food, only reinforced a feeding habit they already had before tool-using, then, it is logical to assume that, at the beginning, tool-using among protohominids only reinforced a feeding habit already present. *To assume that* Ramapithecus *were seed-eaters, and became more efficient seed-eaters by using a natural stone tool, is completely reasonable, a logical hypothesis with solid basis.* Not so the hypothesis that assumes that from seed eaters they turned hunter-gatherers when they *manufactured* tools; or the hypothesis that assumes that the protohominids were mainly vegetarians who ate some insects, before becoming hunter-gatherer or scavenger-gatherer tool-users; since, as we have seen, it is a requirement to assume that before being hunter-gatherers or scavenger-gatherers, in both instances using tools, they must have been hunter-gatherers or scavenger-gatherers, in both instances without tools. Furthermore, these last hypotheses assume something illogical: that hominid tool-using started with the manual dexterity and intelligence required to *manufacture* tools with sharp edges, and not only with the ability to use only one absolutely *natural* tool, as all other unskilled (beginner) tool-user animals do.

(e) It can be stated that if we do not assume a long-ago common ancestor of all living pongids and humans, who was already a skilled tool-user, we are forced to assume a serious mistake: that skilled tool-using, as rare a character as it is in the animal kingdom (it could even be said unique), four times evolved *independently* among hominoids: once in the lineage that gave origin to the orangutan, another time in the lineage that gave origin to the gorilla, another time in the lineage that gave origin to the chimpanzee, and another time in the lineage that gave origin to the hominids.

In parallel in four (or several) related lineages, the same character may evolve when the same genetic basis is present in the four lines; for instance, the knuckle-walking in the respective lineages of the living pongids evolved in parallel from the genetic basis of bipedalism; but the *start* of tool-using is not genetic, and it can't be assumed parallel evolution. We know that the aptitudes for using tools are genetically inherited, but in order for a hominoid to transmit these abilities to descendants, these abilities must have first evolved, step by step, over the long period of time that would be required for these hominoids who were unskilled tool-users to acquire genetically, by cumulative selection, the true ability of expert tool-using. Therefore, to take any of the living pongids as a model for the first hominid tool-users is illogical, since living pongids descend from skilled tool-users, and are accomplished tool-users.

Susman (1988) has found fossil evidence for tool behavior attributable to *Paranthropus robustus (Australopithecus robustus)*, based on the similarity between their finger bones and those of humans. This indicates that *Paranthropus robustus* is most probably the ancestor of the gorilla, as suggested by Kleindienst (1975).

If we do not assume a long-ago common ancestor of all living pongids and humans who was already a skilled tool-user, then, I repeat: Why have all living pongids developed, *independently, at the same time*, the manual aptitude to use tools, *without any selective pressure to generate it*? How can this very rare character be at present in the same evolutionary stage of development in all of them, including the orangutan that is phylogenetically so separated from the African pongids?

2. Interdependence of Knuckle-Walking and Skilled Tool-Using

Let us consider skilled (expert) tool-using and knuckle-walking in living pongids:

The knuckle-walking character is not present in any other mammal species, including primates, except in the living pongids; the same can be said of skilled tool-using (if we exclude humans). Nevertheless, *to find both*, skilled tool-using and knuckle-walking, together, in each of the African pongid species, is an extraordinary occurrence. And that another hominoid phylogenetically separated from the African pongids for more than 4 million years, the orangutan, also presents those two very rare characters together, makes it an extraordinary and unique occurrence (despite the fact that the orangutan sometimes adopts fist-walking, sometimes knuckle-walking, and sometimes palmigrade, in the support of his forelimbs on the ground can be seen a locomotive tendency very similar to that of the knuckle-walking of the African pongids). Then, it can be assumed that these two characters in living pongids are interdependent; that is, that in some way they go together; and this must be explained and not taken as a normal occurrence as it has been thought of until now.

Because of its peculiarity, the development of these two characters in all living pongid species is due only to parallel evolution—that is, because it is genetically inherited, and because it is extraordinarily rare, it is due to the same and unique cause; it is not due to similar causes; and this cause and its genetic origins had to be generated many millions of years before their respective lineages split.

It can be immediately noted that we humans are skilled hominoid tool-users, but we are not knuckle-walkers; we show in isolation one of these two characters. To what is this rarity due? It is not the rarity that it may seem, since humans have the *potential of easily acquiring knuckle-walking* by parallel evolution, if the selective pressure of gathering in the forests or woodlands operates, as we will see later on in this chapter, section 4.

We already have some reasons to suspect that, among living hominoids (except hylobatids), skilled tool-using is present in bipeds, and skilled tool-using together with knuckle-walking is present in former bipeds.

If we do not admit that knuckle-walking and skilled tool-using are two characters present in all living pongids due to the same unique cause, that this cause is genetically inherited, and that knuckle-walking evolved in parallel in each one of their lineages because they are descendants of bipedal skilled tool-users, then we are forced to assume something really illogical: *that in each one of the lineages of the living pongids, these two very rare characters are evolving at present, or recently evolved, independently, as evolutionary novelties, at the same time, and without any selective pressure to generate them.*

3. Ancestral Tool-Using Capabilities and Bipedalism

Another serious oversight currently made by students of human evolution, paleoanthropologists, and paleontologists is the following: to know that tool manufacturing was present among some australopithecines, and not to have assumed the existence of a *remote* ancestor of them that had been an unskilled (beginner) tool-user, since the manufacturing of tools is evidence of a long history of tool using, first as unskilled, later as skilled tool-users. These scientists are not surprised by the tool-using abilities of the orangutan, this ape being so phylogenetically distant from African apes and humans. This mistake

32

partly originates from the false assumption already mentioned in section 1 of this chapter: that the tool-using capabilities of the chimpanzee (and the tool-using capabilities of the orangutan) are that of an unskilled (beginner) tool-user; and partly originates because paleontologists and paleoanthropologists want to see physical evidence, and will not accept logic and deductive reasoning as sufficient: In the fossil record they want to see tools *manufactured* by hominids, since that is evidence of their use; but not natural tools, since these would have to appear in a very particular place and form to *assure*, without any doubt, that they were used by hominid tool-users. Nevertheless, this evidence would be necessarily tenuous, as is the evidence of the Middle and Upper Miocene and Pliocene Eoliths (we will be covering this subject in Chapter III, section 1). Perhaps they are very intent upon making their discipline reliable, and they're right, but with this in mind it will be very difficult to *demonstrate* the existence of hominid tool-using since the Middle Miocene; it can only be *inferred*; that is, it can only be assumed as a logical antecedent to the results and consequences we see, which we also assume are derivative of this character and behavior.

The main problem is that paleontologists have arrogated unto themselves the mantle of final arbiters of our understanding of the evolutionary process—in effect, if we cannot see it in the fossil record, it never really happened. (Sarich, 1983: 143)

In the fossil record that is presently forming, although there is no direct evidence that the Egyptian vulture uses *natural* stones to break ostrich eggshells, still, we know it to be true. There is also *no* manifestation in the fossil record of the Middle and Upper Miocene and Pliocene that the early hominids used *natural* stones for graincollection. If this is also a fact, it has to be demonstrated by indirect methods, but it cannot be arbitrarily discarded simply because of the unavailability of direct proof.

A similar mistake is this: to know that there are perfect bipeds among the australopithecines based, among other facts, on the Laetoli (North Tanzania) footprints preserved in volcanic ash of 3.0–3.5 million years ago (Leakey and Hay, 1979) and on research made by many scientists on some fossil remains of *Australopithecus*, to demonstrate, without any doubt, that 3 million years ago hominid upright walking was well established (Lovejoy, 1988), and at the same time failing to assume a *long history* of full-time bipedalism among their *remote ancestors.*

Incipient bipedalism exists among some mammals, such as bears and baboons; and partial success is very common among those who practice it—success that sometimes is not even a feeding success; however, only humans are perfect full-time bipeds. Perfect bipedalism is unique in mammal evolution, and this implies an *uncommon total feeding success* (I say *feeding* as this is the most probable cause of it; and *total* since it makes its user a full-time biped so he can *continuously* benefit from bipedalism).

Nevertheless, the manufacture of tools and bipedalism are, taken individually, rare in mammal evolution; together, even more rare. Then we are right to suspect that, most probably, in humans, australopithecines, and all living pongids, both characters are inter-dependent and have a *common origin.* Therefore, the real mistake is to know that among the australopithecines there are perfect bipeds and skilled tool-user manufacturers of tools, and still fail to assume a *long history of unskilled tool-using and bipedalism among their distant ancestors.*

4. Hunting; Scavenging; Gathering

"Whether the earliest stone tool-using hominids were primarily hunters or scavengers is a hotly debated issue." (Bunn and Blumenschine, 1987: 444)

If we review recent literature related to this topic (up until May 1990), we will see that the disagreement is enormous. I believe the reason for such disagreement is that neither hunting nor scavenging was possible as a *normal* means of subsistence for human ancestors during *all of their evolution*, except during the last 50 thousand years; therefore, I will attempt to demonstrate that both positions—i.e., the claim that these hominids were hunters, and the claim they were scavengers—are untenable.

Bunn and Blumenschine (1987: 447) arrive at the following conclusion: "We still do not know with confidence how the earliest stone tool-using hominids acquired animal foods and what the relative contribution of hunting and/or scavenging was to subsistence activities."

Both hypotheses assume the early hominids to have been bipedal tool-users, but do not explain how they acquired these characters; they part from unexplainable beginnings. Nevertheless, based on the theory of graincollection, we can explain these beginnings because *it is very easy and efficient to use absolutely natural stone tools to graincollect*, but not to butcher carcasses, much less to hunt, and that is why it is more probable that graincollection, and not hunting or scavenging, represents the start of hominid tool-using.

Most researchers and students of different scientific branches related to anthropology and paleoanthropology accept that our ancestors, the first manufacturers of tools, were hunter-gatherers—this despite the fact that there is no basis for this assumption. Let us analyze hunting in more detail. Lovejoy states (1981: 348 [16]):

> Contrary to popular opinion, there is no evidence whatsoever that early hominids hunted. Bipedality is probably the mode of locomotion least adapted to hunting, unless sophisticated technology is available (or unusually high levels of intelligence, or both) . . . Artifacts do not appear until 2 million years ago, and when they do appear it is difficult to interpret them as hunting implements. In short, if the evidence made available by the fossil record is to be used in reconstructing early hominid evolution, one of its clearest implications is that hunting was not a dietarily significant behavior.

Similar reasoning to the one made in section 1 of this chapter to demonstrate that the chimpanzee, and in general, all living pongids, cannot be taken as models of early hominid tool-users, must be made here in relation to hunting and meat-eating. We cannot take current chimpanzees as models of the first hominid hunters and meat-eaters, since chimpanzees are already skilled tool-users and possess developed manual aptitudes that we cannot assume the early hominids had. In general we may say that much care must be exercised when taking as a model some aspects of the behavior of living pongids for the abovementioned purpose, since *most probably they descend from tool-user hominids*, and that invalidates the model.

Also, to take as a model savanna baboons (the olive, yellow, and chacma) or baboons in general for a protohominid or for an early hominid state of partial carnivorism is not valid, as I will try to demonstrate later in this section. Then, we can only take as a model the gelada baboons because, most probably, their dental-gnathic complex, as well as many other current morphological and behavioral characters, are similar to those *we must assume Ramapithecus* had (Jolly, 1970). But the gelada baboons do not hunt or eat meat; they only occasionally eat some insects (Iwamoto, 1979), since their basic food is seeds and grass blades (Jolly, 1970; Iwamoto, 1979; Dunbar and Dunbar, 1975).

Charles Darwin had long ago indicated the extreme difficulty of approaching flocks, troops, or herds of animals when they have already been threatened or attacked by the approacher. Scared or threatened animals do not allow anyone to come near them.

Washburn and Lancaster (1968: 299) describe that James Woodburn took a Hadza hunter to the Nairobi Park, and observed that this hunter was surprised and excited to see that the animals were not afraid of him: He had never seen so many animals up close. The concept he had of animals was due to the panic he inspired in them, since they reacted to him in accordance with what man is nowadays: " . . . the most destructive carnivore." (Washburn and Lancaster, 1968: 299)

Let us look at the following facts that can now be deduced:

First: If all the animal inhabitants of the savannas of the Old World *do not have an instinctive fear of humans*, this is reason to believe that humans were not hunters. The panic modern hunters inspire in some animals *is not instinctive*, but the result of current experiences.

Second: The unnatural and destructive form in which modern man hunts makes us believe that hunting is not instinctive in humans. Humans do not know how to hunt, since they do not choose their prey from among the sick, old, or slow animals, as natural predators do; instead, humans kill indiscriminately, *therefore decimating the hunted species*. Natural predators benefit the hunted species by eliminating the sick and the less fit. If we add to the aforementioned that humans are slow, and, due to their bipedality, too visible for hunting, we again arrive at the conclusion that our human ancestors were not hunters.

From all the field studies made on current hunter-gatherers that are believed to be most similar to the first hominid manufacturers of tools, such as the !Kung Bushmen of the Kalahari Desert, South Africa, it can be concluded that their nourishment, and therefore their subsistence, depends much more from gathering than from hunting.

The !Kung Bushmen have modern weapons such as knives, bows, arrows, spears and poisons, and it is valid to assume that our distant ancestors did not; however, !Kung Bushmen hunters do not provide more than 37% of the food the tribe consumes; and it takes them up to four days for several individuals to obtain prey when they go hunting (Lee, 1968). It seems that they hunt more for the fun of it, than from a need for meat. Lee (1968: 41, 43) states:

> It would be theoretically possible for the Bushmen to survive entirely on vegetable foods, but life would be boring indeed without the excitement of meat feasts. . . . the basis of Bushman diet is derived from sources other than meat. This emphasis makes good ecological sense to the !Kung Bushmen and appears to be a common feature among hunters and gatherers in general.

If !Kung Bushmen would agree to participate in an experiment in which they would set aside their modern weapons and poisons, and use only stone tools like the Oldowans or Acheulians, animal bones, branches, natural stones, etc., for hunting and butchering carcasses, I can predict they would not hunt or scavenge because in normal times they would not obtain any animals—with the exception of the dry season or in times of drought or scarcity of vegetable food, when large numbers of herbivorous animals die of natural causes, causing an overload of carcasses. Like their ancestors, they would not like to eat carrion, except during *abnormal times* of prolonged drought or scarcity of vegetable food for sheer survival. Therefore, men and women *normally* would devote themselves to gathering full-time.

If we take into consideration that the manual dexterity and intelligence of modern man is far superior to that of the early hominids, and even with this advantage it is not possible at present to survive from hunting using the same tools those early hominids used, we can state, without doubt, that our ancestors were never dependent on hunting for survival, and that their tools were not used for hunting.

Now, let us analyze scavenging in greater detail:

Many researchers consider it possible that our ancestors, the first manufacturers of tools, lived as scavengers, despite the fact that they can not support their argument.

The thought that a terrestrial and bipedal primate, with his slow movements and lacking a sharp sense of smell, could compete with the specialized carnivorous scavenger hyaenids, canids, and felids, plus scavenging birds (Houston, 1979) who find their food with their keen sight from high altitudes and long distances, with their excellent sense of smell, and their capability of moving at great speeds, could not be defended, and would therefore make us reject completely the possibility that our ancestors lived as scavengers.

Nevertheless, the proposition of Sinclair et al. (1986: 307) that " . . . bipedalism developed for long distance migration to scavenge from migrating ungulate populations . . . "—mentioned by Lewin (1987: 969)—has against it all the arguments that Lewin opposes in his article, since the early hominids were mainly vegetarians and not meat-eaters, and also has against it the following:

According to Sinclair et al. (1986: 308) " . . . tool use was an adaptation to speed up the butchering of carcasses and avoid competition with other stronger mammal predators"; that is: tool-using protohominids were evolving toward bipedalism due to the selective pressure of walking behind the ungulate migrations, waiting for an animal's natural death.

Quoting further from Sinclair et al. (1986: 307, 308):

We envisage the protohominid quadruped as a plant gatherer and occasional scavenger, much like the baboon. For this type to follow migrating ungulates two essential adaptations are required simultaneously. First, members of the type must carry their young efficiently. This requires arms for carrying, and an upright stance. . . . Second, they must travel long distances efficiently.

But it would have been easier for them to go ahead of those migrating ungulates, and, when graincollecting with natural stone tools, *passively* compete only with the equines, because those tools were better suited for that type of activity than for butchering carcasses, since they were natural stones. And it would be very difficult for those protohominids *actively* to compete with natural predators and scavengers, using tools that, if used for that kind of activity, should have been manufactured tools; and we cannot assume that these tools could be manufactured by the *first* hominid tool-users.

When commenting on the hypothesis of Sinclair et al. (1986), that Lewin (1987: 969) gives in the title of his article, "Four Legs Bad, Two Legs Good," we might ask: Why is quadrupedalism bad for long-distance migration? Carrying the infant on the rump of quadrupedal mothers (as is done by most nonhuman primate females) is more efficient than carrying him in the arms or on the hips, as is done today by human mothers. Where did the need for bipedalism come from? The mistake is the same: to assume that the first hominids were skilled (expert) tool-users *"like the chimpanzee,"* and tool-manufacturers as well, before being perfect bipeds.

On the other hand, Bunn and Blumenschine (1987: 444) make Shipman see her mistake when she concludes " . . . that carcasses were sufficiently plentiful to supply hominids with a scavenged meat intake comparable to that obtained currently by !Kung San through hunting and by spotted hyenas through scavenging." They support their argument by saying that comparing the availability of carcasses in current habitats with the Bed I times at Olduvai is mistaken, since the availability of carcasses to hominids in those times is not known; and they add:

> Shipman bases her estimate of available carcass biomass on the proportion of carcasses *not consumed* by mammalian or avian carnivores in the modern Serengeti. . . . In fact, carcass availability to a nonhyaenid scavenger in Ngorongoro is virtually nil. . . . The 35% excess, in fact, is not consumed because most of it is available during the stressful last two months of the dry season (Houston 1979), when vertebrate carnivore numbers are simply too low to accommodate the glut of carcasses resulting from high levels of natural mortality among herbivores. (Bunn and Blumenschine, 1987: 444, 445; italics mine)

Bunn and Blumenschine point out that the remaining carcasses are only temporary and there are no leftovers for current humans. That's how it should have been for the first hominid manufacturers of tools if they would have been scavengers: they couldn't have survived all year as scavengers. These researchers implicitly give a glimpse of a fundamental fact—that the probability of *continuously having leftovers* of any type of food for those animals who feed precisely from that type of food is very low, since that leftover food would facilitate, in a population, the survival of many weak, sick, or less fit animals that would not survive otherwise. Therefore, the number of individuals capable of reaching reproductive age would be higher, and consequently that *excess* of food would not last long, and thus the natural balance would soon return.

39

If early hominids occasionally resorted to scavenging, it would probably have been when they, as well as other herbivores, were decimated by drought, cold weather, etc.; but in no way would it have been their *normal* subsistence activity, since they were not equipped by nature to continuously thrive in a niche like that. Under normal circumstances nothing helped them locate carcasses and quickly reach them. Only in abnormal times of extreme drought or scarcity, when many herbivorous animals die, they were able to obtain carcasses without competing with animals who are natural scavengers; but *it is sure* that those early hominids would refrain from eating carrion when there was other food available. Teleki (1981: 328) states:

> With the exception of a few baboon cases observed at Gilgil in recent years (Sturm, in this volume), nonhuman primates that actively prey on mammals do not seem highly motivated to eat carrion (Teleki, 1975: 159). All experiments conducted with collector/predator baboons and chimpanzees at sites where predatory behavior is frequent—experiments in which various kinds of meat, including carcasses of species normally preyed upon, were offered for examination—have thus far failed to stimulate a meat-eating response (van Lawick-Goodall, 1968).

Strum (1981) says that scavenging in baboons is very rare. No primate customarily eats carrion; it is only done in cases of extreme hunger.

The fact that tools manufactured and used by early hominids as well as fossil bones with cut marks from those stone tools are found in many sites, does not prove that those hominids continuously scavenged as their normal and natural subsistence activity. If a tribe of graincollector hominids would, in times of extreme drought or of scarcity of their basic food, remain in a living site for some time, for example, a month or two, they would leave signs of their stay, since adult males would take meat to that place for females and infants to eat. Such signs would include manufactured stone tools, as well as bones with cut marks made with those tools. But this would hold true only until they had evolved and had acquired the manual dexterity to *manufacture* tools with sharp edges. If many tribes of hominids were forced to survive in this way at that same time, each one would leave signs in a different living site. If this unusual occurrence would repeat itself, say, *every hundred years*, the individual tribes would leave signs *in 10 thousand sites for every million years*. If multiplied by the number of graincollector tribes and by the number of millions of years, the total number of sites would be enormous. Furthermore, we should take under consideration that all these living sites should be more or less in the same places—most probably in the hills near the plains where the hominids would normally live as graincollectors, since many natural springs at the foothills would have water even in times of drought, and it can be assumed that grazing animals would approach those places. That is where a great number of weak ungulates die of thirst during drought; so it is in such places that the fossil remains of the early hominids may be found—in the caves they used for protecting themselves from the elements. Therefore, we can conclude that the probability of finding such sites is high. If numerous sites of this type are found, many scientists could accept that those hominids were really scavengers (or even hunters) because it could be affirmed that *"the evidence can be seen in the fossil and archeological record."* However, in fact, early hominids were scavengers—or rather, they resorted to eating carrion *one or two months every hundred years.*

Let us take another look at both hunting and scavenging. If we assume that, prior to tool using, protohominids hunted or scavenged during some periods of the year, and that during other periods they were gatherer vegetarians (this type of seasonally changing diet is similar to the feeding habits of the European wild boar and of some bears), or that they were omnivorous the whole year, we must assume that those individuals who had larger canines and were prognathous had a selective advantage over those who did not. In that case, we must assume something illogical: that when they started to use tools to improve and augment their partially carnivorous diet, the size of their canines adaptively diminished, along with their prognathism. This assumption fails to take into consideration the fact that even with tools to butcher carcasses, whoever had bigger canines and prognathism would be more efficient in feeding from meat. But this advantage was most pronounced for *hunting.* We must assume, as it has already been mentioned, that the first completely natural stone tools weren't useful for butchering carcasses or hunting, and that the largest canines give their possessors, in the long run, a selective advantage over those with small canines. Therefore, the great canines, with either of these selective pressures, would have naturally tended to increase, or at least be maintained. *The truth is that neither hunting nor scavenging is improved with use of natural, or even manufactured, stone tools, since canines are a superior tool.* On the contrary: using tools would make these activities less efficient. Furthermore, where did the need of peeling and butchering the hunted or scavenged animals came from? Baboons tear the skin off with their canines, and then eat the animal from the inside out, doing all this with great efficiency.

Scavenging can only be improved when a hominid with *no* great canines or prognathism uses tools. From this we can infer that *the size of canines and prognathism were first reduced by some cause differing from that of using tools for hunting and scavenging,* and later an attempt was made to improve the access to carrion by the use of tools. That is, we have to unavoidably assume that early hominids were at first graincollectors, and later, once they were able to manufacture tools with sharp edges, *they would scavenge only during unusual times* of great drought, cold weather, or scarcity of gramineous seeds, *pushed to it by extreme hunger.*

The fact that some of the early hominids had used stone tools to butcher carcasses, and therefore had access to meat for feeding, is proof that all hominids were not, and are not natural hunters or scavengers. This fact is evidence against and not in favor to the belief that we descend from hunters or scavengers.

Up to two centuries ago, in the courts of powerful European kings, at grand banquets, the guests would still hold the roasted meat with their hands, and devour it with teeth that were basically useless for this action. This was happening in very special formal occasions and at times when eating utensils, including knives, were available. The aforementioned shows that if the early hominids, manufacturers of tools, would have had to survive, normally, from hunting or scavenging, their canines would have never been reduced during their evolution, since, with or without tools, whoever had larger canines had a selective advantage over those who did not. It can be concluded then that, as a result of the use of tools for hunting and scavenging, the quantity of consumed meat was greater, and therefore their dependency to it as part of their diet increased. That is: if those tools would have been used for hunting and scavenging as a *normal* way of living, and not only occasionally, that behavior would have brought about the selective pressure *to increase the canines, and not to reduce them.*

Lovejoy (1981: 341) states:

As Holloway (7) and Jolly (8) have cogently argued, however, tool use
is not an explanation of canine reduction since there is no behavioral
contradiction in having both functional canines and tools.

These are some of the reasons for which it is not valid to take
savanna baboons, or baboons in general, as a model for a
protohominid state of partial carnivorism; furthermore, the hypotheses
and theories for explaining the origin of hominids with these models
do not explain the origin of bipedalism, tool-using, and tool-manufac-
turing; do not explain the increase of size of the molars and the
reduction in size of the front teeth, particularly the canines, and do not
explain the origin of many other hominid characters. Consequently,
we are forced to conclude that the early hominids, and in general,
hominids of all times, never were hunters or scavengers; and if we also
conclude that the hominids of the Pliocene and Pleistocene epochs,
whose fossil remains have been found in Africa, had already abandoned graincollection as their normal way of living, then we are forced
to admit that they were *exclusively gatherers*, despite the fact that they
were capable of manufacturing tools and resorted to eating carrion
occasionally. If we are forced to admit that their subsistence depended
entirely on gathering, then let us examine the behavior of current
hunter-gatherers, to consider it as a model.

Let us examine gathering. In a gathering niche, both men and
women would gather, and not women only as currently done by the
hunter-gatherers of the Kalahari Desert, South Africa.

When observing the way !Kung women gather, we notice that a
great part of this activity is done squatting or bending down (see for
example the photographs throughout the book of Lee and DeVore,
1976), both very uncomfortable positions. When supporting their
bodies with one or both hands on the ground—a frequent occurrence
when gathering—they support themselves on their knuckles, as all
humans do in similar situations, this being more comfortable and
efficient than supporting ourselves on flat hands. We also can see that
it would be easier for any human being, when trying to gather from the
small trees of the Kalahari Desert, if he could use his hands *and feet* to
hold himself from the tree branches and trunk. This would be even
more of a need if the trees were higher, as they are in the forests.

Schaller (1963: 83) states:

Bipedal locomotion confers no obvious selective advantage in the dense
vegetation and on the precipitous slopes of the mountains. In fact, such
a gait would appear to be undesirable in these situations, *and man too
is often reduced to the gorilla's quadrupedal mode of progression.*
(Italics mine)

In an exclusively gathering niche, in a habitat like the one in the
Kalahari Desert (tree savanna), or in the forests, humans could be
displaced by a hominoid that could bend down and climb trees better;
that is, by a knuckle-walker ape. Gause (1969: 19, reprint of the original
of 1934) states:

It is admitted that as a result of competition two similar species scarcely
ever occupy similar niches, but displace each other in such a manner
that each takes possession of certain peculiar kinds of food and modes
of life in which it has an advantage over its competitor.

Or maybe, and more probably, with this selective pressure con-
tinuing for many hundreds of thousands of years, one would observe
the existence of a survival prize for those humans who would gather
more efficiently. *In this way humans would adaptively evolve towards
knuckle-walking.*

Many quadrupedal primates have abilities for bipedalism even
though it is not commonly practiced, and no one uses knuckle-walking
as an intermediate gait; therefore, it is *not* probable that the knuckle-
walking of the living pongids is an evolutionary intermediate gait
between quadrupedalism and bipedalism, and indeed very probably
it is the resulting evolutionary gait in bipedal hominids that return to
adaptive zones in habitats in which bipedal gathering is inefficient.

I have talked about gathering in a habitat like the Kalahari Desert,
or in the forests, but not of *gathering in the open grasslands.* In the
long-grass grasslands, the human being could displace hominoid
knuckle-walkers, because in these places almost the only food that can
be gathered, without having to resort to digging, are the seeds and
blades of those grasses. A bipedal hominoid, *having the seeds of these
grasses right at the height of his skillful hands,* would remove them
better than a knuckle-walker, since it is difficult for the latter even to
remain upright for long periods of time. In this habitat hominoid
knuckle-walkers would live together with humans, *each one in a
different niche,* if they could also feed from parts of the stem and blades,

not only from the seeds of the grasses, since it is easier for them to remove a greater part of the stem in a knuckle-walking position than only seeds staying in an unstable bipedal position. The problem is that both would use their hands for their respective activities and both would injure them: humans when removing a great number of seeds, and knuckle-walkers when removing part of the stem and seeds all day and every day in a plentiful season, since neither of them performs this activity using teeth as ungulates do.

Let us assume now that they both know they can use a natural stone as grainthresher and that they can protect their hands by using this tool, as well as achieving greater efficiency. By using this tool one would reaffirm its bipedal gait, and the other its knuckle-walker gait. I could add that hominoid knuckle-walkers, in that niche, with that type of food, would tend to giantism, maybe like *Gigantopithecus* did in their times, since it is the niche of some current Equidae, in which their ancestors notably increased their size during the Miocene, Pliocene, and Pleistocene.

Once they had that natural stone tool in their hands and experienced the ease of obtaining their nourishment, humans, as well as hominoid knuckle-walkers, would always tend to look for fresh grasses and try to continue with that same type of diet throughout the year. Perhaps hominoid knuckle-walkers would remain sedentary, as the buffalo, impala, and topi are in the woodlands of the Serengeti (I use the word "sedentary" referring to their staying in limited geographical areas); meanwhile, bipedal humans, because they feed only from seeds, would develop true migratory habits, taking advantage of larger geographical areas, as Thomson's gazelle, wildebeest, and zebra are also in Serengeti (Jarman and Sinclair, 1979).

From the above, we can conclude the following:

(a) Graincollection in the long-grass grasslands is the natural niche for bipedal hominids. I believe there is enough evidence to accept that the niche of migrating graincollectors in the long-grass grasslands fits us humans *as if tailored*. There is enough support to believe that graincollection for humans is like speaking our own language: we could do it *without consciously thinking about it*, and we wouldn't even realize that it has a great degree of difficulty: Currently, no animal could survive in a long-grass grassland exclusively gathering seeds from the grasses, as the tool-user humans could. However, there are many animals that can hunt and eat carcasses better than humans, even when humans have modern weapons, poisons, and tools like the ones !Kung Bushmen have; there are other animals that can scavenge year-round, and do it better than the tool-user humans; and there are some animals that, *in woodlands and forests*, are able to gather more efficiently than humans: apes.

In the niche of migratory graincollectors of the long-grass grassland, humans are to some degree in the niche of some Equidae; ecologically apart from them by the fact that we feed only from the seeds and they feed from seeds and a great part of the stem of grasses; therefore, when migrating, we go ahead of them in the grazer successions.

(b) If the bipedal and tool-user hominids of the Upper Miocene, Pliocene, and Pleistocene had abandoned graincollection, compelled by glaciation or drought, etc., they would have returned to graincollection in the long-grass grasslands, since that is the appropriate niche for their natural characters; or they would have taken to gathering in the woodlands and forests; and in this latter adaptive zone they would have adaptively evolved toward knuckle-walking, as indeed I believe happened.

(c) It is very probable that the orangutan and the African pongids descend from the abovementioned hominids.

(d) The origin of *Gigantopithecus* can be explained if we assume that some already bipedal hominid tool-users changed their graincollector niche to a gathering niche; and also, using tools, they could gather gramineous *stems and seeds* in that same savanna habitat. In this way, those bipedal hominids would tend toward knuckle-walking and giantism.

(e) We can surely state that graincollection did *not* originate until the Pliocene, but in the Middle Miocene. Perfect bipedalism and skilled tool-using seen in the fossil remains of australopithecines and other hominids of the Upper Miocene, Pliocene, and Pleistocene are evidence of that.

(f) A gathering niche in a habitat other than long-grass grassland is not the natural niche of humans.

(g) Hunting-gathering and scavenging-gathering, whether in savannas, woodlands, or forests, are not natural niches of humans.

(h) The niche of all current pongids is that of gathering in forests and woodlands.

(i) Hominid graincollectors, and those hominids who had abandoned graincollection and were evolving towards gatherers during the
Upper Miocene, Pliocene, and Pleistocene, during abnormal time of
prolonged weather, drought, etc., would occasionally resort to
scavenging, but only when they were already expert tool-manufacturers and, not earlier, when they were still unskilled tool-users.

All of this supports the belief that hominids, during the whole
course of their evolution, were never scavenger or hunter meat-eaters.
Our only hunter ancestors, and maybe also scavengers, were those
who were forced into it at the beginning of Würm's Glaciation. Later
they became the manufacturers of tools and weapons referred to as
Neolithic, since they made a regular, *although not natural*, way of living
out of that activity.

One of the most reliable proofs that graincollector hominids
resorted to hunting and scavenging *only during abnormal times of
scarcity*, is the coincidence of the appearance of small stone tools *with
sharp edges and points*, used as weapons for hunting or as tools for
butchering, with the start of Würm's Glaciation. Why didn't the tools
evolve step by step into weapons? Why was the manufacture of
weapons as sudden as the arrival of that glaciation? The answer can
only be: because before Würm's Glaciation human ancestors used
tools only for graincollecting, and not as weapons for hunting, or tools
for scavenging.

5. Evolutionary Reversals

Ciochon states (1983: 834):

In the reconstruction of phylogeny no evolutionary scenario can be
completely parsimonious. The fact that *reversals and parallelisms* are
common features in mammalian evolution is now considered a truism.
Therefore a certain number of characters used to establish any
cladogram or phylogeny can be expected to show homoplasy. In some
cases the occurrence of *reversals, parallelisms,* or convergence can
involve as many as half of all characters (Cartmill, 1982). Parsimony at
this point becomes a relative term. (Italics mine)

Researchers from different scientific areas, mainly paleoanthropologists and comparative anatomists, are aware of the above observation stated by Ciochon; however, many of them do not take evolutionary reversals under consideration.

Zihlman and Lowenstein (1983) give a great deal of importance to the interpretative mistakes caused by evolutionary convergences, Kay and Simons (1983) to those caused by parallelisms; furthermore, these latter authors take great pains in offering excellent anatomic comparisons, based mainly on homologous (primitive and derived) characters, for the " . . . demonstration of significant anatomical (and thus phyletic) relationship of any of these later Miocene taxa to later hominids . . . " (Kay and Simons, 1983: 577); and they conclude: "We believe available evidence is strong enough to indicate that ramapithecines are broadly ancestral to Pliocene–Recent *Australopithecus* and *Homo*, but not to any living ape" (Kay and Simons, 1983: 620).

If, as would be much more parsimonious, we take under consideration that in 14 million years many evolutionary reversals could have occurred in some of the examined morphological characters of all the studied hominoids, during the evolution of their respective lineages, and could have affected the compared anatomical zones, we notice that this conclusion is not valid. Many scientists blindly trust the comparative analysis of morphological characters to establish phylogenetic relationships, and accept conclusions like the last one. If we take evolutionary reversals under consideration, those comparisons give *but little* indication of phylogenetic relationships when dealing with accurate and precise approximations, and are not reliable grounds on which to establish them.

An evolutionary reversal, since it carries changes at a genetic level, can also cause pleiotropic effects (correlative effects) in other anatomical areas; therefore, the evolutionary reversals and their pleiotropic effects must have played a crucial role in the evolution of all living beings; but they are not easily detected when using comparative analysis of morphological characters, because we can think, among other mistakes, that the reverted characters that we see are retained primitive characters.

We know that the return of animal populations to adaptive zones where their recent or distant ancestors once lived is possible, and is very common in their evolution. This is one of the selective pressures enabling a population to reacquire recent ancestral characters or primitive ancestral characters not completely lost (being still deeply fixed in the genoma), and can also lose some derived characters. It is very probable, then, that many evolutionary reversions could have occurred in some characters during the course of the evolution of hominids, and in general of all hominoids, in millions of years, that could cause the reacquisition of primitive characters, such as large canines, prognathism, body hair, etc.; and the disappearance of derived characters, such as loss of pure bipedalism, loss of long hair on the head, diminution of their prolonged childhood, etc. That is probably what happened during the evolution of the lineages that gave origin to each of the living pongids.

Characters that have already passed by the sieve of natural selection in the ancestral phenotype are those reacquired in reversions. Then they can become *rapid* evolutionary adaptations if a strong selective pressure, similar to that endured by the ancestors, is present. Meanwhile, the adaptative evolution toward the acquisition of true evolutionary novelties is necessarily gradual (Dawkins, 1986). As a result of this, such reversions may be the cause of an apparent instantaneous punctuated evolution. Punctuationalists might, *in some cases*, be fooled by the rapid evolutionary reversions occurring in some anatomical areas during evolution in some lineages of different animal species. For example, if we observe the great morphological differences between the African pongids and humans, and assume, based on biochemical studies, such as immunological, molecular (molecular clock), DNA comparisons, etc., that all those species are sibling species because their genetic distance is very short, then we may ascribe this to a punctuated adaptive evolution towards true evolutionary novelties having occurred in the human lineage, when in actuality they are *quick* evolutionary reversals that have occurred in the lineages of each of these pongids, starting from beings similar to humans.

In many cases the fossil record might not be evidence for rapid changes caused by true evolutionary novelties, but may be caused instead by evolutionary reversals. B. J. Williams (1987:107) concludes: "The apparent discrepancy in rate estimates between fossil and living species is due to frequent *micro-reversals* in direction of evolution of traits." (Italics mine)

Many scientists at present ascribe the adaptive changes that many species undergo, in part, to evolutionary reversals; and also ascribe interpretative mistakes of other scientists to these scientists' failure to take such reversions into account.

Kleindienst (1975: 644, 645) states:

> . . . there are *no* fossil ancestors assigned to the African apes for something on the order of *14 million years* (or more) of geological time (using van Couvering's [1972] correlations) . . . . All of this suggests that something about these fossils does not fit the prevailing preconceptions . . . . I think there are sufficient grounds for at least asking my biobehavioral colleagues to consider what I have come to think of as the "unmentionable alternative hypothesis." (I think it is theologically, rather than biologically, unmentionable.) A third class of model, not now acknowledged, is that australopithecines (rather, assigned fossils) are not representatives of a bipedal "experiment that failed" and became extinct (Oxnard 1979: 9); they—or some of them—*are* the ancestral African apes. . . . The knuckle-walking specialisation of African apes can be seen as explained by Tuttle (CA 15: 397; cf. Simons 1972: 236) and/or as a logical adjustment of a specialized form of bipedalism to quadrupedalism. At the logical extreme, it is possible to view the robust australopithecines as potential ancestral gorillas and the gracile forms as potential ancestral chimpanzees. The final divergence of ape and hominid lines may indeed be as recent as the biochemical evidence suggests. This alternative hypothesis would reconcile some of the apparent contradictions, although it certainly transgresses the entrenched views of ape and human evolution. . . (Emphasis author's)

Dunbar (1976: 161) suggests, based on a baboon analogy, that " . . . both gracile and robust australopithecines could have been 'small object feeders' in the sense suggested by Jolly (1970)." They could, then, have been some of the australopithecines I suggest descended from hominid graincollectors of Europe and Asia, and could have been ancestors of the chimpanzee and gorilla respectively, as suggested by Kleindienst (1975).

More recently, Edelstein (1987), based on the fact that knuckle-walking is a gait that is inefficient for serving as a transition from quadrupedalism to bipedalism, has also suggested that African pongids descend from bipedal australopithecines, and that evolutionary reversions must have played an important role in their evolution, since he places *A. afarensis* as their ancestor.

When some hominids from Europe-Asia stopped graincollecting and initiated their migration south, driven to it by extended periods of cold weather or some other cause, they were entering woodland and forest-like regions. Therefore, they began their adaptive transition from perfect bipedalism to knuckle-walking. As a result, those australopithecines developed a mixture of locomotive skills which made them adaptively acquire morphological and functional characters that now we see through their fossil remains, and that at present are incomprehensible to researchers. Regarding them, Oxnard (1975: 67) states:

> We just do not know what the animal is doing; there is some evidence for a type of habitual bipedalism; there is some evidence for climbing and quadrupedal abilities; there must presumably have been some functional mix that has not been determined at this time.

After many studies based on multivariate analysis done on bones of different anatomical areas of contemporary humans and pongids, and of fossil remains of australopithecines, such as shoulder, elbow, hands, pelvis, wrist, knee, etc., Oxnard (1975: 119, 120) concludes:

> The meaning of this result is far more difficult to disentangle. . . . They [the australopithecines] therefore displayed either a totally new and unknown manner of locomotion which would be totally unique and which we will judge rather unlikely; or they displayed such a mixture of locomotor abilities, therefore anatomical adaptations, and therefore bony morphologies, as to be rendered unique through being a mixture of different intermediates. . . . *Australopithecus* may display these morphologies because it had both sets of abilities or because, while performing the one as a new acquisition, it had not yet lost the hallmarks of the other, older, mode.

It is clear that all this is confusing for researchers who still do not take into consideration that the ancestors of the australopithecines were perfect bipedal graincollectors inhabiting the savannas of Europe and Asia, and that in their new adaptive zones in Africa they were forced to practice knuckle-walking.

Oxnard (1975), based on results and studies done by Patterson and Howells (1967) on a human fragment found in Kanapoi in 1965, with a calculated age of 4 million years; based on the work and studies made by Patterson, Behrensmeyer, and Sill (1970) on a jaw and molar found in the hills of Lothagam in 1967, with a calculated age of 5.5

million years; based on the findings of Johanson and Taieb (1967) on jaws, femur, tibia, humerus, and even a quite complete skeleton, all these from 12 different hominids, in Hadar, Ethiopia, to which an age of 3 million years has been attributed; and based on the work, studies, and results done by Leakey and Wood (1973)—concludes that these studies show that the older the remains of australopithecines are, the greater is their similarity to current humans; while the less age attributed to them, the greater is their similarity with present African pongids, and the more different they are from current humans. He then adds (Oxnard 1975: 121, 122):

> The third piece of evidence comes from an even earlier find, the fragment of arm bone perhaps four million years old from Kanapoi. This has already been shown by Patterson and Howells (1967) to be very similar to that of modern man, and some of the demonstrations in this book clearly support that contention (chapter 5). Again, unless arm bones evolved through a cycle of being more like man at an earlier, Kanapoi, stage, less like him at later australopithecine stage, and more like him again at a much later human stage, then the australopithecines had to have lain on an evolutionary side branch.
>
> And these pieces of evidence must also mean that perhaps as long as five million years ago (and the possibility is not lost that future finds may place this yet further back in time) there may well have been creatures living that were generally similar to *Homo erectus* and therefore classifiable as man in a way that we must deny to any australopithecine (whether named *"H. habilis," "H. africanus,"* or whatever else). . . . We may well have to accept that human bipedality is far older than previously guessed. . . .

Oxnard's studies (1975, 1987) show that the australopithecines are not human ancestors. His studies and results demonstrate that during the Middle Miocene, Pliocene, and Pleistocene, different groups of hominids, very similar to contemporary humans, arrived in Africa *several times* in different migrations, each migration being hundreds of thousands, or maybe millions of years removed from the previous one, and that those different migrations, through their fossil remains, show us a confusing evolutionary panorama. We cannot interpret what really happened during the evolution of the lineages of the African pongids, and we erroneously think that our ancestors are among the australopithecines because each hominid migration that arrived in Africa causes fossil hominid remains to appear that are very similar to those of contemporary humans. Such bipedal hominids, through many thousands of years, and due to the fact that they live in adaptive zones in the woodlands and forests of Africa, *unavoidably* tend to evolve towards the acquisition of knuckle-walking, in the same way that hominids of earlier migrations had evolved. This can be the reason why the evolutionary panorama shown by their fossil remains is absolutely confusing.

Kurtén (1972) is of the opinion that the human characters are very ancient and primitive, since *Propliopithecus-Ramapithecus-Homo* already showed canines that were reduced or in the process of reduction 30 million years ago. That is why he assumes that the lineage of the living pongids separated from the human lineage more than 30 million years ago. From biochemical evidence we know this is not possible; it is more probable that an evolutionary reversion in those characters could have occurred in each of the lineages of all living pongids, and that they really descend from beings more similar to humans.

There is some basis to suspect that the living pongids descend from skilled tool-using bipeds; therefore, we are forced to assume that there were evolutionary reversals in each of their lineages. None of the fossil remains found in Africa has been attributed to the gorilla's or chimpanzee's ancestors. Apparently, then, we do not have these kinds of evidences to prove that all living pongids descend from skilled tool-using bipeds. But if we assume, as Kleindienst (1975) suggested so many years ago, that among the australopithecines are the ancestors of the African pongids, then this is solved.

These reversions are very probable in their evolution, since all the species of living pongids present several reverted characters in parallel. I will attempt to prove this assertion as follows:

Let us examine three characters. Humans present polymorphism and heritable phenotypic variation within and between populations in the following characters: size of canines, prognathism, and amount of body hair. If a survival prize would exist for the members of a human population that had larger canines, greater prognathism, and a greater amount of body hair, it would be much more probable that that human population would, adaptively, revert to those characters. That being the case, we should not wonder at the possibility that the ancestors of the living pongids could have reacquired, during the evolution of their respective lineages, in parallel, those same characters, starting from bipedal and naked tool-user hominids with those three *more human* characters.

If we assume that the ancestors of the African australopithecines were bipedal and naked graincollectors in Europe and Asia, and that they found themselves forced to migrate to warmer places during, perhaps, a glaciation, taking refuge in woodlands or forests, those bipeds had the selective pressure such that their whole population would reacquire some primitive characters through evolutionary reversals—since, as I have already mentioned, the primitive characters had already passed through the sieve of natural selection long before in the phenotype of their ancestors, in an adaptive zone and habitat similar to the one they were now going back to. Also, the derived characters that they presented, like bipedalism, reduced canines, lack of body hair, etc., had not been subjected to that selection, since they were not present in their ancestors' phenotype at that time; and these derived characters, now present in the phenotype, do not overcome the sieve of natural selection in the adaptive zone and habitat to which they were returning. As mentioned earlier, in this niche and habitat in Africa, the bipedal australopithecines are also subjected to the selective pressure to acquire the evolutionary novelty of knuckle-walking.

When gene rearrangements occur in small populations during genetic revolutions (Mayr, 1979), it is more probable that those rearrangements that resemble combinations already used in previous evolutionary periods will be selected, since those rearrangements are partly in harmony with the whole genoma; and the phenotype structures that are related to those rearrangements are in better functional harmony with the total structural ensemble of the phenotype. Understandably, those rearrangements are chosen by natural selection if the population has returned to adaptive zones that their ancestors passed through in a previous evolutionary period.

Therefore, the fact that some structures can be reverted, and that they revert adaptively in a small population during genetic revolutions (Mayr, 1979), must be a common phenomenon in the evolution of all living beings. What has happened up to now is that, due to the great difficulty of detecting an evolutionary reversion (as above mentioned, because we can think, among other mistakes, that the reverted characters that we see are retained primitive characters), scientists have not identified the extent to which this phenomenon has occurred.

The students of organic evolution are aware of how difficult it is to *demonstrate*, without any doubt, a single case of evolutionary reversal. But the knowledge that evolutionary reversals are possible should make us doubt conclusions reached by the indiscriminate use of comparative analysis of morphological characters to establish phylogenetic relationships, *when dealing with accurate and precise approximations.* I agree with Sarich (1983: 143) that paleontologists have no basis to be the " . . . final arbiters of our understanding of the evolutionary process. . . . " We have to resort to the concordance and harmony of many studies and facts in order to establish reliable phylogenetic relationships as well as to establish reliable cases of evolutionary reversions.

Darwin considered the occasional reversions in some structures as important. In the prologue of the second edition of *The Descent of Man* he emphasizes that evolutionary reversions must be considered. From the time of Darwin to the present day, many scientists who have carefully studied organic evolution have seen evolutionary reversions as very possible and probable. Simpson (1953) was the first who, after being persuaded of its importance, made a decision to support it.

Simpson (1953: 311) states:

There is nothing in the analyzably separate factors of evolution that prohibits reversion. Back mutations occur. Lost combinations can be reconstituted by recombination. Variation is practically always present on *both* sides of the mode. Selection can reverse its direction. As regards particular characters and trends, therefore, if genetic variation and selection really are essential factors of evolution, evolution should be reversible—and it is. (Emphasis author's)

Mayr (1979: 6) states:

Statements to the effect that "evolution is one more expression of the general principle of irreversibility embodied in the second law of thermodynamics" are based on a facile analogy that has no operational value. Since every individual is unique, strict evolutionary reversibility is a logical impossibility. Yet acquired specializations may be lost again at later stages of evolution and a type may evolve that has in its essential structure reverted to a prior condition although it is obviously not the same as the ancestral type. The processes in physics and evolution labeled by the same term, "irreversibility," are fundamentally different.

Kurtén (1988: 217) states:

There is a graded series of transitions, both in China and in Europe, with overlapping variation in successive populations. This must be regarded as strong evidence that the sequence is a phyletic one and hence that lynxes with metaconid and talonid in M_1 evolved out of ancestral forms lacking both. The main objection to this interpretation would be the fact that the character thus evolved shows a striking resemblance to those found in geologically earlier felids, probably including the direct ancestors of *Felis issiodorensis*, though they are not at present known or at least not identified. A good example is the Miocene genus *Pseudaelurus* (including the Pliocene *Metailurus*) . . . This would then be an example of a structure totally lost and then regained in similar form—which is something that simply "cannot" happen according to Dollo's Law.
   Of course it would be possible to interpret the facts in another more "orthodox" way, as due to repeated migrations of successively more "primitive" forms from an unknown center of distribution. Studied in detail, however, this proposition becomes so complicated as to border on the miraculous. The main argument for the interpretation suggested here is, however, the reappearance of another dental structure of vastly greater geological age, in the living *Felis lynx*. This is the second lower molar, which was lost in the Miocene in all known Felidae. (Emphasis author's)

Dawkins (1986: 94) states:

There is no reason why general trends in evolution shouldn't be reversed . . . Dollo's Law is really just a statement about the statistical improbability of following exactly the same evolutionary trajectory twice (or, indeed, any *particular* trajectory), in either direction . . . There is nothing mysterious or mystical about Dollo's Law, nor is it something that we go out and "test" in nature. It follows simply from the elementary laws of probability. (Emphasis author's)

Note that he says: " . . . the statistical improbability of following exactly the same evolutionary trajectory twice . . . in either direction. . . ." Evolutionary reversions could, more probably, follow a trajectory somewhat different.
   But few concrete cases have been studied because it is not " . . . something that we go out and 'test' in nature." There are still some

scientists who, due to the lack of direct evidence, don't believe in the possibility of evolutionary reversions in some derived structures to *recent* ancestral states or in some *primitive* structures, not completely lost, to states very similar to the originals. "Indeed, what is rare is a concise example of reversible evolution." (Williams, P. L., 1987: 22) And there still are some other scientists who, for the same reason, continue to see evolutionary reversals suspiciously. De Bonis (1982: 510) states:

> He [Wolpoff, 1982] admits, however, that ramapithecines are also a stem group for the African apes, whose tooth enamel is very thin. This would be a full reverse evolution toward a dentition very similar to that of *Dryopithecus*. Is this a parsimonious hypothesis? It does not seem so to me.

However, Wolpoff (1982), when stating what De Bonis mentions, and suggesting that the common ancestor of the African apes and hominids walked more erect than the current African apes, is implicitly assuming in them various other evolutionary reversions (despite the fact that knuckle-walking is not a reversion from bipedalism to quadrupedalism, as I will try to demonstrate below). Therefore, a more logical hypothesis and one that offers more of a complete explanation, seems to De Bonis less parsimonious only because it assumes evolutionary reversions.

In order to state with certainty which characters of living pongids were reacquired through evolutionary reversion and which are true evolutionary novelties, we must make certain observations. Knuckle-walking is a true evolutionary novelty that has evolved in parallel in their respective lineages from the genetic basis of the derived character of bipedalism; it is not a reversion to quadrupedalism: if it was to be a reversion it should present itself in infants and adults, but, being an evolutionary novelty it only presents itself from the age in which this character acquires survival value for the individual; that is, it appears only in juveniles and adults. Furthermore, if it were a reversion, apes would support themselves with their flat hands on the ground, and not with their knuckles, when resting the weight of their body over their arms. Also, many of their reverted characters give the appearance of evolutionary novelties, like body hair, which is sparse on their skin, and which we can think of as being a step toward its total loss and not the reacquisition through evolutionary reversion.

There are more grounds now to see why the living pongids, when infants, show a greater resemblance to human infants and adults: because 3 million years ago their ancestors were more or less like humans are at present. Therefore, we have *no* support to a belief that humans present Paedomorphosis (that we have evolved by retaining the infant or juvenile characters of our ancestors) caused by "heterochrony" (Gould, 1977). We continue being graincollectors, and have graincollector characters acquired by our ancestors some 14 million years ago. The ancestors of all living pongids abandoned graincollection 2 or 3 million years ago. That is why they, when infants, still present some of the characters typical of graincollectors: bipedalism, lack of body hair, nonprominent jaw, etc. Living pongids are, and mainly when infants, who still present some characters typical of humans, but not humans who retain characters typical of living pongid infants or juveniles. I believe I can apply to this case what Mayr (1979: 607) applies referring to similar cases; he says:

> These authors forget that the juvenile phenotype and the adult phenotype are expressions of the same genotype. It is a matter of selection pressure (including that exercised by the epigenetic system as a whole) which determines whether the juvenile or the adult phenotype is modified more rapidly and more drastically.

As a corollary of Mayr's words, we can ask ourselves: Is there a real selective pressure that makes all living pongids bipedals only during their infancy? The answer is categorically *no*; therefore, let's examine the following:

Pongid infants, the same as children, must *struggle* to acquire bipedalism in their first years of life. Why do they make this effort? Why do they later on abandon this aptitude that required so much effort? The human infant, as well as the pongid infant, must learn to be bipedal. This does confirm what we already know: that bipedalism is a more difficult and dangerous gait than quadrupedalism. Therefore, the question is: What is the selective pressure that makes infant pongids *learn* to walk in a bipedal position? This selective pressure does not exist, but there must be a cause. The selective pressure to abandon bipedalism later on, when they are older, does exist: when older, they must survive on their own and not with their mother's help and milk, and they must gather in habitats where knuckle-walking is more efficient than bipedalism; but why must they start out by being bipedals and not knuckle-walkers?

The simple fact that infant pongids *achieve* bipedalism without this being an adaptive need in their current niche, and despite its huge effort, is evidence that they descend from recent bipeds and not from recent arboreals or quadrupeds. We cannot accept that nature would waste abilities without any selective pressure to do so. *Living pongid infants acquire bipedalism because it is still in their genoma*: "It is a matter of selection pressure (including that exercised by the epigenetic system as a whole) which determines whether the juvenile or the adult phenotype is modified more rapidly and more drastically." (Mayr, 1979: 607)

Farris (1984: 692) warns:

Whenever a putative reversal offers a more complete (that is, as already seen, more parsimonious) explanation of observed similarities than does a reconstruction enforcing irreversibility, irreversibility must be discounted.

Dobzhansky et al. (1977: 3) state:

Given a new ecological niche to which it can become adapted, a population can achieve this adaptation in any one of several different ways. Although in many instances the particular adaptation that is adopted may depend entirely upon the chance appearance of certain favorable mutations or gene combinations, generally the direction taken depends chiefly upon *preexisting capacities already present in the gene pools*. (Italics mine)

Zuckerkandl (1976: 421) states:

. . . structural genes are building stones which can be used over again for achieving different styles of architecture . . . *evolution is mostly the reutilization of essentially constituted genomes*. (Emphasis author's)

Harvey and Partridge (1987: 128) state:

For the most part, biologists view adaptive evolutionary change as reversible. For example, when dark moths were selectively favored through camouflage against a background of sooty tree trunks, it came as no surprise that lighter forms became more frequent again after the introduction of smoke-control measures.

To those scientists who think of evolutionary reversions as highly unlikely (due to the fact that we are not used to considering them), I would like to say the following: Evolutionary reversions in the respective lineages of living pongids can be explained; furthermore, their reverted characters are not many. What has happened is that the combination of two very visible reverted characters—the reacquisition of body hair, and the reacquisition of great canines and prognathism—joined with the evolutionary novelty of the acquisition of knuckle-walking in parallel; joined also with the recent loss of manual dexterity; and joined with the fact that in their recent evolution there could not have been great brain development, since their ancestors had left graincollection 2 or 3 million years ago, that is, before the great brain development occurred in the graincollectors' lineage—all this gives, as an evolutionary result, beings that *look very different from humans* in spite of being so close phylogenetically. But reality shows that evolutionary reversions in their lineages have occurred in a very few characters. Those characters are very old, deeply fixed in the genoma, and very difficult to lose in the course of evolution.

Lewin (1989: 40) states:

Andrews's and Martin's conclusions are intriguing and puzzling. For instance, although cladistic analysis of morphological data link chimpanzees and gorillas together strongly, support for a human/African ape clade is surprisingly weak. By contrast, molecular evidence strongly suggests a human/African ape clade, with humans and chimpanzees being linked together within it. One set of data—molecular or anatomical—must be being incorrectly interpreted in some way. Andrews and Martin note that in the molecular data, whatever shape of human/chimpanzee/gorilla tree is selected, there appears to be a surprisingly high degree of parallel evolution (homoplasy), much higher than would be predicted on simple statistical grounds. Its significance remains obscure for the present.

If the human/chimpanzee association is correct, then there are certain implications regarding the common ancestor of humans and African apes: specifically in its mode of locomotion. The notion that chimpanzees and gorillas might have independently evolved the knuckle-walking habit from a nonknuckle-walking ancestor is unacceptable to many anatomists, simply because it is such a very complex set of anatomical adaptations: for it to have evolved twice is thought to be unlikely.

The alternative—that the common ancestor of humans and the African apes was a knuckle-walker, an adaptation that was lost in the hominid line—is equally difficult to accept. Most anatomists who have studied the issue see no vestigial signs of knuckle-walking in the anatomy of living or fossil hominids. Yet, if humans really are uniquely linked with chimpanzees as the molecular evidence seems to imply, one of these alternatives must be correct. It would be a tremendous challenge to comparative anatomy to resolve this one.

If we do not accept in the respective lineages of the chimpanzee and gorilla that evolutionary reversals and parallelisms have taken place, and that they are descendants of a *bipedal* common ancestor, many misinterpretations and some unexplainable facts, such as mentioned above by Lewin, remain.

6. Life in the Savanna; Adaptation to a Diet Based on Gramineous Seeds

There is another oversight that I believe many paleoanthropologists make. Even if we assume as valid all the current theories that try to explain the origin of early hominids through the hunting-gathering or scavenging-gathering hypotheses, without explaining the origin of bipedalism and tool-using, there is in all of them another serious omission: It is inconceivable to think that hominids and their protohominid ancestors lived in the savannas for millions of years, and never developed the practice of feeding from gramineous seeds until the discovery of agriculture, or until fire was used to cook food. If we take under consideration that the early hominids were already bipeds and tool-users, and that *the seeds from grasses would lightly touch their hands as they walked in the savanna*, it would be illogical to assume that, in spite of the many vicissitudes they suffered during so many million years of living in the savannas, they never tried to feed from these seeds; that they never thought of removing the seeds with their hands. Then, when doing it and injuring themselves, they must have tried to *protect* their hands with something; and that something couldn't have been other than a natural small stone. In short, *to think that we are and descend from graincollectors is inevitable*, no matter how you look at the origin of graincollection; and, as I assume, it is very probable that *Ramapithecus* were our first ancestors who practiced graincollection.

On the other hand, it is illogical to think that exclusively from the discovery of agriculture some 10 thousand years ago, up to the present day, the feeding of all human societies has depended for their development and maintenance on gramineous seeds, and that these are a completely new source of nourishment for humans. Humans, like many monogastric mammals that are digesters of cellulose, have cellulolytic organisms in the caecum and colon that break down the cellulose; furthermore, we can digest various plant starches without cooking them (Milton, 1984). Physiologically we are perfectly adapted to feed from gramineous seeds because our ancestors depended on them for millions of years, and not only because grains have been our basic source of nourishment—"thanks to agriculture and fire"—for the last 10 thousand years. On the contrary: feeding from gramineous seeds was much more perfect in our ancestors when they didn't eat food of animal origin or *unfamiliar* vegetables, since, according to Kortlandt (1984), humans have lost some infusoria ciliates, *Troglodytella*, from our intestines, that in symbiosis helped us digest cellulose and starch, and provided us with all types of vitamins, in a similar way to many ungulates. Such *Troglodytella* are present in the intestines of the wild African pongids.

These symbiotic microorganisms, and the bacteria digesters of cellulose, can be easily recovered by humans if we want to; it is not an irrecoverable loss. The most serious problem is that we do not know what species of *Troglodytella* are those which would best live in our intestine. It will probably be researched in the future and we will then know exactly; we must wait.

Many animals that digest cellulose lose their intestinal flora and fauna occasionally due to several diseases or due to the lack of their regular food; but in nature it is easy to recover them: coprophagy is a normal behavior in many animal species, including those so phylogenetically separated as some insects, birds, mammals, and even humans. Sometimes sick and weak horses eat recently defecated dung from other healthy horses, and they are soon back to normal. This instinct probably originated due to the fact that in this way they rapidly obtain the vitamins they are missing, and furthermore, they recover intestinal flora and fauna that had been diminished by disease. Humans could recover the lost microorganisms in this natural way: eating dung of healthy equines; as was surely done by our ancestors during unusual drought, when they lost the microorganisms serving as digesters of cellulose and starch at such times as they were forced to scavenge or to eat unfamiliar vegetables when lacking basic sources of nourishment. This is similar to the way the European wild boar recovers them when it *seasonally* changes its omnivorous feeding habits to become an exclusively vegetarian cellulose digester.

If we were conservative in our eating habits, as is the wild gorilla, it would be enough for a few days to eat only whole gramineous seeds with some of the hulls, followed by dung from healthy wild gorillas, or even from healthy horses, to recover our intestinal microorganisms that are digesters of cellulose. I do not recommend that anyone do this until scientific specialists have performed research on this type of digestion in humans, and obtain true results. I mention it, however, because this or a similar method of recovery must have been practiced by our graincollector ancestors, given all the difficulties and vicissitudes they must have overcome during so many millions of years of life in the savannas. I will again consider this subject in Chapter II, Section 2.

7. Final Notes on Mistakes in Basic Anthropological Concepts

(a) Living pongids lost their tool-using culture, but they haven't lost their aptitude to acquire it, since these aptitudes are genetically inherited. It is very probable that the same tool-using and graincollecting culture that humans lost more than 50 thousand years ago, was lost some 3 million years ago by the ancestors of the African pongids when their respective lineages split from that of humans. The ancestors of the orangutan lost it more or less at the same time, even though their lineage split 6 or 7 million years ago from the one that gave origin to African pongids and humans. The orangutan's tool-using abilities reveal that, most probably, when their lineage split from ours, they continued being graincollectors for 3 or 4 million years. Then they returned to life in the forests and became gatherers, losing their tool-using culture and, by parallel evolution, acquiring in this new niche characters similar to those of the African pongids.

(b) Based on what we have stated in Section 4 of this chapter regarding some hypothetical exclusive gatherers in the Kalahari Desert, we may infer that if human ancestors hadn't used the grainthresher manufacturing technique to manufacture weapons at the beginning of the last great glaciation, pushed and forced to it because of the partial disappearance of the long-grass grasslands in Europe and Asia, their descendants would have never been able to hunt. We would be gatherers (in forests or woodlands) and would tend to be knuckle-walkers. Some human groups, however, might have been able to survive as graincollectors in the few remaining grasslands, as did our graincollector ancestors during *all* the previous great Pleistocene glaciations. However, it is precisely due to their possession of weapons that humans did not survive the last great glaciation as graincollectors. This was because humans, when armed, conquered and subdued other human graincollectors, as we humans have *always* done in modern times against defenseless people (e.g., the conquest of America, the conquest of The West, etc.). I suspect that this is the *main* reason why humans did not maintain their graincollector culture during the last 50 thousand years, not even in some populations, and never returned to graincollection even though the intense cold later diminished, and some grasslands reappeared in South Asia.

Another powerful reason why humans never returned to graincollection is that, in order for graincollectors to be true digesters of cellulose and starch, they need, as Kortlandt (1984) mentions, the infusoria ciliates *Troglodytella* and other microorganisms living in their intestine; but humans do not remember how to recover them, nor the proper feeding conditions needed to do this. It is easy for humans to recover all those microorganisms, but we have already lost our grain-collector *culture*. We no longer remember our natural ecological niche, our natural habitat, or even our natural type of food.

I believe all of the abovementioned facts answer a question put to me in 1976 by Dr. Alberto Folch in a personal communication: How is it that humanity, which has gone through so many shortages, deprivations, and hunger in the past 50 thousand years, never returned to graincollection?

(c) We are forced to assume that our distant ancestors of the Middle and Upper Miocene and Pliocene were bipedal tool-users; therefore, they had a true tool-using culture. Now, I want to revive the name of that culture: *"Eolithic Culture"*; that is, I want to speculate that those first tools that *we are forced* to assume were used by our ancestors at that time were small *natural* stones that they chose as scrapers for graincollection. This subject will again be brought up in Chapter III, Section 1.

(d) Based on what we have seen up to now, we can say that in the Middle Miocene, protohominid part-time seed-eaters must have had, *in some way*, great success in order to turn into full-time seed-eaters and migratory long-distance walkers. This makes us assume a total feeding success, and makes us look for *only one natural tool* that would allow (and force) the quadrupedal part-time seed-eaters to become completely successful full-time bipedal seed-eaters. Furthermore, with this one tool they obtained only one type of food in only one situation and in only one context, and obtained it with the execution of only one action, almost like a conditioned reflex.

Chapter II
Supports

1. Parallelisms and Divergences

The theory of graincollection is based on Jolly's model and interprets the origin of all living hominoids. As already mentioned in the Introduction, *Phase 1* of Jolly's model as the start of the protohominid differentiation, and *graincollection* as an arrival to the true hominidization, are complementary in this theory.

Most of the models proposed up until now that have attempted to explain hominid origins cannot explain their own beginnings—that is, the hominoids chosen as models of the basal hominid trunk already have evolved hominid morphological and behavioral characters that are illogical to assume as a beginning. Jolly's model postulates basal hominid characters logical to assume in *Ramapithecus* of the Middle Miocene, and that is the basal trunk that Jolly proposes as a beginning.

Tattersall (1975: 21) states:

> If we accept that the morphology of the dental/facial complex in mammals is largely determined by the demands of mastication, which in turn depends on diet, we must recognize the very high probability of a similar dietary regime in *Ramapithecus* and *Theropithecus*.

Since Simons (1961) identified and proposed *Ramapithecus* as a basal hominid candidate, many paleoanthropologists support this idea. Others have not supported it due to one fact that up to now seems not to fit: they accept the late divergence (of apes and hominids) hypothesis based on many biochemical studies, such as the immunological and molecular (molecular clock) studies done by Goodman (1963, 1975, 1976), Sarich (1968), Sarich and Wilson (1967), Wilson and Sarich (1969), etc. The theory of graincollection reconciles these two apparent contradictions when it proposes *Ramapithecus* as the ancestor of all living hominoids; so, according to this theory, *Ramapithecus* is the basal hominid as proposed by Simons (1961), and the late divergence took place.

Jolly assumes in Phase 1 of his model, that the characters of *Ramapithecus* are very similar to those of the *Theropithecus gelada.* To support his hypothesis, he points out, among other facts, twenty-two parallelisms out of forty-eight characters among early Hominidae (distinguished from *Pan*) and *Theropithecus* (distinguished from *Papio* and *Mandrillus*), which gives him a . . .

> . . . reasonable *prima facie* evidence for parallelism between them. This hypothesis can be tested by checking the elements of the complexes for cross-occurrence in *Papio* and *Pan*. If the high number of common characters were simply due to chance, rather than to parallelism, we should not expect significantly fewer of the Hominid characters to appear in *Papio* (as opposed to *Theropithecus*), or significantly fewer of the *Theropithecus* complex characters to occur in *Pan*. In fact, none of these cross-correspondences occurs. There are some grounds, therefore, for assuming the existence of evolutionary parallelism, and perhaps some degree of functional equivalence between the differentiation of *Theropithecus* and that of the basal hominids. . . . (Jolly, 1970: 12)

Jolly compares some morphological characters of *Theropithecus* with those of the Villafranchian Hominidae; other characters, for example: the "Accessory sitting pads (fat deposits on buttocks) . . ." (Jolly, 1970: 10) are compared with those of current humans; the same can be said of some behavioral characters. He also points out some important divergences.

Among the characters compared by Jolly I'll consider only those which I believe are more important and helpful for the presentation of the theory of graincollection.

(a) Jolly (1970: 12, 13) states:

> Recent work by Crook (e.g., 1966), including filmed close-ups of hand-use in the wild, has made it clear that the gelada (in contrast to, for instance, *Papio*) uses a precision-grip for most of its food-collecting. Food consists mainly of grass-blades, seeds and rhizomes which are picked up singly between thumb and index, and collected in the fist until a mouthful is accumulated. The index is thus continually used

independently of the other digits. This feeding method is facilitated by the well-developed pollex and the very short index finger (Pocock 1925; Jolly 1965), a combination giving the gelada the highest 'opposability index' (Napier & Napier 1967) of any catharrine, not excluding *Homo sapiens* (J.R. Napier, personal communication). It is significant that the precision-grip of the gelada, which like other Cercopithecinae has not been seen making or using artifacts in the wild, should far outclass that of the tool- and weapon-using chimpanzee (Napier 1960).

From the abovementioned, said by Jolly, we can conclude the following:

First: the geladas, as part-time seed-eaters, have what evolutionists call *preadaptations* for the use of tools; then, *Ramapithecus*, when part time seed-eaters, could also have had them.

Second: the seeds that a gelada is about to eat are accumulated in the fist before taking a "mouthful," since he is removing them, one by one, with the other hand. *Ramapithecus* could have done the same thing, but once they turned graincollectors a fistful of seeds could be obtained by only one-handed action with the grainthresher. What I want to emphasize is the fact that, even before turning into tool-users, *Ramapithecus* could have already been adapted to work with one hand, accumulating and taking a fistful of seeds to the mouth with the opposite hand.

Third: the precision-grip that the geladas have should have developed in *Ramapithecus*. That is why there is support to believe that it could have been very easy to place a small stone tool, similar to a flake or scraper, in one hand, and in between the ball of the thumb (thenar eminence) and such tool, secure the grains that were to be *cut* or *scraped* from the stem of the grasses. This can lead us to think that the change from part time seed-eaters to tool-user graincollectors (full time seed-eaters) could have been a very simple and probable step.

(b) In the Pleistocene, before humans encroached on them, the natural habitat of the gelada baboons was the savanna plains of eastern and western Africa (Dunbar and Dunbar, 1975: 1), and is similar to the grassland savannas in which early hominids lived. What were early hominids subsisting on in that habitat? Hunting and scavenging as subsistence activities are eliminated as we have seen in Chapter I, Section 4; furthermore, we know they were bipeds and not knuckle-walkers; therefore, only one niche remains in those grassland savannas for a gatherer *bipedal* hominid: graincollection (full time seed-eater).

(c) As seen in (a), the food of the gelada baboons is composed not only of seeds, but also of grass blades and rhizomes (Jolly, 1970; Iwamoto, 1979; Dunbar and Dunbar, 1975). Jolly says that the dental characters of the *Theropithecus* adjust precisely to that type of diet, unlike these characters of hominids, and adds (Jolly, 1970: 18):

> We can thus distinguish a sub-complex of unique hominid characters which suggests that the "small objects" of the basal hominid diet were solid, spherical, and hard. Many potential foods fit the description, but only one is widespread enough in open country to be a likely staple. This is the seeds of grasses and annual herbs, *which still provide the bulk of the calories of most hominids.* This is not to say that other resources were not exploited when available, *but that the diet of basal hominids was probably centered upon cereal grains.* . . . (Italics mine)

Jolly concludes that the dental characters of hominids are exclusively of seed-eaters, and that those of *Theropithecus* are better adjusted to a diet that also includes grass blades and rhizomes, which is what they currently have in the wild. This supports my hypothesis that *Ramapithecus*, when changing habits from part-time to full-time seed-eater graincollectors, almost exclusively depended on grains for nourishment, and acquired all their hominid characters in this new adaptive zone.

(d) Jolly also finds that a group of postcranial characters reveals that " . . . *Theropithecus* is a quadruped, at least when moving more than a few paces, the Villafranchian hominids were evidently bipeds of a sort" (Jolly, 1970: 18). Jolly points out that the gelada baboons also use bipedalism quite frequently. He states:

> A gelada-like foraging pattern leads to constant truncal erectness in the sitting position, with the trunk "balanced" on the pelvis, and the forelimbs free. In *Theropithecus*, this behavioral trait (and its associated adaptive features) are superimposed upon a thoroughgoing, cercopithecoid quadrupedalism, producing a locomotor repertoire in which the animal abandons "bipedal" bottom-shuffling for quadrupedal locomotion when it moves fast, or for more than a few paces. (Jolly, 1970: 18, 19)

From this, we can assume that when *Ramapithecus* were part time seed-eaters, they also had aptitudes for an incipient bipedalism, that is: It is not a strange hypothesis to assume that when they turned graincollectors, they could have turned to full time bipedalism; but only if they had the selective pressure to do so; therefore, we have to demonstrate that graincollection demands perfect bipedalism, and consequently, that *that* was the required selective pressure. I will demonstrate this later on in Section 4 of this chapter.

Taking under consideration that bipedalism is a difficult gait, very attractive to possible predators, and not rewarding if a specific and useful cause is not obvious to those who use this gait, we may infer then that the *huge success* obtained from the use of the grainthresher was what pushed and kept hominids into full-time bipedalism, from some 14 millions years ago until the start of the last great glaciation, 50 thousand years ago.

(e) Jolly (1970: 17) states:

> Fatty pads on the buttocks, adjacent to the true ischial callosities, are another *Theropithecus* peculiarity (Pocock 1925) which can be plausibly related to the habit of sitting while feeding, and also occur uniquely in *Homo sapiens* among the Hominoidea.

This is a very important character in explaining the origin of many other hominid characters, such as the origin of the *brachiators* capability that all living hominoids have. Given its importance I will deal with it later, also in Section 4 of this chapter.

Jolly relates the "Fatty pads on the buttocks . . . [with the] habit of sitting while feeding . . . " and I believe this to be wrong: Many monkeys sit while feeding, some *Papio* among them—who furthermore sleep all night sitting on a tree branch. They have adaptively developed ischial callosities—horny epidermal thickenings, but they have not developed similar fatty pads. Furthermore, currently all present-day women have "fatty pads on the buttocks . . . " what we could call a *moderate steatopygia* (steatopygia being the tendency to accumulate fat on the buttocks) more developed than men. And it is more pronounced in women during their childbearing years, and still more when they are pregnant. There are human races—Hottentots and some Andamanese people—where women really present *steatopygia* and men to a much less extent. This character seems to be related with the food reserves needed in times of scarcity, like the camel hump; and, of course, related with *the food reserves needed to breastfeed children.*

The fact that that steatopygia is useful to sit more comfortably is just a fortunate coincidence, since that food reserve is exactly where biologically it should be—where it least affects locomotion, and in general, where it is least bothersome for all of our movements, and doesn't interfere with the loss of body heat—here once again similar to the camels' hump (Rensch's Law).

Once all these characters are analyzed, and without taking under consideration all the others mentioned by Jolly (1970), we can conclude:

Humans have more conspicuous seed-eater characters than Theropithecus gelada; some acquired by parallel evolution and others acquired by divergent evolution. Women have more developed steatopygia than female geladas, humans have a more specialized seed-eaters' dental/gnathic complex, we have developed manual aptitudes that allow us easily to collect gramineous seeds with the aid of a small natural stone, and we are full-time bipeds. We are " . . . long distance walkers . . . " (Kortlandt, 1974: 441); that is, we are migratory grazers. In short, *humans are still graincollectors*. All of our characters demonstrate it.

2. Loss of Body Hair; Human Head of Hair

Paterson (1984: 161) points out that all primates, even those categorized as "folivorous," have been in some degree carnivorous over most of their evolutionary history, and adds: " . . . I can assert that every primate I have studied at least occasionally utilizes animal protein sources."

All nonhuman primates obtain vitamin D almost exclusively by eating animal food, mainly insects. Gorillas, in the wild, are *almost* exclusively vegetarians, since they very seldom eat insects or some terrestrial snails; then, how do gorillas obtain vitamin D? All primates have a *thick* layer of hair over all of their body, except the living pongids on whom it is *sparse,* and humans who are completely *naked.*

Humans depend a great deal on the synthesis of vitamin D in our skin through the action of solar rays upon it. Vitamin D is essential for calcium and phosphorous absorption through the intestine. The lack of vitamin D may cause rachitis. If humans had body hair, the solar rays wouldn't reach our skin and therefore we wouldn't be able to synthesize vitamin D through it.

If our ancestors had had a dependence on animal food for their subsistence, they would not have lost their body hair, since hair has many protective functions on the skin, and in general on the body, and we would not have to depend on the synthesis of vitamin D in our skin in order to satisfy our requirements of this vitamin. From this we may tentatively conclude that *for many million years our ancestors did not depend on food of animal origin for their normal daily nourishment.*

If we assume that our ancestors' diet was composed partially from animal food, then a selective pressure that would have caused the loss of body hair shouldn't have existed; however, that selective pressure does exist if we assume that our ancestors were *exclusively* granivorous graincollectors.

Human nudity is a very important adaptative character that hasn't yet been explained; very little effort has been made to explain it, despite its being a very rare character in primates, and in general in non-aquatic mammals. This nudity makes us consider the following:

(a) Humans' ancestors totally depended, and present-day humans still depend a great deal, on the action of solar rays on their skin for the obtention of vitamin D, differing in this character from all other primates, except from living pongids.

(b) Body hair is a very old character in mammals, deeply fixed in the genome by being linked to many other characters, and very difficult to lose during evolution. The fact that humans are so well adapted to their body nudity is evidence that this character was lost during the evolution of our lineage *many millions of years ago.*

(c) The selective pressure causing our loss of body hair must have worked in one way; that is, in only one direction, for many millions of years, and it kept working in that way until the last great Pleistocene glaciation. Were this not so, body hair would have been adaptively reacquired during the evolution of our lineage, because this is a very useful character, deeply fixed in our genoma, and because humans still show polymorphism and a great phenotypic variation in this character. If, for a long period in the evolution of our lineage, *diminution* of this selective pressure was present; and if, moreover, the existing selective pressures to have all of the skin covered with hair (which would bring down the number of deaths caused by insect-transmitted diseases, as well as from skin infections caused by insect attacks; protection against abrupt changes in temperatures, and so forth), body hair would have very soon been adaptively reacquired by our ancestors, just as it happened, independently; that is, in parallel, during the last 2 or 3 million years of evolution in *all* of the lineages of the living pongids, due to the huge probability connected with its recovery. If modern-day humans did not use clothing, and because our present diet includes food of animal origin, we would currently have great selective pressure to recover our body hair.

At this point I would like to indicate the following to those researchers who, based on the fact that living pongids have sparse body hair, theorize that pongids are now losing their body hair and perhaps suspect that all these apes descend from naked graincollectors and which then reacquired their body hair through evolutionary reversal:

Seven-month-old chimpanzee fetuses show copious hair on the head and not on the rest of their body (Schultz, 1969). All newborn pongids show more hair on the head than on any other part of the body. All this makes us believe that living pongids descend from beings with a head of hair and a hairless body.

A selective pressure that would explain a *gradual* loss of body hair during the evolution of the respective lineages of the living pongids does not exist. It is illogical to believe that the orangutan and the African pongids, who are phylogenetically so distant, are at the same stage in their "*gradual*" body hair loss at this time in their evolution. And in the case of humans (without taking into consideration at this moment that pongids, like humans, also descend from graincollectors), we can categorically affirm that the loss of body hair was not gradual, but punctuated (Eldredge and Gould, 1972) in the evolution of their lineage (see below).

(d) The change from obtaining vitamin D through feeding on insects and meat to obtaining it through synthesis in the skin was an abrupt and sudden change, not a gradual one. If it had been gradual, our ancestors' skin would have adapted, step by step, through cumulative selection, and would have become a more efficient synthesizer of vitamin D. The evolutionary need of losing *all* body hair would not have been present. Maybe the diminution of hair length would have been enough, just as happened in the Equidae lineages. The equines that live in the North Temperate Zone, for example, develop thick and long hair during winter, and shed it in summer, keeping only a fine and short layer that allows enough solar rays to reach their skin. In similar

73

manner, it would not have been adaptively necessary (in this theoretical scenario that did not occur) for the human ancestors to thicken their thermo-insulative subcutaneous fat layers to provide a *substitute* for the insulation given by body hair.

But in the evolution of our lineage *two* other circumstances took place that forced our ancestors adaptively to lose all their body hair.

First, a bipedal mammal, because of its verticality, exposes a lot less skin area to the direct action of those solar rays that fall in a direction close to the vertical of a place. Besides, the morning solar rays, as well as the afternoon ones, due to their great slope, go through a very thick layer of atmosphere. Therefore, solar energy is trapped in that atmospheric layer, and a very low quantity of solar energy reaches those places during those hours of the day. In other words, the time closer to noon is more important for the reception of solar energy on the skin than the morning or afternoon, since in those times of day, the more oblique solar rays could be equally useful to a quadrupedal or to a bipedal mammal if the atmosphere wouldn't hold solar energy. Therefore, the bipedal mammal needs to expose a greater part of naked skin to the sun if it is to achieve the efficiency of a quadrupedal mammal.

Second, body hair is not only ornamental, but also has other important functions. Therefore, some of these functions had to be adaptively *substituted*, even if only in part. Besides the abovementioned insulative function, another function is the avoidance of insects that attack the skin in the area of the shoulders and back, which are not easily reached with the hands. Then, the graincollector *Ramapithecus* adaptively developed a long head of hair that served to protect those parts of the body when attacked by insects. In this way, it has two advantages: back and shoulders are reached by a good amount of solar rays, and the head of hair is able to act when insects attack (similar in function to the tail and mane of horses). But this head of hair also diminishes some of the skin area around the shoulders and back that is exposed to the solar rays; therefore, *Ramapithecus* adaptively had to bare almost all the body.

Along similar lines, let us now consider the following: The liver of vertebrates is an organ in which, among its many other functions, vitamins are stored, especially in times when food is plentiful—for eventual use in times of scarcity. Vitamin D is found in the liver of all vertebrates: in average quantities in the liver of mammals, but in great quantities in the liver of fish. Vitamin D is also found in great quantities in the fat-body of insects, which, in its function of storing vitamins, is similar to the liver in vertebrates. Insects synthesize great amounts of vitamin D in the fat-body. This shows the great importance that feeding from insects has for the obtention of vitamin D, and the ease with which insectivorous animals obtain it.

Almost all primates are insectivorous, thus obtaining vitamin D. If they hunt or scavenge small herbivorous mammals, they also obtain great quantities of vitamin D from the liver, or simply by eating the meat, although the amount of this vitamin in the meat is lower.

Monogastric mammals which are digesters of cellulose do not eat insects or any other food of animal origin, but obtain vitamin D directly through the synthesis of it in their skin by the action of the sun's ultraviolet rays.

Here, I would like to remind the reader of two things:

First, the suggestion made by Kortlandt (1984) that humans have possibly lost some protozoa infusoria ciliates *(Troglodytella)* from our intestines, which are present in the intestines of the wild African pongids, and that in symbiosis help the host digest cellulose in a similar way as done by many ungulates. Kortlandt indicates, in addition, that these infusoria die and are lost from the intestinal tract when the feeding of pongids in captivity is not the same as that in their wild state, and adds:

> One of the intriguing aspects of chimpanzee and gorilla behaviour, both in the wild and shortly after capture, is their extreme conservatism with regard to unfamiliar food . . . In the late 1950s an IRSAC team at Bukavu in the then Belgian Congo found that adult and subadult gorillas captured some 150 km away on the other side of the ridge tended to starve to death rather than accept the kinds of food eaten by the gorillas living in the forests around Bukavu (U. Rahm, personal communication). (Kortlandt, 1984: 158)

Second, let us take note of what Milton (1984) and Stahl (1984) say. Milton (1984: 160, 161) states:

> Many monogastric animals, including humans, have cellulolytic organisms in the gut (caecum and colon) that can degrade some cellulose (e.g., cabbage) (and hemicellulose) quite efficiently.

Stahl (1984: 163, 164) states:

> Studies of nonruminant species have shown that considerable bacterial digestion may occur in the caecum or colon . . . and, as Milton points out, some microbial digestion of plant structural carbohydrates does appear to take place in the human colon (Van Soest et al. 1978). Van Soest (1982: 199) *suggests that the sacculated nature of the human colon may be indicative of an evolutionary adaptation to a degree of fibrousness in the diet.* . . . (Italics mine)

We can assume that *Ramapithecus*, when quadrupedal and a part-time seed-eater, during winter was omnivorous or was partially insectivorous; during summer, when grasses were plentiful, he could depend exclusively on grass seeds—that is: he would behave as an omnivorous during winter, and as a seed-eater *digester of cellulose* during summer. This would be closely comparable to the European wild boar *(Sus scrofa)*, which changes diet during those times of the year (Frädrich, 1972). (This Old-World pig has a digestive system, a tendency to store fat in its body, and skin somewhat similar to those of humans.) Therefore, during winter and before becoming a graincollector, *Ramapithecus* ate insects, larvae, eggs, worms, and small animals, in addition to vegetables such as rhizomes and other roots, due to the lack of seeds and blades. He would, during winter, lose his intestinal cellulolytic organisms, but would store enough vitamin D in his liver to cover his needs of this vitamin during summer. In summer, he would reacquire that intestinal flora and fauna, maybe by eating equine manure, since we can assume that at that time of the year the grazing migrations of ungulates would pass by the savannas and woodlands where *Ramapithecus* lived a sedentary life. Then, in summer, his feeding behavior would be very conservative as a part time seed-eater cellulose digester. Due to those seasonal changes in his digestion, he was able to keep all of his body hair, since it was not necessary to synthesize vitamin D through his skin.

If *Ramapithecus*, when quadrupedal and a part-time seed-eater, was not seasonally omnivorous and a seasonal digester of cellulose, as hypothesized above, we can assume that year-round he had a diet similar to that of the living gelada baboons, which includes insectivorism (Iwamoto, 1979). Therefore, he could obtain through this diet all requirements of vitamin D and, like the geladas, would be able to keep all his body hair.

By suddenly turning into a migratory graincollector and tool-user, and by depending only on seeds for his nourishment all year round, he must *always* keep his cellulose-digesting intestinal flora and fauna. He must then be conservative in his feeding habits all year round, as the gorilla currently is. Then, he stopped the seasonal omnivorism or the continuous partial insectivorism. If we suppose that *Ramapithecus*, when quadrupedal and part-time seed-eater, had a continuous diet that included insects, similar to that of the living gelada baboons, we have to suppose too that, when he became a migrating graincollector, he was now unable to get the insects he was used to and was adapted to eat. Therefore, vitamin D now must be synthesized through his skin, but his skin was quite inefficient for this activity, since never before in the evolution of his lineage had this selective pressure been present. Due to the inefficiency of his skin in synthesizing vitamin D from the action of the solar rays, and due to the rapid change of niche caused by the rapid change of behavior, all of his body hair had to be adaptively lost to permit the solar rays to reach his skin and satisfy his vitamin D requirements. Only those individual *Ramapithecus* who quickly lost all body hair and were able to synthesize in their skin the needed amounts of vitamin D would survive as full-time graincollectors. This skin inefficiency makes us believe that *Ramapithecus*, before turning graincollector, had a thick layer of hair and depended almost totally on a vegetarian and *seasonally* omnivorous diet, or on a continuous vegetarian–partially insectivorous diet.

The vegetarian-*seasonal*-omnivorous diet previously mentioned is not speculative or "forced" so as to fit the theory of graincollection. It is a fact that the diet of many terrestrial mammal species is different during the dry season or winter from its wet season or summer diet. It is also a fact that some mammals, like the European brown bears of Scandinavia and Russia, the Kodiak bears, the Kamchatkan bears, and other mammals, like the European wild boar, can be omnivorous (mainly carnivorous) some time of the year, becoming vegetarian cellulose digesters the other time. (Generally, these mammals have a great tendency to store fat in their bodies in order to have reserves for those times of the year when they are omnivorous-carnivorous.) What has happened up to now is that those peculiarities haven't been highlighted. The fact that special intestinal flora and fauna are needed in order to digest cellulose has not been highlighted either, nor that these special flora and fauna can sometimes be lost when changing diets, and that it can also be reacquired. Additionally, there is the fact that in the same individual animal, the digestive system works differently when digesting an omnivorous diet compared to a cellulose diet.

Mammals capable of digesting both types of diet do not do it efficiently during the season when they are pure cellulose digesters. Furthermore, *they cannot digest in both ways at the same time*, since they need several days to reestablish their cellulose-digesting intestinal flora and fauna lost during the omnivorous period. The time needed by each individual to recover intestinal flora and fauna can be quite different; it depends on the animal species and the feeding conditions of the individual before trying to recover it by eating dung or manure of healthy cellulose-digesting ungulates since, according to those previous diet conditions, their stomach acids might prevent ingested flora and fauna from reaching the intestine alive. During the time of the year when they are cellulose digesters they have to be very conservative in their feeding habits.

Mountain gorillas, in the wild, are digesters of cellulose, and when their diet is similar to that of the equines, their excrement is very similar to that of horses: Schaller (1963) points out the huge similarity in constitution, lobular form, and smell of the dung of wild mountain gorillas and horse manure. However, these same gorillas in captivity become omnivorous like current humans, and their excrement is the same as of humans.

The gorilla's digestive system is very similar to that of humans, even though we know that in the wild they are *almost* exclusively vegetarians, and digesters of cellulose, while humans are omnivorous. From the foregoing we see that, like humans, gorillas *can be digesters of cellulose or omnivorous, but not at the same time.*

Some researchers would object that some vitamins, for example B_{12}, can only be obtained by eating food of animal origin, and that this vitamin is essential for the health of gorillas as well as humans. I believe that once having in the intestines the infusoria ciliates *Troglodytella*, like the wild gorilla has, all needed vitamins can be obtained from pure granivorism, even B_{12}. In support of the aforementioned, I will quote Kortlandt (1984: 160), who states:

Troglodytella: Possibly a symbiont of early hominids? Another intriguing matter is that of two ciliates that live mainly attached to the mucous membranes of the caecum and the large intestine of wild-living chimpanzees and gorillas, *Troglodytella abrassarti* and *T. gorillae* respectively (Richenow 1920). These infusoria ingest and digest chiefly cellulose and some protozoa, reproduce quite rapidly, and are digested by the host while they are still in the intestine. Richenow inferred that they probably had a symbiotic function by converting cellulose into what he called "animal food for a vegetarian that requires nutrients of animal origin." This function would be similar to the digestive processes performed by similar ciliates in the stomachs and intestines of many hoofed mammals. However, after capture of young chimpanzees and gorillas from the wild, the intestinal ciliates soon die as a rule, apparently owing to the new food (usually bananas and boiled rice). Unfortunately, in 63 years since Richenow's paper, no further research seems to have been done on this issue (Kortlandt n.d.; R. A. Prins, personal communication).

Then, my assumptions regarding the feeding behavior of *Ramapithecus* are not extraordinary nor artificial, but very probable.

Let us now consider the European Wild Boar (*Sus scrofa*) as a model. It is not easy to find a wild living mammal that has adaptively and *rapidly* lost all body hair, similar to how I assume *Ramapithecus* did—and in addition also has similar feeding habits, similar skin, similar digestive system, and is capable of storing fat reserves in his body, similar to humans, and therefore, might be similar to the first hominids. Possibly the European wild boar is not useful as a model, since man has enormously interfered in his recent evolution; making it difficult to determine up to what point this interference may have been favorable to what I am trying to demonstrate. In my opinion, all seems to have been favorable to the model I offer, since it seems that when selecting breeding hogs (which are descendants of the European wild boar) it hasn't been important to breeders whether hogs have more body hair or less body hair. Instead, they are interested in the amount of meat and lard hogs are able to produce at the lowest possible cost. If, in the past, pig breeders selected breeding hogs due to their scarce body hair, big ears, and lighter color of skin, then this model would not be valid.

Frädrich (1972: 76) states:

Among the present nonruminants, the pig-like mammals (superfamily Suoidea) are the oldest and the most primitive even-toed ungulates. Most of the species have teeth characteristic of omnivorous animals. Their menu is extremely varied. They eat the parts of plants under ground as well as grass, leaves, sprouts, fallen fruit, seeds, juicy herbs, and mushrooms . . . *Depending on the season*, they may also become carnivorous. Then they will eat worms, the larvae of insects, eggs and young birds, snakes, lizards, and small rodents. They may even attack injured and disabled larger mammals *and eat carcasses.* (Italics mine)

Their complete diet resembles the current human omnivorous diet, except for the great amounts of grass and leaves that the wild boars are able to eat under a cellulose-digesting diet.

I emphasized "depending on the season" to point out that both diets, omnivorous and cellulose-digesting, cannot be mixed, and that wild boars do not mix them. I also emphasized "and eat carcasses" to indicate that wild boars feed themselves in a similar way to current humans, and in addition, they are normally scavengers; but they return, seasonally, to cellulose digestion.

(Hominids of the Pliocene and Pleistocene, already tool manufacturers, that resorted to scavenging during unusual times of extreme drought or other abnormal conditions, could also return to cellulose digestion.)

The wild boar has a thick, coarse, and dense layer of hair, has ears that are short and erect, and the color of his skin is generally dark. From the time in which the domesticity of pigs began up until now, they tended, adaptively, to have scarce body hair, big ears, and lighter skin colors.

Past pig breeders (not current ones, since these use very modern techniques in breeding, and feed pigs with vitamins and minerals; also with blood, meat and bone meal from slaughterhouses) used to feed the pigs with grains, grass, and other vegetables, *since, commonly, people believed, and many still do, that pigs are exclusively vegetarians,* and wouldn't provide them food of animal origin that would directly provide them with vitamin D, nor would the pigs be given foraging opportunities. Therefore, pigs were susceptible to rachitis, and they did in fact suffer from it. But in the past, pigs were allowed to live in pens where they were exposed to the sun; nowadays, they are often confined to closed buildings where the sun can't reach their skin. Therefore, in the past, pigs could live exclusively as cellulose digesters; but this might only have happened at the beginning of their domesticity when it was possible to allow them to reacquire their *natural* intestinal flora and fauna. As those pigs were taken away from their place of origin and transported to faraway places, they were no longer able to reacquire their natural intestinal flora and fauna, but were capable of living only as omnivorous, eating a variety of unfamiliar vegetables, but not food of animal origin that they used to look for on their own and eat in the wild. Therefore, due to strong selective pressure, the pigs that remained healthy, spared from rachitis, were those who rapidly adapted to obtain vitamin D in some other way, that is: through the synthesis in their skin. *When eating gramineous seeds and the fungus (yeast) that these seeds very often have between the seed and the glumes and glumellas,* the pigs would obtain ergosterol, needed for vitamin D, along with the action of solar rays upon their skin *(just as was true of the graincollector hominids).*

In the obtention of vitamin D through their skin, their skin had the same functions as if they were *exclusively* year-round vegetarian cellulose digesters, even though also forced to eat unfamiliar vegetables.

If the pig breeder selected the heaviest and strongest hogs as studs and mothers, they absolutely weren't those suffering from rachitis, since those would be unable to carry their own huge weight on their very weak legs. Rachitis is still one of the main causes of death among suckling pigs, and of rejection as possible studs or future mothers. In the past this was the cause of great losses in the pig breeding business. Many breeding texts still recommend to exposing pigs to the sun to keep them healthy and prevent rachitis.

The pigs that did not suffer from rachitis were those who received a great amount of solar rays on their skin and better synthesized vitamin D in it—that is, those with less body hair, lighter skin color (meaning more efficiency in synthesizing vitamin D), and bigger ears (meaning a wider skin area exposed to solar rays).

The constant practice of this type of selection caused a quick loss of body hair during the recent evolution in the lineages of domestic pigs, maybe even faster than the loss of body hair suffered by *Ramapithecus* when they became graincollectors.

Assuredly, then, the artificial selection of pigs by humans was not focused on choosing them based on their lack of hair, light-colored skin, and bigger ears. It would not have been probable that precisely these three characters, all related to vitamin D synthesis, were chosen by *all* pig breeders: Instead, all pig breeders, when choosing the heaviest hogs with the strongest legs as studs and mothers, were unconsciously selecting those characters that would have been selected by natural selection if all the individuals of a European wild boar population had had to survive in a new niche exclusively as cellulose digesters.

Let's not forget that Darwin thought that humans and living pongids descend from beings with *big* and pointed ears, since six-month-old fetuses of all these species show big and pointed ears; and also because " . . . a little blunt point, projecting from the inwardly folded margin, or helix" (Darwin, 1871: 22) is shown in the ears of many individuals of those same species. He believed this to be vestigial. Perhaps Darwin was right, and *Ramapithecus* adaptively enlarged his ears and lightened his skin, besides losing his body hair when he turned graincollector and exclusive cellulose digester, just as the current domestic pig has adaptively evolved owing to a very similar cause. Later in their evolution, hominids lost their large ears character.

All of the above can support the belief that living pongids and humans descend from the naked graincollector *Ramapithecus*, and that living pongids have reacquired their body hair through evolutionary reversion. This can also explain why they have scarce body hair, and all of them have, more or less, the same amounts (depending on the zone in which they live). It explains why gorillas can survive almost without eating animal food, and why their eating habits are so conservative in the wild. It explains why gorillas sunbathe for so many hours in a habitat in which solar rays generally don't even reach the ground due to the shade and foliage of trees; and why they especially expose chest and stomach to the solar rays (Schaller, 1963)—these being the body parts with the least hair. It can also explain why infant pongids are born with copious hair on their head, and little on their body.

Regarding cellulose digestion by humans and by living pongids, it may seem strange that after 14 million years of digesting cellulose (I should say starch and cellulose) during the evolution of our respective lineages, we, as well as the pongids, should be such inefficient digesters of it, i.e., that our digestive system isn't better adapted for that type of digestion. I believe we are inefficient cellulose digesters compared, for example, with equines, because our ancestors looked for the nutritious seeds of grasses and ate little cellulose and hemicellulose. At any rate, we should not be surprised that after digesting cellulose for so many millions of years, we should be so inefficient in that function. While it is true that equines are better cellulose digesters than we are, they are very inefficient compared with other ungulates, despite the fact that in their evolution, cellulose digestion evolved some 40 million years ago. I believe that the reason for their inefficiency is similar to that of our inefficiency. When migrating, they, too, look for the nutritious seeds on the long grasses, even though they additionally eat a good portion of the stem.

There are now just two more points. First, the human head of long hair is *very obstructing* when hunting, scavenging, and even when gathering, but very useful in graincollection. Those hominids who developed such an obstructing head of hair must have depended on a very easy way of obtaining their food, in a tranquil environment and were not under the pressure of possible attacks by predators, or fights when competing with them. Second, all—absolutely all—animals in their natural habitat and niche are very beautiful. We can picture ourselves beautiful as tool-user graincollectors, and revolting as hunters or scavengers: dirty hands, face, and hair, and adult males with beard and mustache, caked with the grease and blood of animals. Is not this an indication that our real nature is that of graincollectors? *Why can we feel so touched by the beauty of all animals in their natural ecological niche and environment, and not by our own?*

3. Prolonged Maternal Dependency (Prolonged Childhood)

There is a tendency in all primates for a delayed development of infants. Gould (1977: 399, 400, 439) states:

Mann (1975) has now presented evidence for the third element from his studies of dental eruption and skeletal maturation in South African australopithecines—these primitive hominids had already evolved an extended childhood. . . . To begin with, we [humans] belong to a class of animals in which K selection dominates (Pianka, 1970). We evolved in the generally K-selective tropical regime. We belong to an order of mammals distinguished by their propensity for repeated single births, intense parental care, long life spans, late maturation, and a high degree of socialization—a point-for-point agreement with Pianka's listing of traits common to *K* strategists (1970).

Human evolution has emphasized one feature of this common primate heritage—delayed development, particularly as expressed in late maturation and extended childhood. . . . Schultz (1948) recorded the prevalence of single births among primate species. He related this tendency to the difficulty of carrying several large offspring about in trees. Haldane (1932) argued that single births strongly favored (or at least permitted) delayed development since uterine competition among several growing offspring would favor accelerated development.

Compared with other mammal species, the period of time from the start of intrauterine life up until weaning is long in primates; infant maternal dependency is prolonged in all these species. Among them, in Hominoidea, maternal dependency is the greatest; and in humans, is of longest duration.

This important character of all living pongids and humans, different as it is from all other primates, and especially from all other mammal species, may be regarded as *exceptional*.

The theories that assume humans descend from hunter-gatherers or from scavenger-gatherers fail to give a satisfactory explanation for the appearance of this prolonged maternal dependency *in living pongids and humans*. We cannot accept the arguments that are advanced that explain this phenomenon due to the fact that those hominoids assumed in those theories to be the ancestors of the first hominids (hominoids similar to the African pongids), already present it. These theories must be rejected as the explanation we are seeking, since they only postpone the problem: It must now be explained why those *ancestral hominoids* already present prolonged maternal dependency.

Because this extended childhood in humans and living pongids cannot be satisfactorily explained with hunting-gathering nor with scavenging-gathering theories, proponents resort to a very weak argument based on the increase of sociality (increasingly complex intraspecific social relations) that we see in the different primate species, in the degree in which these species ascend the primatological scale.

Let us try to investigate the origin of prolonged maternal dependency in the lineage of the common ancestor of all living hominoids.

Simons (1976: 522) states:

It has long been stressed that some *Ramapithecus* show in their molar anatomy that eruption times of the molars were spaced out, so that differential wear on them occurs. This same phenomenon has been noted for *Australopithecus* and primitive *Homo* . . . What is more important, even, than this similarity of *Ramapithecus* molars to those of later hominids, is that early *Dryopithecus* does not show to the same degree differential wear between adjacent molars.

Leakey and Lewin (1978: 38) state:

The fact that [in *Ramapithecus*] there is a noticeable difference in the amount of grinding down inflicted on the teeth means that there must be a significant lapse of time between the appearance of the first and second, and the second and third molars. And this means a prolonged childhood—we think.

It is a fact generally accepted among anthropologists and paleoanthropologists that the differential wear resulting from a delayed eruption of successive molars, observed in the fossil jaws and maxillars found and attributed to hominids and to other hominoids, is evidence of a prolonged childhood (Simons, 1972: 273, 274; Simons, 1976: 523). Some other researchers doubt it. Wolpoff (1982: 502) says:

The evidence for steep molar wear gradient in *Ramapithecus* was questioned (Greenfield 1974), and in any event the presence of steep gradients in primate species without delayed maturation had already been shown (Mann 1968, Wolpoff 1971b).

But we have the task of explaining the origin of the prolonged childhood *that we are witnessing* in living pongids and humans.

The fact that those fossil maxillars and jaws of *Ramapithecus*, *Australopithecus*, and the current ones of living pongids and humans have the steep molar wear gradient (Simons, 1972, 1976), makes us suspect that their lineages are phylogenetically related to each other, because such a prolonged childhood as *living pongids and humans present* is very rare in animal evolution, and *must have only one origin*. As we know that all these living species have the steep molar wear gradient attributed to their prolonged childhood, then most probably that steep molar wear gradient really is evidence of a prolonged childhood in *Ramapithecus* and *Australopithecus*.

How can we explain the origin of prolonged childhood in all living Hominoidea? It cannot be explained with the increased sociality argument *alone,* as has been done up until now: To ascribe it to an increase in sociality is partially true if we observe that this period of maternal dependency increases from the so-called lower primates up to higher primates and man. The general explanation based on the argument that accompanying an ascent of the primatological scale the intraspecific social relations turn more complex is quite acceptable. The infant must learn more before being able to conduct an independent social life. But I would like to highlight the following: a more complex sociality is not the only direct and proximate cause of an increase on maternal dependency, *since a change in the usual way of getting food (as I assume happened when Ramapithecus turned grain-collectors) causes an increase or decrease of maternal dependency; but, independently, the intraspecific social relations can become more complex or less complex with this change.* That is because there is no cause–effect relationship between the fact that due to the new way of acquiring food, and the fact that the infant depends more, or depends less, on its mother, the effect of a proportional increase or decrease of the sociality, equal to the increase or decrease of maternal dependency, would unavoidably arise. Also, there is the fact that if there is an ascent in the primatological scale, that would not necessarily mean that those intraspecific social relations must become more complex. Thus, the period of maternal dependency is slightly related with sociality.

From the abovementioned, and from what was stated by Shultz and by Haldane, quoted by Gould (1977: 439) concerning " . . . the difficulty of carrying several large offspring about in trees," and that " . . . single births strongly favored (or at least permitted) delayed development . . . " we can deduce that *it was arboreal life and not sociality* that caused the *original* prolonged maternal dependency in primates, and this is the basis of the *preadaptation* that allowed maternal dependency to increase. Thus, if the mother devotes all her efforts to only one infant from the time of conception up until a delayed weaning, then, her infant and herself are adapted to this dependency. As a result of that absolute devotion to the infant, the infant can depend on its mother for *longer* periods of time *if adaptively necessary,* and can learn more from her, especially if there is a noticeable change of feeding behavior in the individuals of the population they belong to—change that can provoke a change of niche and habitat in that population. The infant can spend more time with its mother if the new way of acquiring food demands it; that is, infant dependency on the mother can easily increase, since she is exclusively devoted to her *one infant*, rather than because of an increase in the complexity of social relations.

Nomadic and semi-migratory life was possible when some arboreal primates adaptively acquired more terrestrial habits, *thanks to the preadaptation of mothers always to carry their infant with them.* This caused maternal dependency to increase, or at least be maintained. However, having nothing more than these facts, we still cannot say with certainty if the period of maternal dependency increased due to the change in subsistence strategies or due to an increase in sociality, since, due to the acquisition of more terrestrial habits, social relations did in fact become more complex and maternal dependency also increased.

Let us compare prolonged maternal dependency of baboons with that of African pongids, because of their similar terrestrial habits.

A great and noticeable difference in maternal dependency is found between baboons and living apes, since in baboons it lasts half as long as in apes. Intraspecific social relations in the majority of baboon species are not very different or less complex than the intraspecific social relations in all living Hominoidea species; except, of course, in humans. To assume that humans, when infants, receive more teaching than olive baboons before their independent life is logical if we look at a present-day child's socialization and all that it has to learn; but the infant gorilla and chimpanzee do not seem to have to socialize and learn more than the infant baboon in order to live independently. However, the period of maternal dependency of those pongids is between 4 and 5 years, and sometimes more, and that of baboons is a maximum of 2 to 2.5 years.

The duration of maternal dependency also seems *not* to be related to the complexity of cerebral activities, since baboons and African pongids greatly differ as to the period of dependency but do not differ in cerebral activities (referring here to the *cerebral activities they utilize in their current way of living in the wild,* not to artificial training, since, in this respect, as well as because living pongids descend from skilled tool-users, they greatly surpass baboons).

Leakey and Lewin (1978: 149–150) state:

> You only have to spend a morning quietly watching a troop of *chimps or baboons* to realize what a complex business group living is . . . consort pairs attentively groom; adult males vie with each other for the attentions of a female just coming into estrus; other males challenge each other for social status; mothers keep watch over their frolicking offspring; alliances form between brothers or between "friends" in order to gain an unbeatable advantage over a temporary adversary. The scene is complex, indeed, and much more so than meets the eye. (Italics mine)

Baboon troops, at any time of year, especially when food is plentiful, have more members than gorilla and chimpanzee troops, and their habits are equally terrestrial. Gorillas and chimpanzees do not have predators due to the fact that they are skilled tool-users and can wield branches or sticks, and in this way drive predators away; but baboons do have predators. Baboons present cooperative behavior, not only as a defense against predators, but also when they are the predators and they hunt (Strum, 1981; R. S. O. Harding, mentioned by Strum). In the hunts they behave similarly to chimpanzees. Defense of the whole population, daily walks, formations and assemblies are more complex and strict in baboons than in gorillas and chimpanzees. DeVore and Washburn (1963) have indicated that baboons would not survive isolated from their troop or in small groups the way gorillas and chimpanzees can. Social ties in baboons are of vital importance, since they not only have the natural goal of forming animal attachments, but also of facing the great challenges and dangers to which they are exposed; dangers and challenges that are greater than those the gorilla and chimpanzee face. In brief: baboons are extremely sociable and extremely dependent on their societies.

On the other hand, the skilled tool-using of the African pongids has no relation with their sociality. Currently, infant pongids do not have to learn to use tools to survive, and adults incidentally use tools in the wild. Therefore, if we accept as true the idea that by ascending the primatological scale sociality increases, and as a result the period of maternal dependency also increases, we can conclude that in the abovementioned case something is incongruent and a paradox is present, since it would be expected that maternal dependency among baboons would be even greater than in pongids, and not the other way around.

All the abovementioned supports our belief that it is not valid to explain the increase of maternal dependency in primates with the increase of sociality as a foundation; therefore, in order to explain each increment in the period of maternal dependency, and in each particular case, we must look for the change of life-style—*mainly the feeding behavior*—that triggered it; specially when we find a great increase in the duration of that period, since, in this case it would necessarily be a result of noticeable changes in feeding habits.

Pongids are genetically endowed with a long period of maternal dependency, and this is a character that currently has no functional or survival value for them, but instead is a bother: there is no current visible selective pressure that demands it.

In light of what we have seen up to now, and because prolonged childhood is genetically inherited in all living pongids and in humans, we must accept that even though currently the orangutan, the gorilla, and the chimpanzee do not have the selective pressure for a prolonged childhood, their common ancestor did have it. If living pongids are genetically endowed with a prolonged childhood very different from that of all other nonhuman primates, and if it is a character not directly related to sociality and to complex cerebral activities, we can suspect that their ancestors, when infants, were not able to get food on their own for many years, depending on their mother for that. And we can suspect that it was the same selective pressure that gave origin to such an extended childhood in *Ramapithecus* and *Australopithecus*; then, the common ancestor of living pongids and humans is unavoidably among them, since it is erroneous to imagine that such a rare character in all mammals, and particularly in all primates, appeared *independently*, due to similar or different causes, *during the evolution of each one of the lineages of the living Hominoidea.*

Mayr (1974: 651) states:

We can ask what differences exist between genetic programs responsible for behaviors formerly called innate and those considered as experientially acquired. A genetic program which does not allow appreciable modifications during the process of translation into the phenotype I call a *closed program*—closed because nothing can be inserted in it through experience. Such closed programs are widespread among the so-called lower animals. A genetic program which allows for additional input during the lifespan of its owner I call an *open program* . . . (Emphasis author's)

If we do not assume that a common ancestor to all living pongids already had the prolonged childhood character genetically programmed as a *closed program*, that is now evolving to the opening phase in all species due to the present lack of that selective pressure that originated and maintained it for millions of years, then we must assume something illogical: that this character is evolving *at the same time, and that it is now in the same stage of evolutionary development* in each species and in all the species of living pongids, including the orangutan that is phylogenetically so separated from the African pongids. It is illogical to assume that for the different stimuli that each species now receives, according to the different life-styles and selective pressures they undergo, there is only one and the same adaptive response, and this response is now evolving *simultaneously* in all species. Why the same adaptive response? Why simultaneously? Why are *all* the living pongid species at present in the same stage of evolutionary development of this character, *without any visible common selective pressure to generate it*?

As we have seen, because primate females give birth to only one infant and carry it during all of its dependent childhood, baboons were able to develop new nomadic or semi-migratory habits; that is, all the troop, including infants, would stroll during the day in search of food in a not very wide geographical area similarly to the way gorillas and chimpanzees now do in other habitats.

This same semi-migratory or nomadic habit of current baboons can be assumed in *Ramapithecus*, and it may be seen as a preadaptation to graincollection, since, without this preadaptation, the human ancestors would have never turned into migratory graincollectors. Their transition from part-time seed-eaters, sedentary in reduced geographical areas, to full-time seed-eaters, migratory in wider geographical areas could only have occurred if the mothers were adapted to carry their infant while this infant depended on its mother for nourishment, and for an even longer period of time than their ancestors had when arboreals, because the period of maternal dependency would be *even greater* in the graincollecting populations than in part-time seed-eater populations, since the infant cannot be separated from its mother until it is able to graincollect on its own. This is because it cannot depend, even partially, on other types of food as it did before, since they were now migratory grazers, and in their new habitat there wasn't a sufficient variety of food, inasmuch as the mothers only looked for seeds in good quality grasses. There was not much food to choose from within the infants' reach in the long-grass grasslands. Furthermore, since they were now exclusively cellulose digesters, infants learned from their mothers to be very careful and conservative in their feeding habits (just as infant and adult gorillas currently are). They were excluded from varying their type of food intake—being confined to breast milk and the seeds given to them by their mothers, whether in their natural state, or already chewed by her: maternal dependency was then complete and very prolonged.

I would like to highlight the difficulty for infants, not only in learning the use of the grainthresher, *but, above all, I want to highlight the great difficulty for a small infant to survive independently in the long-grass grasslands.* The infant might have been able to learn about and to use the grainthresher, but the grasses of the savanna in which the graincollector tribes thrived were long, and the infant, though able to reach the seeds with its hands, would not have been capable of pulling them off while holding the tool in one hand, since it would have to make a horizontal movement when pulling the seeds with that hand (assuming that this is not yet a tall infant), and it would have to take one or two steps backwards or sideways. If it used one hand to hold the stem while holding the tool and scraping the stem with the other hand, he would cut or scrape the seeds without making that horizontal movement, and would gradually injure the hand that held the stem. Furthermore, for the infant it was a much more difficult operation to execute than the one done by the mother, because she scraped or cut the seeds with the grainthresher in one hand, and moved this hand *upwards. But the real problem for the bipedal and small infant wasn't graincollecting, but walking in the long-grass savanna*—first, because his head couldn't rise above the grass and he was not able to see his surroundings; and second, because the stems, blades, seeds, spikes, spikelets, awns, etc., of the grasses, were hitting his face and getting tangled in his hair as he walked. The infant may have walked a few steps protecting his face with his hands and arms, but he couldn't do this all day long during the unceasing grazers' migration, not to mention the great enjoyment of looking around and satisfying his curiosity, having direct contact with adults, and receiving the necessary feedback to learn to make an independent life for himself later on. Even newborn equines' heads reach above the long grasses, so that they are able to see all of their surroundings, and their faces and eyes are not hurt by the blows of blades, seeds, spikes, etc. Like humans, equines migrate at the head of the grazers' successions, and, by means of their feeding action, improve the access to the long-grass grasslands to other smaller grazer ungulates that follow them in those successions (Bell, 1971; McNaughton, 1976).

All of this goes to show that the infant had to have a certain minimum height in order to graincollect with one hand and pull up the seeds in each action, and also to be able to lift his head above the grasses and see his surroundings.

It can be concluded that the increase in the period of maternal dependency in protohominids when they turned graincollectors was not related to an increase in the complexity of their social relations, since we can't believe that their social relations would become more complex as a result of wider migrations. It is not valid to think that complete migratory habits, developed out of semi-migratory nomadic habits, would cause an increase in maternal dependency. In other grazer mammals with migratory habits, these habits have not been seen to exert the selective pressure for them to acquire more complex social relations. Nor is it plausible that an increase in the complexity of social relations is attributable to the use of one tool for obtaining their food, since it is seen that in other unskilled (beginner) tool-user animals, tool-using has *not* caused an increase in the complexity of their social relations. It is, however, probable that with respect to these unskilled tool-users, and more so with the skilled (expert) tool-users, learning to use tools would have brought about a *small* increase in maternal dependency. Owing to this, their childhood could have been extended until they mastered the use of the tool. *But it is even more probable that such dependency had enormously increased in early graincollector hominids due to the fact that the small infant was unable to walk in the long-grass grasslands, and had to be transported and fed by his mother until he was tall enough for his head to come above the grasses.* Thus, it may be seen that prolonged childhood was a need and a functional character within the context of perpetual migrations by the graincollectors in those long-grass grasslands.

The question now arises: Why was it specifically graincollection, rather than gathering, hunting-gathering, or scavenging-gathering that caused such prolonged maternal dependency?

It is obvious that maternal dependency has genetic bases. *Ramapithecus*, australopithecines, living pongids and humans present this character, which also means that this dependency either has been modified during the evolution of the lineages of each one of the living hominoids or has remained without modifications in their evolution. But we must unavoidably assume an origin; that is, a certain behavioral modification (Mayr, 1976) in a common ancestor that originated the prolonged childhood of hominoids and retain it during their evolution for million of years—that is to say, the selective pressure that originally caused it must have worked and continues to work, starting from the common ancestral hominoid in which it first appeared, until the present-day humans, who are the Hominoidea that exhibit that character even more strongly. Mayr (1976: 106) states:

> A shift into a new niche or adaptive zone requires, almost without exception, a change in behavior . . . It is now quite evident that every habit and behavior has some structural basis but that the evolutionary changes that result from adaptive shifts are often initiated by a change in behavior, to be followed secondarily by a change in structure . . . The new habit often serves as the pacemaker that sets up the selection pressure that shifts the mean of the curve of structural variation.

The prolonged childhood is genetically determined in all living hominoids, *and does not allow* for modifications during the period of translation into the phenotype; this is what Mayr (1974) calls "closed programs"; however, the size of the groups and the more complex or less complex sociality in all primates, and particularly in hominoids, *does allow* for modifications during the life of an individual. Mayr (1974) calls this "open programs." The social organization and the size of groups of primates depends on many factors. (None of the present theories concerning the function of groups explains the social organization and the distribution of the size of those groups in primates [Clutton-Brock and Harvey, 1977] because sociality is not purely determined by maternal dependency, or vice-versa; therefore, we must search for the change of habits that originated the prolonged childhood and made the old genetic program change, and *whose stimuli asked for only one adaptive response.*)

However, the importance of it all lies here: the genetically determined prolonged childhood, which demands only one adaptive response to only one stimulus, *would have been very difficult to develop among omnivorous hominoids* (in the case of hominids I refer to hunter-gatherers or scavenger-gatherers) *since their feeding habits are very flexible and allow for opportunistic adjustments and changes.* Along with that, it may also allow for the modification of their social habits (Clutton-Brock and Harvey, 1977); and, *independently*, allow for the modification of the period of maternal dependency in each one of those opportunistic adjustments and changes. Consequently, prolonged childhood is more likely to develop in those hominoids whose diet is rigidly subject to cellulose digestion and which excludes variations in their feeding habits. Additionally, such hominoids must have a life-style with almost no change in feeding habits because they are very successful in the way they get their food, since the same subsistence strategies and diet had to remain continuous, with no change, for millions of years. That is to say: In those hominoids in which prolonged childhood was developed, the selective pressure that originated it and allowed its continuance had to be invariant, as was the unique adaptive response, throughout the many millions of years of their evolution, because *all* living hominoids present this character.

As mentioned, some anthropologists have accepted the idea that prolonged maternal dependency is caused by cerebral activities (culture, spoken language, complex social relations, etc.). The differences in cerebral activities between humans and pongids are indeed very noticeable and the difference in the period of maternal dependency is also marked. This could justify our acceptance of a relationship between maternal dependency and the development of the brain. But there is another fact that militates against it, and is equally final in its opposition.

In a recent study on the differential wear on molars of several australopithecines, Smith (1986) found that some of them show a childhood almost as prolonged as that of humans, and some others as that of pongids: *A. africanus* and *A. afarensis* tend to present the wear like pongids do, and *A. robustus* and *A. boisei* tend to present it more similarly to humans. Since we cannot assume cerebral activities similar to humans in *A. robustus* and *A. boisei*, then we cannot link maternal dependency to cerebral activities. From what Shipman (1987) states in an article published in *Discover* (a magazine of science and technology for the general reader) about the results found by Smith (1986), we are made aware that a mistake was made in linking them. Shipman (1987: 62) states:

This shows that we've been fooled into linking prolonged immaturity with these brain-related characteristics simply because we possess both.

If we accept that prolonged maternal dependency was caused by graincollection, and based in what Smith (1986) found: *that many fossils of australopithecines show in their teeth that their prolonged childhood was similar to that of humans, and many others show that it was governed by a relaxed genetic program*, we can think that all of them had left graincollection sometime before and were living as gatherers, in the same way pongids are living currently. We cannot say to what degree this character is relaxed in some australopithecines and to what degree in others, since, as mentioned, we do not know how much time has elapsed since each of their respective ancestors abandoned graincollection. We can conclude:

(a) It is much more probable that the much longer duration of maternal dependency of living pongids and humans is due more to their common ancestor's migratory character in the long-grass grasslands, and to the use of tools—that is, to graincollection—and less to an increase in sociality and cerebral activities.

(b) In the existing theories that try to explain the origin of the first tool-user hominids, their ancestry is assumed to comprise hominoids that already show a prolonged childhood. Illogically implicit in such an assumption is a surmise that those ancestors were already graincollector tool-users before giving origin to the first hominid tool-users—otherwise, what other selective pressure could have caused such an enormous period of maternal dependency in Hominoidea?

(c) If humans and living pongids present a prolonged childhood, the selective pressure of graincollection must have acted, without changing, for millions of years during the evolution of the lineage of a common ancestor, and this character could not be present in all living Hominoidea for any other reason. That common ancestor is *Ramapithecus.*

4. Infants' Throne (Steatopygia)

What was the *main* selective pressure that forced protohominids to abandon quadrupedalism and the incipient bipedalism as part-time seed-eaters, and to adopt the perfect bipedalism as full-time seed-eater graincollectors?

Let us consider the following two stimuli:

First: It was easier for the early hominids to pull out seeds from grasses with a natural small stone tool in hand, and to scrape or cut those seeds from the stems by pulling them with an *upward* movement instead of a horizontal one.

Second: While they were walking in a quadrupedal position and carrying a small stone grainthresher in one hand, it was very difficult to support the weight of their body with this hand on the ground while grasping this stone tool; therefore, it was easier to graincollect, eat seeds and walk in a bipedal position than in a quadrupedal position.

However, neither of the two stimuli, nor both of them together, appear to exert sufficient selective pressure that would force early hominids to adopt the insecure and dangerous gait of full-time and perfect bipedalism, since, among many dangers and problems, they had the following: perfect bipedalism makes females *permanently* carry their infant in a different, difficult, and strange way, and not merely during the occasional times when they used bipedalism as part-time seed-eaters.

But why would graincollection demand full-time and absolute bipedalism? Why would *Ramapithecus* need to turn to absolute bipedalism? Might they not have continued being quadrupeds with bipedal abilities the way the gelada baboons are? It doesn't seem very convincing that just by using tools to obtain the same food they obtained before, even if more easily, they would have had to abandon a secure gait used successfully for millions of years—one that would allow females to carry their maturing infant easily on their rump during the already long period of maternal dependency, as is done by the female gelada baboons.

I believe that the proximate and main selective pressure that brought about hominid perfect bipedalism was the same that made childhood a prolonged one: If early hominids were to survive now as migratory grazers, feeding exclusively on gramineous seeds grown in the *long-grass savannas, the adults would not be able to walk through those long grasses in a quadrupedal position, the same way that a small infant couldn't do it in a bipedal position.* When walking in a quadrupedal position adults were not able to see their surroundings, and the long grasses were hitting their face. (We must remember that

96

graincollectors go at the head of the migratory grazers' successions, and that they initiate openings and form the paths through the grasses.) This was the proximate and true cause of hominid bipedalism; the other two abovementioned stimuli were minor contributors in arriving to full-time perfect bipedalism in this abrupt change of behavior.

The transition from quadrupedalism and part-time bipedalism to full-time bipedalism had to be rapid in evolution, since an intermediate gait would have been inefficient and difficult for the protohominids, now inhabitants of and migrants through the long-grass savannas. Lovejoy (1981: 349 [26]) states:

> I have elsewhere pointed out (23, 24) that the resting lengths of the major propulsive muscles about the hip and knee in quadrupedal primates are so substantially altered by the adoption of erect posture that the regular effective use of both quadrupedal and bipedal locomotion is not possible. Thus the transition to bipedality as a habitual mode of locomotion must have been relatively rapid.

Therefore, the transition from an incipient to a permanent bipedalism had to be an evolutionary novelty that we could call punctual evolution (Eldredge and Gould, 1972)—in this case, step by step, by cumulative selection, but *rapid* due to strong selective pressure.

Due to this sudden, permanent, and severe change of behavior, adaptive evolution in protohominids had to find support in several previously existing *preadaptations*—incipient bipedalism and manipulative abilities among many others—since it is not likely that any animal population, due to a sudden and severe change of behavior, will evolve rapidly based only on several new favorable genetic mutations, recombinations, or chromosomal changes.

Let's analyze some other of these important preadaptations. When *Ramapithecus* became full-time biped graincollectors, many new selective pressures appeared:

First, females had to store a lot more fat reserves in their body than they did before in order to nurse an infant who would be heavier than before, since he was going to remain dependent on his mother for many more years. It was going to take him many more years to be able to feed himself using the grainthresher and to walk in the long-grass grasslands. Here was an infant whose childhood was necessarily prolonged in the new adaptive zone, having neither the manual dexterity to graincollect, nor the required height to raise his head above the grasses and see his surroundings. The infant's life-style had suddenly changed: he would now have to depend for seven or eight years on his mother. The mother's life-style had also suddenly changed: she had to breast-feed her infant for those seven or eight years.

Second: worst of all, since they were already *migratory grazers*, the mother had to carry her infant the greater part of the day, every day, during the seven or eight years of his prolonged childhood. This mother, now bipedal, had to carry her infant in her arms; otherwise, the infant would have to cling, holding on to her hair all the time. Neither the mother's hair nor the infant's hands and arms could be equal to this task. Nor was it possible for the mother to carry her heavy infant in her arms for so many years every day while walking in the unceasing grazing migrations. Nor could she have her arms and hands free for graincollecting and eating.

But in the same way nature solves all problems, this one was solved too, by natural selection: Only those infants whose mother (even before discovery of the grainthresher) already had the tendency to develop a greater steatopygia (tendency to accumulate fat on the buttocks) during the times when grains were plentiful would be able to survive and grow to an age when they could feed themselves. Steatopygia could now be greatly developed all year round, since the mother ate grains most or all of the time, in this way guaranteeing the infant's nourishment during prolonged childhood. Moreover, if the steatopygia was big enough, she could also carry him comfortably seated astride it while he held on to her head of hair—not supporting all of his weight, but only that necessary to keep his balance when seated on that *infants' throne* (see plate 1). (That has been my term for steatopygia, since that is its *second* great biological function. I also thought of that name due to the fact that in some dictionaries "steatopygia" is defined as a deformity, an abnormality, or an *excessive* development of fat on the buttocks; and this is a mistake.)

This is why many women even now present this character in a more pronounced way than female gelada baboons.

Also, the infants that survived when protohominids turned grain-collectors were those who could lift their arms above their head and had a strong hand grip, so they could travel partly hanging to their mother's head of hair and not to her body hair, since all body hair in

Plate 1   Graincollectors in the savanna harvesting oats.

early hominids had been adaptively lost, as mentioned in Section 2 of this chapter.

This character of lifting the arms above the head and clinging to the mother's head of hair, acquired by our ancestors when they turned graincollectors, in addition to the pronation-supination of our hands of about 160°, also acquired as an adaptation to the use of the grainthresher, presently confuses us and makes us think that gibbons, pongids, and humans (living Hominoidea) descend from brachiators. Living hominoids do not have this character as a result of the practice of their ancestors of hanging from tree branches and brachiating, since their size and massiveness didn't allow it; neither the actual size of humans nor that of living pongids would allow it. The *common ancestor* to all living Hominoidea left arboreal life 20 or 25 million years ago, and probably he never brachiated, since the hands of his descendants, in this case, would have never been fit for handling tools. Due to the fact that the orangutan now leads a more arboreal life, supporting himself with feet and hands on tree branches (not brachiating), his hands are losing the adaptive shape to handle tools, although he still handles them with dexterity. Gorillas and chimpanzees are more or less in the same stage of losing manual dexterity. Even though all living pongids have a partially arboreal life, none of them is brachiator.

As we have seen, a very useful *preadaptation* so that the mother could carry her infant in a much easier way, leaving her arms free to graincollect when they turned bipedal graincollectors, is steatopygia. Females surely already had this character, even though not very developed, as quadrupedal part-time seed eaters, just like the *Theropithecus gelada* females presently have (Jolly, 1970). The infant, seated astride that infants' throne *and holding onto his mother's head of hair,* could be comfortably transported, while his mother retained her freedom of movement (see plate 2). The long hair on the mother's head probably could also have been a useful preadaptation; or maybe the loss of body hair, suffered when they became full-time seed-eaters, was adaptively substituted with the growth of the head of hair, useful to repel insects and to protect the bare back, besides serving as a handle to her infant. Also, the mother's effort in carrying her infant was minimal. Most probably the only infants who survived were those of bipedal graincollector mothers with steatopygia that gave the infant the seat, and with a long head of hair that gave the infant a handle that the hairless body didn't.

Part-time seed-eater protohominid females can, in fact, have the preadaptative small steatopygia character; then, when becoming graincollectors, it can enlarge adaptively if the selective pressure is suitable; but the protohominid *omnivorous* females cannot have this preadaptation due to the same cause hominid hunter-gatherer females cannot develop steatopygia. That is because it is a character that can only be adaptively developed by those females who need to store food reserves to feed their infant when they are very conservative in their feeding habits (because of the digestion of cellulose) and, due to this, they are rigidly attached to a certain kind of vegetable diet. Specifically, steatopygia can be developed by hominid females who depend all year round on an exclusive diet of gramineous seeds, because those seeds are sometimes abundant and sometimes scarce, depending on the seasons.

If early hominids had been hunter-gatherers, they would have had the opportunity of being flexible in their feeding habits, and could have been *omnivorous the whole year*. They would not have been rigidly attached to a certain kind of vegetable diet, nor have strongly marked periods of food scarcity, because they would have had vegetable food as well as the meat from hunted animals available in the wet season, even though during this time of the year these savanna animals are not easily obtained; and in the dry season, when vegetable food is scarce, they would eat mainly meat, since many animals of the savanna weaken, get sick, and die of natural causes at this time of the year. Therefore, at this time they could easily have obtained carrion or weak animals. In that case hunter-gatherer hominid females would not develop steatopygia, nor the tendency to store fatty tissues in some part of their body. Current hunter-gatherers, even though their survival isn't easy since hunting for humans is very difficult, don't have a life-style with pronounced periods of food scarcity; instead, they have a difficult but stable life-style throughout the year *due to their flexible omnivorous eating habits*.

Therefore, bipedalism and constantly transporting their infant with them is exclusively a character of graincollector hominid females, and not of hunter-gatherers or scavenger-gatherers. Current hunter-gatherer females carry their infant with them in an *sling*, because they descend from graincollectors *and they have that instinct in their genome*, but

Plate 2 Graincollectors on a hill. (When grasses were scarce for some abnormal reason, graincollectors would climb the hills near the open plains where they normally migrated and graincollected. The same grass species that in the open plains has the correct height to allow graincollectors to gather it in an erect posture would, in the hills, grow to a lower height; there, graincollectors had to bend down to reach the seeds. This happened very seldom.)

their steatopygia is now less (it is in the stage of evolutionary regression) due to some 50 thousand years of non-adherence to an exclusively vegetarian granivorous diet, and freedom from the selective pressure that demands and keeps this character.

Some predators in the wild, like some bears and the European wild boar, who during winter are omnivorous, and during summer are exclusive vegetarian digesters of cellulose, have the tendency to store fatty tissues in some parts of the body. If we assume in our ancestors a similar subsistence strategy, we would have to assume that they also changed diets twice a year, depending on the seasons. In this case they would also develop, adaptively, the tendency to store fat in the body; but even though accepting it, many facts would remain without an explanation:

Let us now analyze the *hypothetical* ecological niche of changing diets of our ancestors—the seasonally changing niche of omnivorous feeding—being mainly hunter-scavengers part of the year, and exclusively vegetarian gatherers and digesters of cellulose the rest of the year.

In this niche, our ancestors should feed only on certain kinds of vegetables during the rainy season, and be mainly hunter-scavengers, maybe complemented by insectivorism, during the dry season. Depending on the season, they must change from cellulose digestion to omnivorous digestion.

Here I will repeat and add to some arguments made earlier against the hunting-gathering and the scavenging-gathering theories, to try to demonstrate that this new assumed niche could not have been exploited during hominid evolution.

(a) If early hominids had survived in the changing diets niche right from their origin, they wouldn't have lost their body hair, since they could obtain vitamin D directly from meat (mainly from the ungulates' liver) or from the ingestion of insects, and store it in their liver to be used during those times of the year when they were vegetarians.

(b) When using tools to improve their ability for surviving, their canines would have not been reduced in size, since they were now able to depend more heavily on a carnivorous diet; thus, large canines would be far more useful.

(c) If, due to some unexplained reason, their canines had already been reduced even before they entered this new niche, we must accept that, while tools would be indispensable for hunting and scavenging, they couldn't have been absolutely natural tools, but tools needing to be manufactured with sharp edges. If we assume that early hominids were manufacturers of tools, we must also assume that the ancestors of those early hominids had been exclusively tool-user graincollectors for many millions of years, to be able adaptively to acquire the manual dexterity required to manufacture tools; but in this scenario, when graincollectors, they would have lost their body hair, and would have adaptively reacquired it when turning to the seasonal changing-diets niche.

(d) If, when they were already bipedal inhabitants of the savanna, subsisting from gathering vegetables one part of the year, and from hunting-scavenging the other, they necessarily tended towards knuckle-walking and sedentarism (living and migrating in small geographical areas), and would have end up living in the forests, like orangutans, gorillas, and some chimpanzees; or in the woodlands, like some other chimpanzees; or they could only gather gramineous seeds; that is, they would be graincollectors part of the year, and hunter-scavengers the remaining. But this life-style cannot be accepted as probable among early hominids, since, in order to graincollect, they must go ahead of the grazers' successions, and in order to hunt and scavenge, they must follow those migrant grazers, as proposed by Sinclair et al. (1986); or maybe they would reside semi-permanently in sites this part of the year. These seasonal changes are not probable: either they lived one way or the other—that is, if they were graincollectors part of the year, it would be most probable that they would continue being so all year round; and if they were hunter-scavengers, they would probably be hunter-scavenger-gatherers all year.

Almost all of the abovementioned statements regarding this hypothetical niche have been said in reference to the hunter-gatherer and scavenger-gatherer (full-time omnivorous) niches as well; I presented it in this way because I believe it is more adaptively probable that the hunter-scavenger-gatherer and seasonal vegetarian females would develop steatopygia than the hunter-gatherer or scavenger-gatherer females, precisely because the latter are omnivorous all year round and have opportunistic changes in diet; therefore, they do not have the selective pressure to develop steatopygia. I presented it so, also, because I take as my basis the similarity of diet and the similarity of the fat reserve storage capability in some parts of the body, with the

European wild boar and with some bears, which are adapted to seasonal diet change.

Based on what we've seen so far, neither the changing diets niche nor the hunter-gatherer or scavenger-gatherer niches previously mentioned were ever *normally* exploited during hominid evolution; furthermore, our human characters and those of living pongids show that their respective lineages never went through an evolutionary stage that was developed in any of these niches.

Let us now return to our main topic. If present-day women retain the tendency to develop steatopygia and steatomeria (the latter being the tendency to accumulate fat on thighs and hips), it is because humans are still graincollectors not hunter-gatherers. Gramineous seeds are the food that allows men and women to acquire fat reserves in certain parts of their bodies. This is not just a fortunate coincidence but an adaptation for feeding on gramineous seeds.

The *close* ancestors of the Hottentot (people of Southern Africa: relatives of the !Kung Bushmen) probably were, until recently, exclusively vegetarians and granivorous, since these women still present steatopygia.

The fact that the steatopygia is in the stage of evolutionary regression (decreasing) in all the women of the world is due, among other deficiencies, to the following: to the lack of feeding exclusively from grains and particular kinds of vegetables, to the lack of being exposed to the seasonal periods of scarcity and abundance of this food, to the lack of long daily walks carrying a large infant, to the lack of nursing that infant for seven or eight years, etc. In short, this regression is due to a current lack of selective pressure to keep it. If we were again exclusively granivorous, and if the selective pressure to maintain a true steatopygia could now act on us again, this character would be adaptively reacquired in a few thousand years due to its polymorphism and phenotypic variation within and between populations in all women of the world.

The evolutionary regression of the steatopygia character in all women commenced after the start of the last great Pleistocene glaciation, when our ancestors stopped being graincollectors and turned hunter-gatherers, and therefore, omnivorous; even though, as stated above, many women of different races still decidedly present that character.

Many figurines and sculptures of 20 to 30 thousand years ago, found recently in Europe, show the infants' throne in women—such as the Venus of Willendorf of the Danube Valley in Lower Austria, the Venus of Sireuil in Dordona, a similar figurine found in Savignano, Italy; the Venus of Lespugue of the Upper Paleolithic, and numerous others. Campbell (1974: 398) says regarding these figurines: "Relics of this kind suggest that steatopygia was widespread in Europe in prehistoric times."

Let us now shift our topic to the examination of two human traits: one related to the composition of human milk, and the other related to the salivation of adults—both exclusively connected to graincollector characters.

Blurton-Jones (1972: 315, 316) states:

Within the ungulates for example, milk composition relates closely to whether the species has cached young or following young (with cattle being intermediate). Extremes are found in other groups. For instance in the lagomorphs (rabbits and hares), feeding occurs every twenty-four hours (Zarrow, Denenberg and Anderson, 1965) and they have milk with very high protein and fat content. *Tupaia belangeri* goes even further (Martin, 1968a), feeding every forty-eight hours and having still higher protein and fat content. Higher primates feed nearly continuously, having constant access to the nipple, and they have very low protein and fat content. Human milk is almost identical to that of the other apes, and typical of a continuous feeder in any taxonomic group.

Blurton-Jones (1972) states additionally that this adaptation in the human mother is due to the fact that she has to nurse her baby continuously, and this implies that she cannot leave her infant for a long time, but instead has to carry him always with her. He also says (1972: 317):

Possibly the frequent vomiting and "posseting" of human babies is a result of our insistence on the very early development of a four-hourly schedule rather than the quarter-hour to two-hour interval suggested by comparative data on milk composition, and by the rapid cessation of suckling early in a "meal" . . .

We notice that the human infant must remain for many years by his mother's side depending on her for his nourishment. Thus, mother and infant are adapted to living together for a long time: such infant is already adapted to eating continuously, and his mother is adapted to nursing him continuously. During graincollection, owing to the infant always being by his mother's side, she sometimes feeds him also from the food she eats, whether prechewed or in the condition in which she collects it. The Papua women (people of New Guinea) feed their children mouth to mouth quite often (Markl, 1977). This way of feeding infants must have been very common among graincollectors.

On the other hand, our salivation is *continuous* at all ages; in adults it is very abundant during the day, approximately 1 to 2 liters per day, with a minimum of 0.5 ml. per minute in the absence of stimuli, and almost nonexistent when sleeping.

What I wish to highlight here is that humans are continuous eaters from the time they are born and throughout life. Both abovementioned characters can only be of graincollectors, not of hunter-gatherers or scavengers, since the frequency of feeding in graincollector *infants and adults* was almost constant during the daytime.

Returning now to the topic of the "infants' throne," I will quote Caro (1987: 275):

A third, intriguing hypothesis postulates that pendulous breasts [in women] allow infants to nurse while being carried on the hip (LeBlanc & Barnes, 1974). This is the only hypothesis that does not demand that breasts be a signal to males. The argument states that in bipedal hairless hominids infants cannot use hair to cling to their mothers and are thus carried on the hip. In this position, a pendulous breast gives them the opportunity to nurse on demand . . . Most female mammals exercise strict control over suckling attempts at the time of weaning (e.g., Altmann, 1980). Furthermore, during the period after birth when mothers might well allow infants unlimited nursing, infants would probably be unable to reach the nipple while perched on their mother's hip.

Konner (1972: 288, 289) says:

. . . a [!Kung] woman cannot nurse more than one infant at a time, and in order to grow strong and healthy an infant should nurse for at least two to three years. A mother's only responsibility is to the infant alive and growing, and therefore births must be well spaced. . . . There is some evidence that lactation itself may reduce the likelihood of conception (Birdsell, 1968). . . . A new infant born at an opportune time does not restrict a woman's life, it expands it, drawing attention and help to her from everyone around. A woman of child-bearing age without an infant on her hip or toddling behind her most of the time is an unusual and somehow awkward sight.

Altmann (1980: 177) says:

Most of an [baboon] infant's requirements for care increase proportionately with the infant's increase in weight.

The tendency of carrying their child on their back is seen in all the women in the world—but mainly, however, in those who have a more simple and natural life-style, except that they are now aided by a sling of animal skins or pieces of material or something similar (Kaross by !Kung women, and in general by the women of many South-African tribes; Rebozo by the peasant women of Mexico, etc.), due to the fact that their infants' throne has currently been reduced. In many human races, due to their braided and short, curled hair, like the !Kung, it no longer can serve as a handle for the infant.

Women today—as well as their infants—have all the characters, instincts, and reflexes needed for that type of infant transportation. These facts are evidence that infants traveling on the infants' throne is not a fantasy of mine, but an indisputable fact providing proof that we still are graincollectors. Let us now examine some of the reflexes present in all human infants, to support the above.

Konner (1972) states that !Kung infants start their life with the same repertoire of basic reflexes as European babies, and points out that among !Kung infants, many of those reflexes still have survival value, such as the Moro Embracement Reflex or Moro Reflex, and the Palmar Reflex or Hand Grasping Reflex; although very few of those reflexes have survival value for present-day European infants.

Konner states further that !Kung newborns are carried in a sling that keeps them upright and pressed against their mother's side, and that the baby's skin is against their mother's skin. When the babies sleep, they are seen with their faces pressed into their mother's flesh. Furthermore, he says that from time to time, instinctively, the infant turns his face from one side to the other, and appropriately moves his legs and arms in such a way that his mother needs not to readjust him, and that those instinctive movements may even prevent him from smothering in her skin. We notice that all these movements of mother and child are instinctive and reflex movements.

The Palmar Reflex or Hand Grasping Reflex helps !Kung infants to support themselves from the necklaces used by their mothers, since Konner says (1972: 290): "Almost all Zhun/twa [!Kung] women wear many long strands of small beads which are ideal for grasping *in the same way the hair is.*" (Italics mine) We notice something very important here: *!Kung infants still have the Palmar Reflex perfectly developed, despite the fact that their mothers no longer have long hair on their heads, or body hair.* Quantitative tests show that the Palmar Reflex *in all human babies is stronger when touching the palm of the hand with hair.* Many scientists have considered this reflex as vestigial, since they believe it is no longer useful, since during the evolution of the human lineage, we have adaptively lost our body hair millions of years ago. I think this theory is mistaken, since that reflex is currently present because we are still graincollectors. If body hair was lost in the evolution of our lineage many million years ago, we can only accept that this and other linked reflexes are still present if we assume that the selective pressure that developed them is still present in humans; or that, at least, it was present 50 thousand years ago—that is, before Würm's Glaciation.

The Moro Embracement Reflex is linked to the Palmar Reflex. This is another fact that supports the abovementioned. Konner points out that these reflexes do not provide support for all of the infant's weight, and that it doesn't happen in the transportation context of the first months. He believes that their function, in those first months, is to stabilize and keep the mouth at the breast, allowing the mother to reduce her constant watchfulness, and he adds (Konner, 1972: 290, 291):

Some light may be thrown on the origin of this behaviour by the fact that spontaneous Moro reflexes during feeds sometimes terminate in one- or two-handed grasping and clinging, and, also, that when Moro occurs during one-handed cling, the extension-adduction phase engages only the free arm, while the other continues to cling. This is in keeping with the findings of recent electro-myographic research on Moro reflex (Perchtl, 1965; Perchtl and Lenard, 1968) demonstrating that if the infant is grasping with both hands at the onset of the reflex, only the flexion-adduction phase occurs. These authors argue that this finding returns the reflex to the phylogenetic status Moro originally assigned to it, that of a vestige of the embracing reflex of infant monkeys . . . *Our research suggests that Moro was wrong only in considering the reflex in humans completely vestigial.* (Italics mine)

Konner says that the infant !Kung is treated by his mother in the way all mothers of the world should treat their children; he believes that, with civilization, infants have lost something that they instinctively need and are lacking. A civilized mother only feeds her child about every four hours, and she is away from him; thus losing the body contact that would allow her to anticipate a wish or problem the baby might have. Conversely, the !Kung mother notices even a change in the baby's rate of breathing, which is very meaningful to her developed sensibility; furthermore, she can have easy and immediate access to her infant.

Traveling always with his mother, and keeping a vertical position is essential for the development and *mental health* of the infant; Konner (1972: 292) states:

> In connection with this posture [seated vertically], it is worth noting some remarks of Gesell and Amatruda concerning the 6-month-old sitting up: "His eyes widen, pulse strengthens, breathing quickens and he smiles when he is translated from the supine horizontal to the seated perpendicular. This . . . is more than a postural triumph. It is a widening of horizon, a new social orientation" (1947: 42). Zhun/twa [!Kung] infants are held in this position virtually from birth. The horizontal is almost unknown to them during their waking life. From their position on the mother's hip they have available to them her entire social world, the world of objects *(particularly work in the mother's hands)* and the breast, and the mother has immediate easy access to the infant. (Italics mine)

Konner says that the curiosity and exploring desire of !Kung infants is actively encouraged by adults.

All of the abovementioned happens in the !Kung tribes, because the mother devotes three to eight years of her life exclusively to one infant, not just one to two years as civilized women do; but she does not remain celibate during the seven or eight years of infant dependency. Very often, the !Kung mother gets pregnant long before weaning, unlike the seven or eight years of devotion and celibacy that the graincollector mother used to give to her child. My assertion is based on the long period of genetically based maternal dependency that humans have, and on the fact that female gorillas, chimpanzees, and orangutans remain celibate from 3.5 to 5.5 years (with this celibacy occasionally extended up to eight years) while their infant depends on them—despite the fact that in all pongids the period of maternal dependency is now shorter than the human maternal dependency period (Schaller, 1963; van Lawick-Goodall, 1973; Galdikas, 1979).

In short, when humans lost their graincollecting ecological niche, along with loss of traveling on the infants' throne, children lost the absolute, total, celibate and complete devotion that mothers used to give them, of necessity, from the time of conception up to seven or eight years of age. Children lost all these manifestations of affection due to (as will be seen in Part Two of this book) the sexual demands by the mother's spouse (the father), since, in the natural life of grain-collection, women were never obliged to those demands. Children have also lost the direct contact with adults that had been theirs from their birth; they have lost their natural way of socializing and of alerting their curiosity; with that, they have also lost a calm and pleasant life-style in which, due to it, the great development of the brain and intelligence took place during evolution in the human lineage, as we'll also see in Part Two of this book.

The infants' throne is a biological need of a quadrupedal female primate who turns bipedal, even assuming that this primate does not lose body hair in this transition.

The selective pressure for developing steatopygia is higher in bipedal naked graincollector female hominids than in current quad-rupedal *Theropithecus gelada* females, due as much to the steatopygia food reserve storing function as to its function of providing easy transportation for infants. However, gelada females currently present a small steatopygia, despite their being quadrupeds and partial bipeds, despite seed eating by them only part of the year, and despite there being no selective pressure favoring survival of infants whose mother can carry them on her steatopygia, thereby additionally guaranteeing them better and extended nourishment. The gelada females' steatopygia is small despite the additional fact that the infant can hold himself from the mother's body hair, and despite the fact that her infant's childhood is not as prolonged as that of humans. It may be clearly seen, then, that steatopygia really is a biological need for graincollector bipedal females, and they can develop such steatopygia more easily than gelada baboon females.

We may summarize by saying that the change of behavior from part-time seed-eaters to full-time seed-eater migratory bipeds forced early hominid females adaptively to develop steatopygia, since, without it, the mother would have been unable to nourish her infant throughout his extended childhood and *to transport him securely*. Lovejoy (1981: 344, 349 [54]) states:

> In her essay on mother-infant relationships among chimpanzees, van Lawick-Goodall (54) noted two primary causes of mortality among infants: "inadequacy" of the mother-infant relationship and "injuries caused by falling from the mother. " . . . *It should also be pointed out that falls as a consequence of mother-infant travel would be a more critical selection factor in early hominids than other primates.* (Italics mine)

It is probable that the ischial callosities in living pongids, which in females are truly *fatty sitting pads*, the development of which increases during puberty and during infant bearing years, are vestiges of a true steatopygian past (see plate 3).

Plate 3   Female gorilla with her infant.

Chapter III
Miscellany of Objections and Supports

1. Where Is the Archeological and Fossil Evidence? Eolithic Culture

One objection that can be argued against the theory of graincollection is this: Where is the archaeological and fossil evidence of the graincollectors of such an extended period of time?

It is improbable that graincollectors left archaeological and fossil evidence. Only near ancient rivers, puddles, or lakes where they used to go possibly twice daily to drink water, would accumulated fossil remains and possibly tools be found. The probabilities of finding other places with evidence of their existence are slim, except in those sites where, in *abnormal* times of prolonged drought, cold weather, or scarcity of seeds, they were reunited and resorted to scavenging. This, however, does not happen until they have acquired the manual dexterity to manufacture stone tools with sharp edges—that is, from the Lower Pliocene to the present.

In very recent modern times, some tribes lived in a somewhat similar way to graincollectors, such as the Shoshoni-speaking Paiutes of the Great Basin of North America. They collected gramineous seeds and threshed them in winnowing baskets, and even though they also hunted with modern weapons and methods, Birdsell (1975: 358) says of them: "Such people leave so little evidence archeologically that their presence in the Pleistocene is difficult to detect."

Only the *Eoliths* found in some Middle and Upper Miocene, Pliocene, and Pleistocene deposits can be counted as evidence of the hominid graincollectors' presence in these epochs. At the beginning of this century it was widely debated whether or not the eoliths were tools used by our ancestors, and they were not accepted as such because they were confused with absolutely natural stones; and also because at the beginning of this century, hunting, scavenging, and gathering were thought of as the subsistence activities of our ancestors. It is logical that these tools could be mistaken for absolutely natural stones, because, first, at the beginning of graincollection, absolutely natural stone tools must obviously have been used, having been very well selected to serve as scrapers, because the manual dexterity to improve (manufacture) those natural stones to enhance their usefulness as grainthreshers must have been greatly delayed in the evolution of the hominid lineage; and second, because for graincollecting it wasn't required that such stones have sharp edges or points. Pond (1930: 132 [taken from Johnson, 1978: 347]) states:

> "A careful study of the edges and points of these so-called tools [eoliths] will convince anyone who has used flint tools that an extremely small percentage could ever have cut or penetrated any solid substance more resistant than soft butter. [Pond 1930: 132]"

At the beginning of this century this had been argued as evidence that those stones were not the tools of hominid hunter-gatherers. Today I use exactly that same argument, but as evidence that they *could* have been tools of hominid graincollectors. If, at the beginning of this century, anthropologists, archeologists, etc., would have thought of graincollection, it would have been very probable that the Eolithic Culture would have been acknowledged since then.

Even if we do not accept that graincollection is our origin and our nature, and if we do not have any evidence of an Eolithic Culture, we have to necessarily presume it, since, when acknowledging the Oldowan Industry, we are acknowledging implicitly a very rudimentary previous lithic culture that must have lasted millions of years, because it is not valid to admit that a stone tool *manufacturing* culture was the first one in hominid evolution. The adaptive evolution *towards truly evolutionary novelties* does not make jumps; therefore, the hominid *manufacturers* of tools necessarily descend from hominids that used absolutely natural tools for many million years before. They would not have adaptively acquired in any other way the cerebro-muscular coordination required for such advanced work. The confusion is caused by the same mistake: to think that our early hominid ancestors were manufacturers of rudimentary tools *"as the chimpanzee currently is"*; without explaining why chimpanzees can manufacture some *very rudimentary* tools.

2. Are Humans Savanna Inhabitants?

An objection made by Verhaegen (1987) that opposes the suggestion mentioned (Chapter I, Section 4) by Sinclair et al. (1986) that bipedalism evolved because early hominids used to scavenge following migrant ungulate grazers, and which also opposes the theory of graincollection, is the following:

Verhaegen (1987: 305) states:

> . . . it is highly unlikely that our hominid ancestors ever lived in the savannas. Man is the opposite of a savanna inhabitant. Humans lack sun-reflecting fur but have thermo-insulative subcutaneous fat layers, which are never seen in savanna mammals. We have a water- and sodium-wasting cooling system of abundant sweat glands, totally unfit for a dry environment. Our maximal urine concentration is much too low for a savanna-dwelling mammal. We need much more water than other primates, and have to drink more often than savanna inhabitants, yet we cannot drink large quantities at a time. The fossils of our hominid ancestors or relatives are always found in water-rich environments.
>
> It is difficult to understand why most anthropologists keep believing in the savanna theory (possibly because it goes back to Charles Darwin) . . .

I will now present my opposing argument, in which I defend the theory of graincollection, which states that we descend from savanna-living hominids, since our ancestors lived in them from 14 million years ago up to some 50 thousand years ago, and does not confirm the suggestion made by Sinclair et al. (1986).

(a) Humans are inhabitants of the savanna precisely because we find our natural foods in that habitat, *and it is there that we receive an abundance of solar rays on our body*. Human ancestors adaptively lost their body hair in order to receive more solar rays directly on the skin. Human nakedness shows our huge need to receive an abundance of solar rays on our skin; therefore, the fact that humans do not have body hair is a benefit for us when living in the savanna and does not harm us.

(b) Humans descend from hominid inhabitants of the European and Asian savannas. Due to the fact that these savannas are geographically located at higher latitudes than the African savannas, the solar rays in those places reach the ground with much more slope; therefore, less solar energy is received per square meter of ground in those zones than in the African savannas, which are closer to the earth's equator. Consequently, we receive less solar energy (solar rays) per square centimeter of skin in those high latitudes than in those closer to the earth's equator. That was one of the selective pressures that brought about the situation in which only those protohominids survived as graincollectors in those latitudes that had lost *all* of their body hair when they adapted to synthesize through their skin all their requirements of vitamin D.

(c) The fact that humans have " . . . thermo-insulative subcutaneous fat layers, which are never seen in savanna mammals," is also an adaptive result of living in higher latitudes (colder weather), than in Africa. The only human ancestors who survived in these colder zones were those who were able adaptively to acquire a better body thermo-insulation, while still receiving solar rays on their skin. Adaptively, they substituted the insulation provided by body hair for the insulation provided by subcutaneous fat layers. Furthermore, they were able to synthesize in their skin their huge requirements of vitamin D. The adaptive acquisition of these subcutaneous fat layers that thermo-insulate the body, along with the adaptively acquired thermo-regulatory eccrine sweat glands that efficiently cool the body as necessary, were a complete hominid evolutionary success.

(d) Regarding our need for more water than other primates, it might be true, since those other primates eat leaves and vegetables that contain water. Furthermore, some of them live in shaded places. But let's not compare ourselves with other primates who inhabit such different regions, but with other migratory grazer mammals that are inhabitants of the savanna: wildebeests, zebras, etc.; they go to drink water at least two times a day, usually at dawn and dusk. Those humans who nowadays are already adapted to life in the savanna can do the same and do not cover most of their bodies with clothes (more about this in "g" below).

Concerning the wildebeests of the Serengeti, Maddock (1979) states that the migration is different each year, and adds: " . . . the wildebeest preferred fresh green grass and avoided muddy ground, but tended to move through areas where there was likely to be permanent water" (Maddock, 1979: 105–106). I believe that human ancestors tried to migrate close to those areas that permanently had water, as wildebeests and zebras do.

(e) Zebras sweat as humans, since they also have abundant sweat glands over most of their body surface, and like humans, are inhabitants of the savannas.

(f) The fossil remains of our ancestors *must be sought* in places which were ancient puddles, lakes, or rivers where they went to drink water like all the ungulate grazer inhabitants of the savannas do, and it is more probable that their remains would fossilize in those places than in the open fields. Verhaegen, however, says (1987: 305), "The fossils of our hominid ancestors or relatives are always found in water-rich environments"; that is, in regions of higher humidity than the savannas. This is because he is probably referring to some fossil remains of australopithecines, which are not our ancestors, but ancestors of the African pongids, which lived in more humid regions than the savannas, as their pongid descendants do at present.

(g) Let us see the endurance of some human individual inhabitants of semidesertic areas. Devine (1985) states that Tarahumares (a Taracahitian people of southern Sonora and Chihuahua, Mexico) can *run*, not only walk, *without experiencing fatigue* and without stopping, 270 kilometers. That Papago women (of the Piman people of southwestern Arizona and northwestern Sonora, Mexico) can walk all day *in the desert* carrying her child, and drinking only a small amount of water.

Humans, due to the lack of the suitable selective pressures during the last 50 thousand years, have survived and multiplied; but, if exposed to the diverse selective pressures of living in the savanna, very few would have reached reproductive age; so, humans presently would be better adapted to life in the savannas, as the abovementioned Tarahumare and Papago people.

We must also consider that the dark pigmentation of our skin can protect us, and has indeed protected us from an excess of solar rays when it has been adaptively necessary.

3. The Human Diet

Modern research regarding human diet shows the truth about the current lack of vegetal fiber in our diet. I believe that sometime in the not too distant future, it will be concluded that our true nature is granivorous, and that researchers will find which are the Protozoa infusoria ciliates *(Troglodytella)* that in symbiosis can live in our intestines (Kortlandt, 1984), as they probably lived in our ancestors' intestines and as they presently live in the wild gorilla's intestines, so that these microorganisms, and all the intestinal flora and fauna, will provide us with all the required vitamins. In this way we would not need any animal food in our diet, with the proviso that we also allow an abundance of solar rays to reach our naked skin.

I believe gorilla is the living hominoid whose present diet resembles that of our common granivorous ancestors, since gorillas in the wild are cellulose digesters. Humans presently have a very strange diet for our true nature. We suffer from many diseases related to our teeth and to our digestive system, and we very often suffer diarrhea.

For now, the work done by microorganisms in the human intestine and colon, even if very important, is not as basic to our digestion as if we were exclusively cellulose digesters, since at present we are omnivorous; that is why this issue has not been studied in detail. This is a deplorable delay. More ruminants and monogastric mammal digesters of cellulose have been studied than humans. I believe this will change in the future.

4. Viability of the Theories

Living African pongids are very close genetic relatives of humans; that is why any theory that explains human origins must also explain, in a congruent and harmonious way, the origins of these pongids, to consider it viable.

5. Speculation; Harmony

Some readers might object to the theory of graincollection on grounds that it is primarily speculation without any reasonable backing; that unrelated facts are culled as evidence when they could as well be used for quite different interpretations. Of them I would ask: Isn't there more speculation and lack of reasonable backing in all the arguments that support hunting-gathering and scavenging-gathering theories? Isn't there more speculation in carelessly taking morphological comparisons as a basis for deducing phylogenetic relationships when dealing with accurate approximations, since, when doing this, possible evolutionary reversions and parallelisms of the compared anatomic areas are not taken into account? Isn't there a total lack of harmony in such explanations?

I do not believe I have forced any "unrelated facts" into harmony, but instead, they are in harmony because they are truly related to each other: that relation is graincollection in the common ancestor of all living Hominoidea lineages.

6. Two Logical Hypotheses Support the Theory of Graincollection

From the abovementioned we can derive another support for graincollection, and it is that this theory is probable, harmonious, congruent with facts and with recent research regarding biochemical studies, such as immunological, and those dealing with molecular clocks, etc. It explains facts that other existing theories up to now haven't explained; furthermore, it makes sense and reconciles apparent contradictions. It is very simple, since it only makes two logical hypotheses: that protohominids were part-time seed-eaters (Jolly, 1970), and that hominids were and are exclusively graincollector seed-eaters. One hypothesis leads to the other; they complement each other and are consistent with the facts; therefore, my theory is parsimonious.

7. The Small Size of the Human Mouth

The size of the human mouth is very small for almost any type of feeding. Our teeth are not those of carnivorous or omnivorous mammals. All baboons present prognathism that allows them to hunt animals and to eat meat, despite the fact that they rarely eat meat, since their main source of food is *rhizomes, stems, blades, gramineous seeds, and some insects.* The reason why our mouth is so small and our teeth so specialized for grinding seeds can only be due to the fact that our natural diet is granivorous. Our small mouth and powerful teeth are other graincollector characters. Linked to these characters is the ease with which we can handle small seeds and take them to our mouth, which makes us see granivorism as our true nature.

8. Life Stability and High Energy Diet

According to Martin (1981), brain development must present itself in mammal species subject to *K*-selection; that is, when species live in stable environments without a selective pressure to reproduce themselves in great numbers, but rather in great quality; and furthermore, when there is easy access to food high in energy that will enable the mother to feed her infant, first in the uterus and later through breast milk, the necessary nutrients for the development of his brain.

A diet based on seeds, like the one obtained through graincollection, offers all these; furthermore, due to the use of tools, the capability to wield branches and throw rocks is adaptively developed in graincollectors; therefore, they do not have predators.

Graincollection gives a totally tranquil way of life in a stable environment, along with food high in energy. I believe *graincollection* is the answer to the following question Lewin (1982: 841) asks:

The whole picture, Martin suggests, is still far from clear. "Given the fact that brain size, energy levels, and reproduction are so intimately tied together, I feel we have yet to find a satisfactory explanation for how the human brain reached the size it did during evolution. I need to have an explanation of where the stability and high energy came from."

PART TWO

Chapter IV
Animal Intelligence; Animal Instinct

Charles Darwin, when still a very young evolutionist, asked himself:
Is happiness an adaptive advantage in the struggle for survival?
In his "M" notebook, Darwin discussed the source of happiness in animals. In several of his books he also discussed happiness in birds, monkeys, etc. In *The Origin of Species* (1860: 39) he states:

> All that we can do, is to keep steadily in mind that each organic being is striving to increase in a geometrical ratio; that each at some period of its life, during some season of the year, during each generation or at intervals, has to struggle for life and to suffer great destruction. When we reflect on this struggle, we may console ourselves with the full belief, *that the war of nature is not incessant, that not fear is felt, that death is generally prompt, and that the vigorous, the healthy, and the happy survive and multiply.* (Italics mine)

1. Survival Value

The *Webster's New Twentieth Century Dictionary*, Unabridged Second Edition, defines Intelligence as:

> **Intelligence, n.** . . . 1. (a) the ability to learn or understand from experience; ability to acquire and retain knowledge; mental ability; (b) the ability to respond quickly and successfully to a new situation; use of the faculty of reason in solving problems, directing conduct, etc. effectively;
> . . .

Jerison (1973: 17) defined biological intelligence as " . . . the capacity to construct a perceptual world." Later, in 1975, Jerison clarified: " . . . my concept of 'perceptual world' implies a kind of consciousness, or at least an intervening process that transforms stimulus-information into action." (1975: 415)

The two preceding definitions will be implicit in the meaning I will be giving to *animal intelligence* throughout this book.

That same dictionary defines Instinct as:

Instinct, n. . . . 1. (an) inborn tendency to behave in a way characteristic of a species; natural, unacquired mode of response to stimuli; as, suckling is an *instinct* in mammals. . . .

Some authors have tried to establish the "Laws of Brain Evolution." Jerison (1973: 15) has replaced such laws; he states:

I would replace Marsh's laws by a simple general principle (Jerison, 1970b; 1971a):

"The brains of all animals have evolved in ways appropriate to life in their niches or adaptive zones, in accordance with principles . . . that describe the relationship to behavior of the structure of the brain as an organ of the body."

After studying the problem of brain evolution, its relation with behavior, and the evolution of mind, Jerison (1973) establishes that among vertebrates the ratio of brain mass to body mass, as proposed by Karl Lashley in 1949 to measure what he called "behavioral capacity," reflects more or less the degree of what Jerison has defined as biological intelligence, and adds:

It is easier to appreciate now why gross measures of the brain should be most closely related to biological intelligence. The number of neurons and the complexity of their interconnections should reflect the degree to which sensory systems have become elaborated and interconnected; it might make little difference from the point of view of intelligence which systems have actually been emphasized in a particular species. . . . The implication is that the integrative functions of the brain, which will define intelligence for us, are limited by the amount of brain that is typical for an animal of a particular species . . . the amount of neural material available for information-processing and integration is related to the gross brain weight or volume . . . it is for this reason that I approach the evolution of intelligence by analyzing the evolution of the brain, in particular, the evolution of its size. (Jerison, 1973: 24–25)

Some authors state that just taking as a basis the ratio: brain mass/body mass, to measure animal intelligence, presents difficulties. Bindra (1976: 2) states:

The level of development of the brain (see Jerison, 1969, 1973) may appear to be a more meaningful basis for deciding how intelligent a species is, but this criterion too presents difficulties. The question is, which index of brain development is best correlated with our intuitive estimates of species differences in intelligence? The index of brain development that is now widely used for species comparisons is the relative size of the neocortex (Stephan & Andy, 1969) . . . However, what is probably more important than the relative size of the neocortex is the relative size of the different functional areas of the neocortex . . . Man's neocortex differs from that of other primates in having an enlarged angular gyrus, which is implicated in language (Geschwind, 1971).

Some researchers, like Beck (1982), believe that in order to reconstruct the evolution of intelligence in animals, other facts should be taken into account, and not to just consider the genetic closeness that living pongids have with humans when looking for an answer to the problem of acquisition and evolution of intelligence. Beck (1982: 3), in the abstract of his article, states:

Observable attributes of predatory shell-dropping support inferences that the gulls are capable of extended concentration, purposefulness, mental representation of spatially and temporally displaced environ-mental features, cognitive mapping, cognitive modeling, selectivity, and strategy formation. Identical cognitive processes have been inferred to underlie the most sophisticated forms of chimpanzee tool-use.

Advanced cognitive capacities are not restricted to chimpanzees and other pongids, and are not associated uniquely with tool use. The chimpocentric bias should be abandoned, and reconstructions of the evolution of intelligence should be modified accordingly.

Among other researchers, Hodos (1988a, 104) believes there is a low correlation " . . . between overall brain size and intelligence in humans . . . " and adds (Hodos 1988a, 104):

Our search for the biological bases of animal intelligence may progress more rapidly if we abandon the general-intelligence model and general brain indices such as total weight or total volume. My recommendation is that we concentrate our efforts on determining the relationships between specific morphological components of the brain and specific intellectual abilities. By accepting the multidimensional natures of both the brain and intelligence we will have better opportunities to uncover the relationships between the two.

Jerison's (1988b, 459) summarized answer to Hodos (1988a) is the following:

Hodos's proposal that one can partition a brain into visceral, somatic, and intellectual components may have some heuristic appeal, but, as he makes clear, these are not located in completely different places in the brain. If the medulla is a visceral center it is also a somatic center involved in analysis and transmission of sensory and motor information. If frontal neocortex is an intellectual center, it is also a visceral center and a somatic center. I do not believe that the analysis of intelligence can proceed as if it has no significant visceral and somatic dimensions. And I take Hodos's use of this almost Aristotelian vocabulary as intended primarily to indicate weaknesses in the global approach rather than as proposing those as serious categories for partitioning either brain or behavior.

Hodos's (1988b, 463, 464, 465, 466) summarized comments are:

Jerison's definition of encephalization is a good one and I see no problem in it. My point is that it should be applied only to the intellectual brain if one is attempting to correlate intelligence and brain size. . . . I was especially impressed with the very high correlation between neocortex surface and total brain size. On the other hand, I was concerned by the considerably lower correlation between the volume of the olfactory bulb and brain size. . . . I have difficulty with Jerison's definition of biological intelligence as a tool to understand the relationship between the size of the brain and the amount of intelligence because this definition logically locks the independent variable (brain size) and the dependent variable (intelligence) together. It does not permit the one to float freely so that we can determine whether it is related to the other. . . . An analysis based on specific regions and specific abilities would reveal these differences more clearly than a global analysis. . . . My position is that intelligence is a human concept, and when we look for intelligence in animals it is to find features equivalent to human intelligence. I have written elsewhere about the dangers of this approach. Bias is introduced because the tests are made by humans based on traits that they value. We should look at what animals use in their own environments. But we will find it very hard to get away from the notion that being intelligent means doing something clever. My list of specific abilities aims to do that bearing in mind the caveats just raised.

I hope that readers will conclude, as I have, that Jerison and I are not very far apart on most of the major issues in the area of the brain and intelligence. We differ mainly on questions of definition and the relative weights to be given to global versus local indices of brain size. Even here, we seem to differ more in emphasis than in substance. In any case, we have had a useful exchange of views and perhaps have revealed additional facets of these issues.

To sum up, Jerison explains what his objective, methods and basis have been. Jerison (1988a: 1) says:

My objective has been to place intelligence in as broad a biological framework as is consistent with its identification with a specific phenotypic expression. My scientific tactic has been to examine the evolution of that "expression" as a concrete problem, and I solved (or more or less solved) that problem by analyzing measurements of the "expression" in fossil and living animals. For this reason, I have studied encephalization, a morphological trait, because there was evidence (Dubois, 1897; Lashley, 1949) that it could be used as a measure of animal intelligence for evolutionary purposes. Encephalization is not a behavioral measure, of course. It is a simple transformation of a relationship between brain and body size. The measure works (as far as I can tell) because the numbers that it yields are fairly directly related to the capacities of animals to handle information. As a first approximation, information handling capacity is related to body size according to the allometric brain:body relationship. Encephalization is the residual capacity that remains after basic allometric requirements are satisfied, and it represents additional information that an animal handles, beyond that used in routine control of body functions. Encephalization is my phenotypic "expression" of intelligence.

Regarding the abovementioned, Jerison (1988a: 2) says: "I am not especially satisfied with it myself. I present it, because I think most of us would agree that at least in some ways, intelligence in a biological sense is equivalent to residual processing capacity."

Jerison (1973) presents a complete panorama of brain evolution in vertebrates and mainly in mammals; some of his final conclusions are the following:

> The evolution of intelligence occurred mainly within the mammals and only in a casual way in birds, if one defines intelligence as the capacity to learn new response patterns in which sensory information from various modalities is integrated as information about objects in space.
> _ These trends reached their most elaborate development in the evolution of primates, a group of mammals adapted toward adaptability, in which skeletal specialization was minimal and adaptations were more completely determined by the enlargement of the brain and the development of learned behavior mechanisms than in any other vertebrates. The trend culminated in man, and we know it as the capacity for imagery, for language and for culture. (Jerison, 1973: 433)

In all his studies, based on the evolution of the brain of vertebrates, Jerison demonstrates that intelligence began to develop in them since their origin, some 500 million years ago. He also demonstrates that all vertebrates, mainly mammals, have a high degree of intelligence; and among mammals, primates have even greater intelligence, culminating in humans.

A number of conclusions can be drawn from all of the above quoted:

First, what Darwin had already pointed out: that various degrees of intelligence are present in many animals.

Second, that intelligence in the evolution of all vertebrate species is very old.

As I have already said in the Introduction and throughout the preceding chapters, it is very probable that the fossil remains of australopithecines, found in Africa, do not belong to our ancestors, but to the ancestors of the African pongids; in any case, those australopithecines descend from graincollector inhabitants of the savannas of Europe-Asia, who are our ancestors, and their brain size, at that time, was probably more or less the same as that of their African relatives. Knowing, then, that the great enlargement of the brain during the evolution of the human lineage happened in the last 2 or 3 million years, we may conclude:

Third, that the development of intelligence in the ancestors of the human lineage was very slow until 2 or 3 million years ago, and that in the last 2 or 3 million years something *very strange* happened that caused that great development, since it happened only in the human lineage. (According to Jerison [1973:351] something similar happened in the dolphins' lineage during evolution in the last 15 or 20 million years, to which I will refer in Chapter IV, Section 6.)

Based on the preceding, the following additional conclusions can be drawn:

Fourth, that having *suitable* selective pressure, which is not very common, intelligence can quickly become highly developed.

Fifth, and most important: intelligence, during the whole course of the evolution of all vertebrate lineages has developed *very slowly*; and that *slow* development in all mammal lineages is confusing; furthermore, it is amazing that it has been *so slow* in all primate lineages; therefore, *as we cannot assume that there have not been favorable selective pressures for its development, we can suspect that there is an unexplained factor that is holding back and slowing the development of animal intelligence since the first sign of intelligence originated in animal evolution—maybe even since the origin of animal life, or at least since 500 million years ago when the early vertebrates appeared.* I state this based on the following:

To humans, that presently make use of our intelligence for survival purposes, it would *"seem" evident to assume that if intelligence has survival value, more intelligence should have greater survival value;* that is, it *"seems"* evident for us to assume that an animal that is more intelligent than another of the same species and population, with all other circumstances equal, has more opportunities of survival and for reaching reproductive age than the less intelligent one. Then, a small increase in intelligence—caused by mutations, favorable genetic combinations, recombinations, or chromosomal changes—in one or several members of the following generation(s) of that same animal population, and in the additional presence of a favorable selective pressure, will work to support natural selection constituting a basis for future building, and so on. This kind of selection is the fundamental part of the Darwinian evolution through variation and natural selection toward true evolutionary novelties, and it has been called cumulative selection. Dawkins (1986) explains it clearly in the example he uses in relation to the sense of sight in animals: Many animals have sight organs in a very advanced state of functional efficiency. They reached that state, step by step, as all true evolutionary novelties did during the evolution of all living beings. Each species has the sense of sight in a degree of efficiency that would be difficult to increase adaptively through cumulative selection.

Similarly, intelligence can be increased, step by step, until it reaches a high state of efficiency, at which point it would be very difficult adaptively to increase its efficiency.

Taking into consideration all of the above, an obvious question arises: *Why has intelligence not increased in other vertebrates to a degree greater than or equal to that in humans, and why hasn't there been an adaptive radiation of intelligent vertebrates in 500 million years of using their intelligence?*

Even though intelligence shows all the characteristics and properties that would enable it to become more efficient through cumulative selection, it has been only in the evolution of the human lineage, and only in the last 2 or 3 million years, that intelligence has greatly increased through cumulative selection. Why? It cannot be said that intelligence in the rest of the vertebrates failed to advance because it had already reached so great a developmental stage as to preclude any further increase its efficiency, since we are witnessing that in humans, with human intelligence far greater than in the rest of the vertebrates. On the other hand, if the rest of the vertebrates had no intelligence whatsoever, we could assume that, since intelligence never emerged during evolution in any of their lineages, then a character that could adaptively increase its efficiency by cumulative selection never existed; but the fact is that it emerged at least 500 million years ago and its efficiency has not increased even to a state comparable to human intelligence in such an enormous period of time. As the selective pressure to increase intelligence always exists for all animals, it is not possible to believe that the rest of the vertebrates, and, above all, the rest of the mammals, or the rest of the primates didn't have favorable mutations, genetic combinations, recombinations, or chromosomal changes during the evolution of their respective lineages that would enable them to develop intelligence, and that only humans had them. Dobzhansky and Boesiger (1983: 30) state:

Mutations are far more numerous, and on the average less drastic, than supposed by classical geneticists. The speed of evolutionary change does not depend on mutation frequencies. The situation is far more complex and interesting. Mutational raw materials are probably always

128

available. The old idea that the evolutionary conservatism of species that failed to evolve for long geological periods reflected an absence of mutations is certainly wrong.

Noticing the great difference in intelligence between humans and the rest of the vertebrates makes us think of something important: Favorable mutations, genetic combinations, recombinations, chromosomal changes, and the appropriate selective pressure for the development of intelligence, have always been present in all animals through their evolution, and they still are present, but only under extraordinary circumstances do those animals who have them obtain a survival prize with them.

However, we must be aware that intelligence in the course of vertebrate evolution has not increased its efficiency so much and so rapidly as to originate an adaptive radiation, but it has adaptively and *slowly* become more efficient, *even though it has reached a developmental degree quite low throughout 500 million years.* But due to a *powerful cause* its efficiency hasn't increased more rapidly, by cumulative selection, in any other vertebrate species to a developmental stage comparable to that of humans, or even greater. Due to a *powerful cause* its efficiency during the evolution of hominids did not increase rapidly in so many million years, but only in the last 2 or 3.

Let's observe now something very important: We see that *all, absolutely all, animals, even all the human ancestors up until the last great Pleistocene glaciation; that is, up until 50 thousand years ago, followed, and all other animals still follow their natural instincts and not their intelligence in order to thrive (to obtain a material benefit) within their natural niche and ecosystem.* They sometimes follow, in addition, specific actions that have been transmitted *culturally* and which are imitated and repeated by their descendants, who imitate them in such a way that *those actions are no longer intelligent actions, but conditioned reflexes.* They also follow genetically inherited aptitudes that enable them to perform these cultural actions. Survival based on their natural instincts, and, in addition, on their cultural actions and on their inherited aptitudes, is present in the case of all the skilled and unskilled tool user animals we saw in Chapter I, Section 1; and among the skilled tool user hominoids, *in the case of hominid graincollectors during 14 million years of their evolution, including the period of their great brain development that started 2 or 3 million years ago.*

In the case of the hominid graincollectors of the last 2 or 3 million years, when the great brain expansion occurred, the above statement might appear surprising, but the facts show that our ancestors, while being graincollectors during so many million years, never made use of their intelligence in order to thrive within that niche and ecosystem. Instead, they used their instincts, in the same way all other animals do, and as done, I repeat, even by all skilled and unskilled tool-user animals. Thus, when our ancestors used natural stones to graincollect for a period of 9 or 10 million years, similar to the way the Egyptian vulture uses stones to break ostrich eggs, they never used their intelligence to improve the efficiency of such tools. The artificial and intelligent improvement of their natural tools, 3 or 4 million years ago, in order to increase graincollecting efficiency, after 9 or 10 million years of practice, was not a surprisingly intelligent act. The use of only one type of tool in only one situation and context, despite the fact that that tool was artificially improved, is not an intelligent action. It might have been an intelligent action for the first hominid user of that improved tool, but not of those who imitated him and used that improved tool almost as executing a conditioned reflex.

As we have seen, the use of a natural tool by some animals does not make us think of them as performing intelligent acts. With very low intelligence and very little culture, our graincollector ancestors, for the last 14 million years, survived as they had always survived, and as all other animals survive: using their instincts, not their intelligence. *In the last 2 or 3 million years*, and despite the great increase in intelligence that our ancestors experienced during that period of time, *intelligence was not used for survival purposes*, since they only repeated graincollecting actions that their ancestors had been executing for the previous 12 million years; *nor it was used to thrive in any other way.*

Let's now analyze intelligent actions. Each intelligent act is new, and therefore a *temporary change of behavior*. The great majority of intelligent acts executed by an animal are unique, since they depend on the will and on the particular skills of each animal; therefore, it is most probably *not* disseminated in a population, nor culturally transmitted to their descendants. A very small part of all intelligent acts can originate culture. As we saw in Chapter I, Section 1, in the case of unskilled tool-using animals, when a population *is within its natural niche*, an intelligent act of an individual, in order to thrive, can create a habit in this individual and spread by imitation throughout the population, *only if it eases a previous normal action performed by all or mostly all of the members of that population, because an intelligent action performed by an individual with the purpose of obtaining a totally "new" material benefit is very unlikely to spread among many members of that population.*

In the event that due to an abnormal disturbance, a population remains out of its natural ecological niche, then, due to the now very different and abnormal needs of the members of that population, a new and intelligent act executed by an individual in order to obtain a completely new material benefit could spread throughout that population. It should be remembered, however, that a population remaining out of its natural niche has a high extinction likelihood, and furthermore, the probability of forgetting that new intelligent act is high if the abnormal disturbance disappears and this population comes back to its natural ecological niche.

But let us assume that a new intelligent action used to thrive eases and improves one action already known and performed by all the members of a population, and, due to this, spreads by imitation in that population. Therefore, that new action has a high probability of becoming part of the descendants' culture, if, in addition, it is backed by natural selection. If that action has survival value, it will receive such backing.

If by an imperious need of an individual, a new intelligent act *is used to thrive*, not used in an incidental way or to satisfy a momentaneous curiosity, it is very probable that the executor of such an act, at that moment, is going through an abnormal phase that only occurred to him (as in the case of the first *Ramapithecus* female tool-user, that I assume had her hands injured from pulling so many seeds and blades before protecting them with a small stone), or has encountered something out of the ordinary in his habitat that has affected the whole population or all the ecosystem. After all, *when everything remains normal*, the individual is guided mainly by his instincts, because, in this case, to use an intelligent act *to thrive* is unnecessary. If his intelligent act is only incidental or executed to satisfy his curiosity, the executor will most probably soon forget it and no one will imitate him.

If the new intelligent act of an individual is imitated and used to thrive by various members of the population, it is probable that it will only be momentarily beneficial to the executors, because it is most likely that those individuals who performed this act are using it to obtain food that naturally belongs to other species that are members of their ecosystem, and not to them. So it is going to disturb the natural balance of the whole ecosystem and its members. The effect, in that case, inverts and hurts the executors as well as all the members of the population to which they belong.

Let's consider some other related topics to show a paradox. It would *seem* evident that the individual who performs an intelligent action also harms himself in another way. Let us take the following example: In the predator-prey relationships, *any intelligent action* of many individuals of a predator population that would improve their way of obtaining a prey will be detrimental to them and to the whole population of predators if, after some time of practicing it, this action leaves the prey population very decimated. Those predators that now obtain the prey more easily are then able to leave more offspring because it is more probable they can reach reproductive age. In this way, in a short time the habitat and ecosystem to which both populations belong will be saturated with these predators. That action can also be harmful for the predators if only those individuals of the prey population capable of overcoming the intelligent action of the predators survive through an *equally intelligent reaction* on their part. Now, *all* of the individuals of the predator population must perform another different or a more intelligent action in order to obtain a prey. Generally not everyone can do it; therefore, only those predators capable of improving the first action will survive. In this way, adaptively, intelligence should keep *spiraling upward* among the predator population as well as in the prey population.

But it should catch our attention that this has never happened in animal evolution, since we are witnessing that, in all animal populations, intelligent actions of the predators and reactions of their prey have *always* been balanced by natural selection that has left them with quite a low degree of intelligence, *since natural selection does not allow that, due to these actions and reactions, an imbalance of the natural equilibrium of the whole ecosystem results*, as shown by the following facts:

First, animals in their natural wild life, within their natural ecological niche, have always been guided and guide themselves by instinctive actions and not by intelligent actions. Thus, when everything is normal in their ecosystem, or when the individual is not suffering because of some abnormal happening, animals act guided only by their natural instincts and not by their intelligence in order to thrive. However, when their ecosystem has been disturbed, or the individual is suffering from something that has upset his normal life, animals may resort to intelligence. But, *from the results we are witnessing* in all existing animal populations, this hasn't increased animal intelligence, since the more intelligent animals *have not radiated or displaced* (Gause's principle of competitive exclusion) those less intelligent. Most probably, in the case of long-lasting abnormal environmental disturbances affecting the whole ecosystem or only the individual, death of the individual or extinction of the population is, and has always been, throughout the course of animal evolution, the most probable result.

Second, intelligence in all animals (with the exception of humans and dolphins) *has not* increased to very high levels in a way that could make us think that a *spiraling* increase of intelligence has in fact happened.

(The intelligent action performed by a *Ramapithecus* female when she first used the grainthresher, and once it spread and was culturally transmitted within all of the population, *was accepted by natural selection since all the members of that population had already the habit of feeding from gramineous seeds, and the use of the grainthresher did not cause much of an imbalance to the original ecosystem, nor to the migratory grazing ecosystem to which they entered when acquiring the habit of tool-using and the new migratory habits.* This is true because, even before the use of the grainthresher, that *Ramapithecus* population already interfered in that migratory grazing ecosystem; and the migratory grazer ungulates also interfered in the original ecosystem to which this *Ramapithecus* population belonged.)

Self-damaging and therefore limited by natural selection are also those complex social actions intelligently performed by some primates, like establishing networks of friendship and social alliances among several individuals of their group in order to triumph over a stronger individual, or to establish such alliances to socially manipulate other individuals in a humanlike interaction. Such actions, however, also bring about intelligent reactions from the damaged individuals, and, in this way, intelligence, through several generations, keeps spiraling upwards in that group or population. Lewin (1989: 129, 130) says:

"Alliances are far more complex social interactions than are two-animal contests," says Alexander Harcourt of Cambridge University. "The information processing abilities required for success are far greater: complexity is geometrically, not arithmetically, increased with the addition of further participants in an interactions. . . . In sum, primates are consummate social tacticians." . . . Why have primates found it advantageous to indulge in alliance building and manipulation? The answer, again from field studies, is that individuals who are adept at building and maintaining alliances are also reproductively more successful: making alliances aids in access to potential mating opportunities.

Once a lineage takes the evolutionary step of using social alliances to bolster reproductive success, it finds itself in what Nicholas Humphrey, a Cambridge University psychologist, calls an evolutionary ratchet. "Once a society has reached a certain level of complexity, then new internal pressures must arise which act to increase its complexity still further," he explains, "for, in a society [of this kind], an animal's intellectual 'adversaries' are members of his own breeding community. And in these circumstances there can be no going back."

Complex social interactions in primates are characters that appeared during their evolution a long time ago, since almost all living primate species present these characters; but we must notice that some of their respective lineages diverged more than 30 million years ago. We can assure, then, that those characters appeared at least 30 million years ago in their common ancestor, and that these characters were already present, at least 30 million years ago, in the ancestor of the human lineage. We can also assure that those characters are evolutionarily rather conservative due to the way of life of primates, since almost all living primate species present them.

We can, therefore, deduce the following: if complex social actions and reactions do in fact increase intelligence, then, *all*, or at least many primate species should currently have a higher degree of intelligence, not only humans. Why has intelligence in the rest of the primate species remained at such a low degree of development after so many millions of years of using and practicing such complex social interactions? Why has intelligence developed *rapidly* in the human lineage only in the last 2 or 3 million years if such complex social interactions have been used at least 30 million years ago? The answer is the same: because such complex social actions and reactions are not a selective pressure that fuels the development of intelligence. That is because natural selection does not allow for a spiraling increase of intelligence to originate in the members of a population when an imbalance of the natural biological equilibrium of the whole ecosystem results. Therefore, we see that primates execute those complex social interactions because they are intelligent, and they are not intelligent because they execute those complex social interactions.

Instinctive acts of animals, by being genetically and not culturally inherited, overcome all of the natural requirements because they fit, "step by step," in the natural balance of the whole ecosystem, if they have survival value and are approved by natural selection in the phenotype of each individual. But the majority of intelligent acts, by being almost always new and so numerous, cannot fit step by step or in such a way as to avoid unbalancing the whole ecosystem. Just a few repetitive intelligent acts that are spread among all the members of a population have probabilities of passing through the sieve of natural selection; that is, of not unbalancing the equilibrium of the whole ecosystem, of becoming part of the culture, and of benefiting the executors and the whole population.

Natural selection, in the whole course of animal evolution in this planet, chose, among billions of intelligent acts performed by individuals of very different animal species, only a minute number to be spread and culturally transmitted among their respective populations in all the ecosystems of this planet; and only if those acts were beneficial to the general balance of all the ecosystems and to each ecosystem in particular. A great number of intelligent acts were rejected as being damaging, even though they were spread or transmitted culturally; and the *great majority* of those acts didn't even pass the first natural requirement needed; that is, to spread and be transmitted culturally in a population.

Furthermore, an intelligent act can create culture in an animal population (since it is never instinctive), *but when creating culture it isn't any longer an intelligent act, but rather a conditioned reflex acquired by imitation.* Culture in animals, then, *does not* mean greater intelligence. Besides, when a prolonged crisis of lack of food previously obtained with that cultural act occurs, *this act can be very easily forgotten by the members of that population* due to the absence of cultural transmission. (After our ancestors practiced graincollection for 14 million years, humans have lost and forgotten our graincollecting culture.)

Intelligent acts transmitted culturally can easily be forgotten. Instinctive acts *are not* forgotten, even in times of crisis—but they can become useless, as in some cases when a population suffers a change of adaptive zone.

Due to this, we can affirm that animal intelligence, *when used to thrive, and applied to several acts and in different ways by various members of a population, causes damage to the individuals, their population, and their ecosystem.* We can also affirm that intelligence is a character which *helps* beings to learn from experience and to receive culture by imitation, even though in this last case conditioned reflexes have a greater influence than does intelligence. Intelligence also *helps* to "construct a perceptual world" (Jerison, 1973: 17), but is not a character which benefits animals *in a material way* through the execution of new acts in order to thrive.

In the case of an individual executing an intelligent and new act to thrive, and being imitated by other individuals, that act can be of equal or greater benefit to those who imitate it than to the originator of that act. It is *improbable* that in nature the originator of a new and intelligent act, *having used it to thrive*, will be the one that benefits most from it. Thus, it is not the most intelligent inventor who leaves more offspring. We see, then, the difficulty that exists for animals adaptively to increase their intelligence in this way.

We can conclude then that, throughout the whole course of animal evolution, animals have never improved their intelligence by performing new and intelligent acts that could give them *some kind of survival advantage*. That is, it has never happened that an animal obtains a survival prize with the execution of novel intelligent acts in order to thrive. *But, what can be said of those new and intelligent acts that do not cause damage to anyone or to the biological balance of the whole ecosystem and do bring certain nonmaterial satisfaction to those who perform it, or even to all the population to which the executors belong?*

If an individual member of an animal population performs a new and intelligent act that *does not* damage other individuals or interfere with the natural balance of the whole ecosystem, which can be called *neutral act*, it might be learned by other members of the population if that act brings them certain satisfaction, and therefore it may or may not be passed on as culture to the following generations.

We can suspect that new and intelligent acts, or repeated old ones, which are *neutral*, might not fulfill the natural requirements of having survival value and passing as culture to the following generations, even though this may occur and indeed it does occur. That is, these acts might not be sanctioned by natural selection. These are generally acts of individual or group satisfaction: *recreation, entertainment, play, satisfaction of natural curiosity, communication, sports, artistic activities, etc.* These intelligent acts might be learned by imitation as repetitive actions, or may be actions that are *always new* and cannot be disseminated by imitation; therefore, they may or may not form part of the culture in a population; *but it is necessary that the greater intelligence needed to perform those actions be genetically inherited by each individual of that population.* How can this happen, if, from what we have seen so far, it is *unlikely* that an animal more intelligent than others of the same species and population will obtain a survival prize in the form of more offspring?

Let's look at something very important which resolves this problem:

In a population, those animals who *communicate*, play, satisfy their idle curiosity, etc., are generally more vigorous and healthier than those who don't and, despite the disadvantages due to the enormous risks and dangers that exist when performing these actions (have accidents, get in trouble through curiosity, forget about predators, etc.), *it is probable that, due to their healthier and more vigorous constitution, and the fact that they fully enjoy and want life, a small survival advantage would remain to them on balance.* On the other hand, those individuals, generally apathetic, less healthy, and less vigorous, who do not play, satisfy idle curiosity, practice sports, communicate, etc., do not have this *small* favorable balance; and, because of this, the more vigorous and healthier individuals leave *more offspring* than these others; but communicating, playing, being involved in sports, satisfying idle curiosity, etc., are *not* characters, in and of themselves, that have survival value.

Due to this, animal intelligence has increased, *but very slowly* in the whole course of animal evolution.

For the abovementioned reasons, intelligent animals have not had an adaptive radiation: *intelligence does not have survival value, not even when it is used to thrive (to obtain a material benefit), nor when it is used to "enjoy life" (to obtain a non material benefit).*

And it is due to all these reasons that *all* animals survive following their instincts, not their intelligence.

Jerison (1988a: 2) states:

Cladistic analysis of encephalization generally demonstrates that this trait has remained stable and unchanging in related species and in phyletic lineages. Stability, or conservation, is one of the most important facts about the evolution of encephalization: encephalization is a conservative trait.

Based on what Jerison states, we can realize that once intelligence has increased in the evolution of the lineage of any animal species, it has not decreased, and it generally has been retained or increased step by step.

The obvious question, then, is: How was it that for the last 2 or 3 million years in the evolution of the human lineage, intelligence increased so rapidly and in such enormous proportions, without it having survival value—since our ancestors have *always* survived following only their natural instincts? After what we have seen up to now, we can deduce the answer: Based on the extended mother-infant relationship (as we will see in this chapter, Section 6), communication through vocal sounds in our human ancestors of 2 or 3 million years ago had become efficient enough to serve as a medium for their entertainment, play, satisfaction of natural curiosity, etc., but then a selective pressure that had never before fueled the development of their intelligence started to act upon them—a very particular form of *sexual selection*. The members of a population that played, practiced sports, performed artistic activities, knew more, and above all, *were able to speak and communicate better* (notice these actions didn't affect the natural balance of their ecosystem), were preferred by the members of the opposite sex as companions and consorts. Then, it is *in this one case* that intelligence *rapidly* acquired survival value during the evolution of the human lineage, *and kept increasing, step by step, "in spiral," through cumulative selection, during the last 2 or 3 million years*. Those who spoke and expressed themselves better, and were better able to enjoy life, left *many* more offspring than those who were apathetic. This has never happened in the evolution of any other animal species, except in the evolution of dolphins, as we will see in Section 6 of this chapter. We will see how and why the coincidence of many factors makes the human case unique in animal evolution. We will also look at the origin of human speech, and see that the development of spoken language is linked to the development of intelligence.

It is important to point out that being able to speak and communicate expertly was the most important hominid quality, since without this one, all other qualities could not be properly shown, to receive the appreciation of members of the opposite sex.

The conclusion reached in this matter is based on the analysis made by Strum (1987) and Smuts (1985) of sexual consort partners and male-female relationships, as well as, in general, on all their studies made on the social life of the olive baboons *(Papio cynocephalus anubis)*. It is additionally based on the fact that the social life of those troops of baboons (as will be seen in Chapter V, Section 1) most probably is very similar to what the social life of the hominid graincollectors must have been (despite the fact that those graincollectors had true migratory habits and baboons don't). On the basis of all of the above, it is *not* valid to think that the greater *status* acquired in the tribe by the male or female hominid who spoke and communicated better had a greater influence in leaving more offspring, but, instead, that those who spoke and were able to communicate better left more offspring *mainly because they were preferred by members of the opposite sex as consort partners.*

The fact that human males during puberty change their tone of voice, acquiring deeper tones, indicates that a deeper tone of voice is a secondary sexual character important for courting females as well as acquiring respect from other competitor males (acquiring *status*) since, in addition, the graincollector male changes tribe at that time of his life and must display his physical attributes in order to attract females and surpass the other resident males of the unfamiliar tribe which he attempts to enter. This character was probably adaptively acquired by the human ancestors previous to the acquisition of spoken language, since many animals use their voices to woo and attract females. If it was acquired previously, this indicates the importance that the capability of *speaking well* had in the sexual life of human males. If it evolved later, it still indicates the importance *speaking well* had for the human male in order to be accepted by females. Darwin (1871: 337, Vol. II) states:

Bearing in mind that the males of some quadrumanous animals have their vocal organs much more developed than in the females, and that one anthropomorphous species pours forth a whole octave of musical notes and may be said to sing, the suspicion does not appear improbable that the progenitors of man, either the males or females, or both sexes, *before they had acquired the power of expressing their mutual love in articulate language, endeavoured to charm each other with musical notes and rhythm.* (Italics mine)

Dobzhansky and Boesiger (1983: 116) state:

Darwin . . . thinks that, even more than weapons that males use in obtaining mates, all sorts of ornaments and sound-producing organs have evolved under the pressure of sexual selection.

Then, to assume that spoken language developed greatly, and this made intelligence develop greatly, *due to sexual selection*, is a very acceptable and congruent assumption.

Now I would like to remind the reader about a historical controversy that has caught my attention, regarding the *excessive* human intelligence.

Both discoverers of biological evolution through variation and natural selection, Charles Darwin and Alfred Russel Wallace, supported their discovery on many common grounds, but they also had two important issues on which they disagreed: sexual selection, as proposed by Darwin, was denied in its totality by Wallace; he also denied that the great human intelligence was developed through natural selection, as proposed by Darwin, since Wallace thought that humans' great intelligence exceeded the requirements they must fulfill in order to survive in their natural environment. Based on all the material previously covered, we can state that Wallace was right. It is surprising that only Wallace perceived *consciously* at that time that human intelligence must have another origin, since it couldn't be sanctioned by natural selection. But it is also surprising that human intelligence had a great development in the last 2 or 3 million years due to the natural mechanism that only Darwin discovered: sexual selection (present-day evolutionary biologists view sexual selection as a particular phase of natural selection).

Maybe it was a mistake on Darwin's part not to consider Wallace's point of view; but it was Wallace's mistake to argue that human intelligence could have a nonbiological origin. I believe that if Darwin had considered Wallace's point of view, and with it in mind had looked for the *natural, biologic* origin of the excessive intelligence in humans, *he would have put in writing* what he had already concluded *unconsciously* in his mind: that that great development of human intelligence was fueled by the pressure of sexual selection, since in *The Descent of Man*, Darwin (1871: 57, Vol. I) states:

> But *the relation between the continued use of language and the development of the brain has no doubt been far more important* . . . A long and complex train of thought can no more be carried on without the aid of words, whether spoken or silent, than a long calculation without the use of figures or algebra. (Italics mine)

And in another part, Darwin (1871: 337, Vol II) states:

> The *impassioned orator, bard,* or musician, when with his varied tones and cadences he excites the strongest emotions in his hearers, little suspects that he uses the same means by which, at an extremely remote period, his half-human ancestors *aroused each other's ardent passions, during their mutual courtship and rivalry.* (Italics mine)

Many of those who have studied human behavior and human evolution since the times of Darwin and Wallace have seen, and many still see, the difficulty of explaining the origin of human intelligence and spoken language from an adaptationist perspective. That is because they are aware that that origin cannot be reasonably explained if we assume that intelligence and spoken language have survival value. But some persist in trying to relate the development of intelligence with the manufacture and use of tools by the early hominids. We have already seen that they are not related; and know that during the 2 or 3 million–year period of great brain expansion and great development of intelligence in the human lineage, tools remained almost unchanged (Wynn, 1988). Great changes occurred in them recently, no more than the last 50 thousand years when, pushed by Würm's Glaciation, our ancestors applied the ancient technique of grainthresher and hand axe manufacturing to the manufacture of hunting weapons.

As noted in Chapter I, Section 1, Susman (1988) recently found fossil evidence for tool behavior attributable to *Paranthropus robustus*.

"*Paranthropus* is the term he prefers for the robustus." (Bower, 1988: 344). Susman bases his conclusions in the great similarity of finger bones, including the thumb bones, of *Paranthropus robustus* with those of the human hand. This fact supports the belief that brain expansion is not related with the use of tools. Furthermore, if *Paranthropus robustus (Australopithecus robustus)* is the ancestor of the gorilla, as suggested by Kleindienst (1975), then all living pongids are skilled (expert) tool-users because they descend from skilled tool-users; which confirms that the use and the rudimentary manufacture of tools is not related with the development of intelligence. Susman (1988: 783) states:

> . . . the new evidence from Swartkrans demands a reassessment of traditional views of the robust australopithecines and long held notions that the advent of tool behavior and "culture" distinguished early *Homo* from other early hominids, that tools initiated the human career, and that, because of the lack of tool behavior (or the morphological potential for it), *Paranthropus* became extinct.

From all of the abovementioned, we can conclude the following:

First: *Intelligence is used by all animals to enjoy life, not to thrive.*
Second: *For all animals who are within their ecological niche, life in nature, such as it is, has much enjoyment and is not full of hardships.* Darwin (1860: 39) states:

> When we reflect on this struggle [for life], we may console ourselves with the full belief, that the war of nature is not incessant, that fear is not felt, that death is generally prompt, and that the vigorous, the healthy and the happy survive and multiply.

Third: If our graincollector ancestors did not forget their graincollecting culture for 14 million years, this shows that during those 14 million years they didn't go through long periods of scarcity of gramineous seeds. But it also compels us to suspect that *the relatives of our ancestors* who abandoned graincollection for long periods of time *did* forget it. Some of them resorted to the use of their intelligence to thrive; some others survived as gatherers.

Fourth: It is very probable that all the *relatives of our ancestors* that started using fire, and in general, using their intelligence to thrive, *became extinct,* since those actions show *they were out of their natural niche,* or that their habitat and natural ecosystem were, for some reason, disturbed. The same can be said of many of the graincollectors that, at the Pliocene and Pleistocene, resorted to scavenging in times of drought or long periods of cold weather, since this caused them to forget their graincollecting culture. In cases like this, probabilities of extinction are huge even without their use of intelligence to thrive. Using it for that reason would worsen their chances, since those intelligent acts have greater probabilities of accelerating the imbalance of the ecosystem in which they are, whatever ecosystem it happens to be, whether previously disturbed or not, whether their own or not.

Maybe cultural oblivion, to which our ancestors were *always* exposed to during the last 14 million years of their evolution, explains why *very few graincollector populations survived as such.* Maybe this is *one* of the reasons why we have not yet found any fossil remains of graincollectors, or why we find fossil remains of the ancestors of the living pongids, and not of ours. Thus, in 14 million years, many indeed could be the populations of hominids who, having forgotten how to graincollect, could only survive as gatherers: such was the origin of *Gigantopithecus,* of all australopithecines, and of living pongids.

Fifth: *Because presently we humans are not living within our natural ecological niche and ecosystem, we use our intelligence to thrive. We are, then, creating an imbalance in all the ecosystems of the whole world and are going rapidly towards extinction, dragging along with us many innocent living beings.*

It should not seem strange that after 14 million years of being graincollectors, humans, 50 thousand years ago, forgot their graincollecting culture. We possess all the genetic aptitudes and instincts to be graincollectors; but since graincollection is a cultural and not a genetic inheritance, if we are not taught to graincollect we won't. It's the same as learning a language: we have all the genetic aptitudes to learn it, and we even know its grammar without having learned it, as we inherited it genetically (Chomsky, 1967, 1972, 1975a, 1975b); but if we are not taught how to speak it, we'll never do it, and so, that language, that culture, is forgotten. That also happened to the gorilla's, chimpanzee's and orangutan's ancestors 2 or 3 million years ago: All of their tool-using aptitudes to graincollect were perfect, but when they lost that culture they only kept those tool-using aptitudes genetically inherited. Furthermore, they have been losing those aptitudes little by little during the recent evolution of their respective lineages over such a long period of time, and their hands have had to adapt to other needs since they entered other adaptive zones. If there were someone who would teach humans, gorillas, chimpanzees, and orangutans to grain-collect, and we could all live our lives as graincollectors. We all could return to it, despite the fact that pongids have lost, in addition, their aptitude of walking in an upright position.

We will now review some facts that have given support to the aforementioned conclusions.

(a) If many intelligent members of an animal population at the same time perform several new and different intelligent actions *in order to thrive* (as is the current case with humans), how can such a diverse quantity of voluntary acts result in benefit for all or most of the members of that population and, at the same time, not be damaging to all the members of their ecosystem, including themselves? This can only happen when all those actions are *neutral*. Intelligence has increased its efficiency in animal evolution only when its consequences and effects have been neutral.

(b) Intelligence is a very old character in the evolution of the vertebrate species, which, moreover, can increase its efficiency by cumulative selection. If intelligence had survival value, and if some vertebrate species had used it to thrive, then, *only* those species should still be alive now, since they would have radiated and displaced those animal species that only use instincts to thrive and survive. If the human ancestors had used their intelligence to thrive since 2 or 3 million years ago, when the beginning of the great brain development occurred during the evolution of their lineage, and (as earlier stated) if intelligence had survival value, humans would, since then, have displaced (under Gause's principle of competitive exclusion) many animal species out of their niches because an adaptive radiation of intelligent hominids would have occurred. If the abovementioned has not occurred, it can be assured then that vertebrates, in the whole course of their evolution, never used their intelligence to thrive.

(c) Let us now compare the huge biological success and radiation that the macaques in Asia and the baboons in Africa have had, with the near disappearance of the human species at the start of the last great Pleistocene glaciation, and the fact that the living pongids are currently close to extinction (Strum, 1987). From such juxtaposition of

144

facts, it can be assured that animal intelligence did not originate the biological success of the more intelligent species over those less intelligent at any time in the course of animal evolution. This goes to show that the most intelligent members of an animal population never got a survival prize for being so. Strum (1987: 74) states:

Baboons are ubiquitous in Africa, from the arid regions of Ethiopia all the way down to the tip of the continent. If numbers and distribution count, they are second only to humans in their success as a primate. [Strum states in a footnote on the same page, that " . . . Asia has its baboon equivalent—the macaques, sometimes called the baboons of the East."]

It seemed that baboons could adapt their behavior to many different kinds of environment without having to change much of their basic anatomy. They are definitely a primate success story. *By comparison, chimpanzees are on the verge of extinction, so where has all their near humanness gotten them?* (Italics mine)

Jerison (1973: 412) states:

There is nothing in the fossil record of lower vertebrates to indicate that their lives were less "rich" than those of fossil birds and mammals that lived in similar environments. And we know that, despite their relatively small brains, fish and reptiles have not become extinct as a result of the radiation of larger-brained mammals and birds that appear to live in similar niches. We may emphasize therefore, that *vertebrates do not live by brains alone, and, although large brains may signify certain styles of life, the selective advantage associated with an enlarged brain has rarely been a major one.* It is really anthropocentricity that leads us to emphasize the brain and its evolution. (Italics mine)

The abovementioned confirms that animal intelligence does not have survival value.

(d) We must take note of the disastrous effects that the intervention of human beings has had over all the ecosystems of the world, due to the fact that we have used our intelligence in order to thrive and survive during the last 50 thousand years. It may be deduced that hominid populations that have, for long periods of time, used their intelligence to thrive, have become extinct. They used their intelligence to thrive only when pushed by severe and abnormal circumstances that took them out of their natural niche.

In order to support the idea of the extinction of *our ancestors' relatives* who used fire, and used their intelligence to thrive in other ways during the last million years, let us consider findings related to our mitochondrial DNA by Cann, Stoneking, and Wilson (1987). They affirm that most probably all current humans descend from one tribe that lived somewhere in the Old World, possibly in Africa, some 200 thousand years ago. "The question is: what happened to all the other populations around the world? For their women's mitochondrial genes apparently all vanished." (Tierney et al., 1988: 51) Additionally, they state (p. 47):

> "If it's correct, and I'd put money on it, this idea is tremendously important," says Stephen Jay Gould, the Harvard paleontologist and essayist. "It makes us realize that all human beings, despite differences in external appearance, are really members of a single entity that's had a very recent origin in one place. There is a kind of biological brother-hood that's much more profound than we ever realized."

Based on the abovementioned, we can conclude that in order to hunt and scavenge, it was necessary for the early hominids to have *manufactured several suitable types of tools*, made either from stone or other materials. This action indicates they were using their intelligence to thrive; and all this confirms that hunting and scavenging was *not* their normal way of living, but actions they carried out due to severe abnormalities in their natural environment and ecosystem. It is very probable, too, that the relatives of our ancestors who hunted and scavenged became extinct; or, if our ancestors were those who hunted and scavenged, they performed those activities *during short periods of time*, but always returned to their normal graincollecting life-style; since, if they had continued those practices for longer periods of time, they would have forgotten the cultural transmission of graincollection.

I would like to remind the reader that if hunting-gathering or scavenging-gathering had been the normal subsistence activities of our ancestors, instead of graincollecting, then humans wouldn't have in our body all of the graincollectors' characters: we would have those of hunter-gatherers or scavenger-gatherers.

2. Intelligence and the Enjoyment of Life

Citing Erasmus Darwin and Charles Darwin, Gruber (1981: 65) states:

> *Compassion for All Living Things.* While Erasmus [Darwin] came close to a pure utilitarian position, since he believed that the sum of happiness of all living creatures is the prime good, Charles, guided by the theory of natural selection, really substituted *survival* for happiness as the prime good. For him, happiness, or in lower organisms sensual pleasure, had adaptive value in that each species has evolved in such a fashion that the quest for happiness and pleasure contributes to its survival. Although the two positions are slightly different, both are based on a feeling of oneness with all of nature—all creatures enjoy and suffer; it is hard to imagine even an oyster or a plant as insensible.

Life, at the beginning, probably began in several ephemeral forms, but only those forms that could keep obtaining energy to live, to reproduce, and, in addition, to take all benefits from nature without disturbing their primordial ecosystem, survived. But did reproduction, at the beginning, carry a pleasure for those early living forms? We know that reproduction in humans carries a pleasure in itself—the pleasure of satisfying the sexual instinct. We may think then that reproduction *in all* living beings carries a pleasure. There is no reason to believe that that pleasure is exclusive to the so-called higher animals.

Would the higher animals reproduce themselves if there weren't a pleasure in reproduction? Is that pleasure alone enough to desire life? There are many questions very difficult to answer, even for specialist scientists, but let's analyze the problem:

The animals that we have called lower animals generally reproduce themselves at very short intervals of time. Higher animals perform sexual acts and reproduce at *very* long intervals of time. Therefore, it is very probable that the pleasure of the sexual act alone isn't enough for higher animals to *desire* and instinctively defend their life in such a tenacious and strong way as they do.

How are all instincts linked with the pleasure of satisfying them? Do only those individuals who feel pleasure when satisfying their instincts survive because that pleasure attracts animals to perform them, or are instincts linked in a natural mechanical way to the pleasure of satisfying them? Any way we want to look at it, the reality is that *animals feel pleasure when satisfying their natural instincts.*

The satisfaction of natural instincts conveys its pleasures; then, life itself conveys pleasures. Is it *compulsory* for living beings to *live,* only because at the time of conception a series of unavoidable chemical and physical actions and reactions occur in their bodies, or do living beings live for the pleasure of living? Are the pleasures obtained from satisfying instincts the reason why living beings desire life and defend it? *If the fulfillment of instincts were a natural obligation, an inevitable natural mechanism in living beings, then, the appearance of pleasure when satisfying them wouldn't have been adaptively necessary.* Then, the pleasure of reproducing appeared adaptively in all living beings because reproduction *is not a natural obligation* for them; instead, living beings reproduce themselves in order to obtain pleasure from the sexual or asexual act. If, in addition, reproduction later on brings with it pleasure in the satisfaction of other instincts, such as the maternal instinct, etc., it represents another advantage, but the act of reproduction by itself conveys pleasure in the satisfaction of the reproduction instinct.

If animal life was, in a natural way, compulsory to live, and didn't have the pleasures obtained from satisfying instincts, it wouldn't be desirable; and when the need of overcoming difficulties would appear, animal life would end due to a lack of *motivators.* Life without motivators would be monotonous and boring. Humans know that for individuals of human populations who currently live closer to nature, their pure and simple life has many attractions and is not monotonous or boring. In addition, we notice that many animals who live in their natural ecological niche and habitat, play, explore, sing, enjoy, and groom themselves; and they do all this *instinctively.*

Animals have *instincts* with which they thrive and survive, and they also have instincts that do not give them any material advantage, but pleasures that could be called of a *higher* nature.

But right here there is something very important: The fact that the development of intelligence in all animals was generated by instincts and actions whose satisfaction gave them useless benefits, and were only pleasures, makes us think that animal life is, and always has been, desirable; it compels us to think that animals live not simply by predetermined physical and chemical impulses in which their taste, pleasure, and individual satisfaction have no influence. The appearance of intelligence in animals shows that *life* has always given all animals, and still gives them, not only what is necessary to survive, but also satisfactions that go further. These are the nonmaterial satisfactions—not necessary for living and surviving, but which make life desirable, livable, and pleasant. Otherwise, intelligence would have not developed in animals, since, as we've seen, it is not necessary for survival or to thrive; and instincts alone are necessary *and sufficient* to survive. All animals have always survived, and still survive, based on their instincts and not on their intelligence. In the whole course of animal evolution the need for survival based on intelligence never appeared. When intelligence appeared in animal evolution it had nothing to do with survival, *but with the need all living beings have of enjoying life.*

However, life is not only pleasure and enjoyment; survival also carries along with it suffering and problems. Everything as a whole makes animal life attractive and desirable, since, if life were only enjoyment, animals would not be able to appreciate or be aware of that enjoyment; enjoyment alone would be monotonous and boring. In the same way, suffering or obedience to predetermined physical and chemical impulses alone would make for an intolerable life. Therefore, *life, the way it is in Nature, is perfect for all living beings.* If life isn't currently perfect for humans, it is because we live in an environment that is not natural for us. Within this alien environment we obtain very little enjoyment *from the true pleasures of life;* we do not understand the way in which the rest of the animals enjoy their life; and we have lost the natural way of enriching our intelligence the way our graincollector ancestors did: without assaulting nature and our ecosystem.

Animals have developed intelligence to enjoy life, and it progresses in animal evolution due to actions that do not harm or diminish the power of survival of other individuals, of other populations or of other species, whether or not they belong to the same ecosystem—that is, they do not harm anyone, and the performers obtain some nonmaterial benefit and satisfaction. Then, *enjoyment of life is an instinct in all animals,* and *is an instinct that predates the development of intelligence: intelligence developed due to the animal instinct of enjoying life and not vice-versa.*

But, do all animals possess the instinct of enjoying life? We can surely state they do, since those which enjoy life want it, and those who want it have better probabilities of surviving than those who are apathetic to it. Therefore, those who enjoy life have better probabilities of leaving more offspring. Even though enjoyment of life does not, in itself, have a *precise* and *definite* survival value, it does carry a *small* survival prize; this *small* survival prize is for those animals who want life.

Let us analyze some of the natural *motives* animals have for wanting life.

Why do animals instinctively refuse to die? Why do they defend their lives with such perseverance? Animals wouldn't have the desire of defending their lives, nor the desire of living, if life itself didn't *always* give them many desirable reasons for wanting it. If animal life, in the past, had been full of hardship, animals would not defend their life with perseverance. The pleasure of reproduction alone is not strong enough to attract animals to live and to defend their life. *Many of the animals jailed in zoos do not wish to reproduce themselves despite the pleasure of the sexual act, and despite the fact that "they have all they need for living." This is why it's difficult to have them reproduce themselves in such an unnatural environment.* Would dogs, horses, pigs, chickens and cows defend their life *instinctively* if their ancestors, in their wild life, had always lived jailed, almost motionless, even "if they had had all they need for living," as we currently keep them as pets, guarding our property, in the horse stables, or in the meat, egg, and milk *factories? All animals will instinctively defend life because they instinctively expect the pleasure that their ancestors had in their wild life.* If life was only mechanical, consisting only of eating and reproducing, all animal species in this planet would long ago have ended.

A great part of the animal wild life is pleasure, even with all its dangers and risks. *Life within their natural niche is mainly pleasure for all living beings.* We all are made of the same building blocks: the same type of cells, the same molecules, the same matter.

Humans feel pleasure when looking at the flowers in the fields, and when smelling their fragrances. Can we think that insects, at whom these floral attractions are aimed, do not enjoy them the same way we do? We would probably be wrong if we thought that they seek flowers due to physical and chemical impulses *alone*, while humans seek them as a result of higher pleasures. How did the diversity and beauty of forms, colors, and perfumes in flowers appear in nature if insects were incapable of appreciating them? Aren't those attractions a rivalry among flowers to captivate insects? Why must those floral attractions seem beautiful to humans and to other animals "if they only produce physical and chemical reactions" in some part of the body of insects? If those physical and chemical reactions that take place in some part of the body of insects are the selective pressures that generate those diverse forms, colors, and perfumes in flowers, I repeat: Why must those floral attractions seem beautiful to humans and to other animals if they do not even seem beautiful to insects "because they are only simply physical and chemical reactions" in some part of their body? How is it possible that if humans are so phylogenetically apart from insects, we are attracted to those flowers in such a similar way? We do not go to them with utilitarian ends, but insects do.

Humans are not only attracted to grasslands as our source of natural food; grasslands are not only attractive to us for the seeds we collect from grasses, but their beauty also attracts us. Do insects approach flowers due to utilitarian benefits alone and not also captivated by their beauty? We would be wrong and presumptuous if we think that, as humans, we are the only animals who possess that capacity. Dobzhansky and Boesiger (1983: 116, 120, 122) state:

Most persons derive pleasure from contemplating a flower, a butterfly, a bird, or a gazelle. Are these forms, patterns, and colors that we find so beautiful simply tricks of nature, without *functional value*? Or do they have a biological role that could have been established by evolution? Darwin (1871) claims the latter in his theory of sexual selection—at least for certain decorative characters which one finds among animals. He thinks that, even more than weapons that males use in obtaining mates, all sorts of ornaments and sound-producing organs have evolved under the pressure of sexual selection. . . . If we argue that higher vertebrates exhibit elements of perception and that they appreciate esthetic harmonies, we do not necessarily claim that these animals also create works of art. . . . Granted that man alone produces works of art in the usual sense of the word, it is nevertheless unrealistic to claim that an absolute difference separates man and other organisms when art is a question of perceptions or even of esthetic sensations. Forms, colors, patterns, and bodily expressions play an important biological role in the great majority of organisms. From the absence of the perception of forms and colors among plants and among primitive animals, one passes to more and more advanced means of perception. This is related to sensory organs. Man does not possess the most advanced sensory organs of any sort. But "progressive" evolution has led to a central nervous system which alone is capable of integrating sensorial perceptions, thereby producing an esthetic emotion . . . we think that one can also speak of an esthetic in certain higher animals, and of an evolution of esthetics . . . among birds and mammals, colors and patterns have a part in the choice of partners. It is not anthropocentric, then, to attribute to higher vertebrates a degree of esthetic sense. (Italics mine)

What seems most important from the quote just mentioned is: those forms, colors, perfumes, etc., that seem beautiful to a bird, to an insect, to a gazelle, are also beautiful to humans and to other animals; and *most probably seem beautiful to all living beings*. If those attractions have *functional value* to those living beings who possess them and to those to which such charms are directed, they do not have it to members of other species; then, why do they look beautiful and even moving to humans if for us they do not have any functional value?

All the abovementioned shows that all living beings have more or less the same motives for living, the same tastes and higher pleasures, even though they have different ways of living.

Life as part of a group is another natural motive animals have for wanting life. One of the true pleasures of life is living in groups, to belong to an animal group and, in general, to be together with other living beings. Why do animals try to live in groups, such as troops, flocks, schools, etc.? Could it be for the mere pleasure of being together, or is there a probability that when living in groups they obtain other benefits we can't easily perceive? Lewin (1989: 47) states:

Highly social creatures ourselves, it may seem odd to ask, "Why should animals live in groups?" But it is in fact a very good biological question, because there are many costs to gregariousness. For instance, a lone individual doesn't have to share its food with another individual, but in a group there is competition for all resources. A lone individual is not exposed to diseases that flourish in communities, which provide a viable host pool for pathogens. A lone individual is much less conspicuous to predators than is a group of individuals. And so on. Clearly, as most primates do live in groups, the benefits must outweigh the costs.

Does life becomes easier by being together? Is life more fun to live among many congeners? Well, *that is precisely what enjoying life in groups means: making it easier, defending it collectively, enjoying it, etc.*

Animals are instinctively attracted to life in groups; proof of that is that many flocks, herds, etc., have so many members that it appears they bother each other. Through our direct observation of all living beings in nature we may infer that, in some way, they attract each other and try to form groups as big as possible, since living in groups eases and makes life more enjoyable; but the size of the groups is limited by the inconvenience they are to each other within the group in their search and competition for food and sexual partners. Then, these two forces exist: attraction and repulsion. In the case of a complete ecosystem, their equilibrium, according to the unique way of survival and reproduction of its members, gives the optimal size of each population. And in the specific case of a population, the equilibrium of those two forces determines the size of tribes, troops, etc. Forming in this way great colonies of microorganisms, great swarms of migratory locusts, great flocks of birds, and even the lonely life of some spiders; but it seems that all living beings try to live together with as many living beings as is possible while they are able to fulfill their lives.

When life appeared, maybe the only pleasure by which it was desired was reproduction. But after biological evolution created a great variety of beings, and life in groups eased the survival of its members, life among groups required the appearance of other instinctive actions that, once satisfied, produced in turn other pleasures in addition to the one obtained from reproduction alone. Then, life forced individuals to perform actions that satisfied those instincts. But such instincts and their satisfying actions are sanctioned by natural selection, which rejects those damaging the population and the ecosystem. Allowing, first, the arrangement, step by step, in the phenotype of each individual, and in the whole ecosystem, of those instinctive actions that are necessary and essential for the survival of the members of that ecosystem, even though, *at the beginning,* some members are hurt and others benefit from them; and second, the free access of those *neutral* actions that give satisfaction to their performers but do not damage or diminish the survival power of other members of the ecosystem.

In this way, the potential appearance of intelligence was latent almost since the appearance of life itself. Therefore, the satisfaction of those instincts and of those higher neutral actions, in addition to the material ease that life in groups gave animals, dictated that groups be formed instinctively and naturally. Life in groups increases the development of social instincts and higher pleasures, and therefore the gradual development of intelligence.

3. Play Behavior

Play is a *higher* action for the enjoyment of life that several birds and almost all mammals perform, and has been, in the course of their evolution, one of the solid bases in the development of their intelligence.

Darwin (1871: 65, Vol. I) in *The Descent of Man* states:

But not only can we perceive how it is that man is capricious, but the lower animals are . . . capricious in their affections, aversions, and sense of beauty. There is also good reason to suspect that they love novelty, for its own sake.

Asimov (1984: 3) states:

Almost in the beginning was curiosity.

Curiosity, the overwhelming desire to know, is not characteristic of dead matter. Nor does it seem to be characteristic of some forms of living organism, which, for that very reason, we can scarcely bring ourselves to consider alive.

A tree does not display curiosity about its environment in any way we can recognize; nor does a sponge or an oyster. . . . Early in the scheme of life, however, independent motion was developed by some organisms. It meant a tremendous advance in their control of the environment. A moving organism no longer had to wait in stolid rigidity for food to come its way, but went out after it.

Thus, adventure entered the world—and curiosity.

Fagen (1981: 494) says:

In the play of animals we find a pure aesthetic that frankly defies science. Why kittens or puppies chase and vigorously paw at each other in reciprocal fashion without inflicting injury, repeating this behavior almost to the point of physical exhaustion, is not known. Yet this behavior fascinates, indeed enchants. Ernest Hemingway's Santiago, an old fisherman who had fought human and marlin and had known adversity, remembered, above all else, the play of wild lions. With

Santiago, we may well ask "Why are the lions the main thing that is left?" . . . But when . . . Santiago . . . looked back over [his life] . . . remembered play—dreamed, regretted, cherished, and hopelessly poignant—was the sole thing that mattered any more.

Mere nostalgia for childhood is not the issue. The basis of these responses is that suggested by human delight in animal play.

Fagen (1981) makes an exhaustive study of play among animals. The above words are in the epilogue of his book. If all of his book has helped us to better understand play behavior in animals, these final words mean that, up to now, a total understanding is out of our reach.

Caro (1988: 50) in the title of his review article: "Adaptive Significance of Play: Are We Getting Closer?" is telling us that up to the present time the reason of play among animals has not yet been explained, or that we still haven't analyzed and explained it correctly; this becomes evident after reading his article.

In the preface to his book, Fagen (1981: vii) mentions the following:

Animal Play Behavior addresses a major biological paradox. Why do young and old animals of many species spend time and energy, and even risk physical injury, performing the apparently unproductive behaviors colloquially called play? What makes this "useless" activity so important that animals literally risk their lives for it? And, even more curiously, why are humans both enchanted and enraged by play? . . . Animals that play would seem to be at an evolutionary disadvantage. By sacrificing time, energy and safety for play, they negatively influence their chances of surviving to reproduce, all in order to perform behavior that lacks an obvious beneficial product.

Asimov (1984: 4) states:

An organism may be sated with food, and there may, at the moment, be no danger in sight. What does it do then?

It might lapse into an oysterlike stupor. But the higher organisms at least still show a strong instinct to explore the environment. Idle curiosity, we may call it. Yet, though we may sneer at it, *we judge intelligence by it.* (Italics mine)

Why do we judge the intelligence of animals according to their idle curiosity and capability for play? The answer is simple: Because there is no other *direct* way of judging it. Because those are almost the only animal characters in which intelligence is fully evident, since it can't be judged by the capability each animal, each species, or each population has in order to survive or to *face* their environment, since animals never use their intelligence for those purposes. It cannot be judged, either, by the capability of learning by experience, since conditioned reflexes play a major role in this process. No animal uses its intelligence to thrive or to face its environment; however, it uses it when displaying inquisitive behavior, for free play at idle times, and at times of relaxation.

All the material benefits that animals can obtain from playing, and we may think that these are the adaptive reasons for their play, are circumstantial and secondary. That is why, after 110 years in which many scientists have been dedicated to explaining the adaptive meaning of play behavior in animals, a solution to the problem has not yet been found: we want to find a material reason, a utilitarian reason, a reason that in fact does not exist. Probably the only true reason for play is *living—enjoying life.* Thus, play behavior is favored by natural selection, even though it has no survival value, only because it doesn't hurt anyone; that is, it does not influence the natural balance of any ecosystem, *and it benefits the individual or individuals who perform it: It makes them desire life. Maybe the only adaptive meaning of play and of exercising idle curiosity is the will of the animal to live.*

The mother is the first one to play with her infant. I'll repeat the quote Herter (1975) makes from Georg Wilhelm Steller's report of 1741–42:

> "Females [sea otters] carry the young in their mouth, but in the sea the mother lies on her back and holds the baby between her fore feet just like a human mother holds a baby in her arms. The mother otter plays with her baby, tossing it in the air and catching it like a ball, putting it in the water so it learns to swim, and taking it back when it is tired and kissing it in a very human way." (Herter, 1975: Vol. 12, p. 86)

Is it not play that makes those two beings love and want life with all their strength?

The adult animal who watches infant animals playing in the wild also wants and enjoys life, maybe as much as they do. Which is the happiest being: the infant who plays or the mother watching him?

Darwin (1871: 39, Vol. I) states:

Happiness is never better exhibited than by young animals, such as puppies, kittens, lambs, etc., when playing together, *like our own children*. (Italics mine)

Adults experience greater joy when watching children or animals play than that experienced with their own play, or with the memories of their childhood play. This is a character that has been sublimated in humans.

Spencer (1878: 627) states:

Many years ago I met with a quotation from a German author to the effect that the aesthetic sentiments originate from the play-impulse. I do not remember the name of the author; and if any reasons were given for this statement, or any inferences drawn from it, I cannot recall them. But the statement itself has remained with me, as being one which, if not literally true, is yet the adumbration of a truth.

The activities we call play are united with the aesthetic activities, by the trait that neither subserve, in any direct way, the processes conducive to life. [From a reprint in Muller-Schwarze, 1978: 10]

Caro (1988: 50) says that in 1898, Karl Gross " . . . attempted to link the biology of play to human artistic activity. . . . " Spencer also viewed that link as an acceptable possibility. Besides Spencer and Gross in the past, presently Caro and Fagen, in several of their articles and books, link play behavior with artistic activities. Currently there are many other scientists who accept it as well, or consider this link to be probable. This is very important, first, because it explains the origin of our artistic tendencies through play, since play behavior has its origin in animals' primitive curiosity and in their instinct to enjoy life, which pushed the development of intelligence during animal evolution, and later, is intelligence, which pushes the development of artistic sense; and second, because it strongly supports *that all the "human" virtues we possess (intelligence, artistic sense, moral sense, natural ethics, scientific curiosity, etc.) were acquired by our ancestors when and while being animals, and not when and while being "civilized" people.* That is, it demonstrates that all the virtues that humans have were acquired by our ancestors before Würm's Glaciation, following only their animal instincts when being graincollectors, *and not* following their intelligence during *the cavemen age* that *they* lived during that last great Pleistocene glaciation—*the cavemen age that we are presently living.*

Artistic activities have been very important in human evolution. There is evidence that our ancestors performed many artistic non-utilitarian activities. Judging by our artistic aptitudes (since we are genetically endowed with these kinds of capabilities), our ancestors had been practicing them for millions of years: they enjoyed music, dancing, painting, drawing, sculpture, etc.

I believe it is a mistake to attempt to explain all animal *behavioral* characters thinking that natural selection is only *differential reproduction in favor of the fittest*; that it is only a *material* victory of those individuals or groups of individuals best adapted to the conditions under which they live, taking into account only material advantages and disadvantages. Within all the cases sanctioned by natural selection there must be special cases that we can't explain if we have in mind only *material* outlines of convenience or inconvenience, since that narrowing of our mind doesn't allow us to see the true reasons by which animals are moved to live and enjoy life. *Even though, in reality, those reasons generate behavioral actions that are special and very important cases sanctioned by natural selection,* all of these actions might not require the success of the fittest, but the simple survival of those desiring life the most, and who fully enjoy it. Animals play despite the risk of losing their lives in an accident, and when playing they do not obtain any benefit; play behavior is not a character that adaptively appeared in animals to prepare them for their future life, as some investigators believe. If by playing they obtain this or other advantages, such advantages are incidental; but natural selection cannot sanction play behavior in this way. Singing, playing, satisfying idle curiosity, communicating, etc., are performed by animals from their desire to *live and enjoy life*, and *no* visible survival benefits are obtained from it. If these kinds of actions provide insufficient explanation for the origin of our intelligence, *or do not seem to be cases sanctioned by natural selection*, it is probably because we still have not begun to understand animals; it is probably because we still have not begun to understand humans. We don't know or understand ourselves anymore because, for the last 50 thousand years, we haven't lived within nature; therefore, *we think that life for humans and animals was, and has always been, this present misery that we humans have brought about throughout the whole world.*

Based on the material covered up to now in this chapter, it can be assured that a great part of the life of animals living within their natural niche is pleasure, and that the life of those animals who are out of their natural niche has no pleasure, since they are struggling against extinction. Since the last great glaciation, humans do not know the natural and simple joys of life. Since that time, we are *fighting against nature and working to avoid extinction.* The worst part is that, in this way, we do not satisfy all of our natural instincts, and this drives us crazy. *Enjoying life, satisfying all our natural instincts* (not repressing them as we are currently doing), *can only be achieved if we live within our natural ecological niche, the niche in which our ancestors lived for the last 14 million years, the niche for which all of our anatomical, physiological, and behavioral characters are "made to measure":* graincollection.

4. The Origin of Food Sharing; the Origin of Informal Gatherings

The time at which brain development occurred and intelligence greatly developed in the evolution of the human lineage is marked by the predominant use of a stone tool: the so-called *hand axe.* What does this mean? Is the use of this tool related with the increase in intelligence, or is it just a coincidence without relation? Before the start of that rapid increase in intelligence, our ancestors used hand axes very seldom, and the few they used were rudimentary. It can be noticed that there seems to be a relation between the use of hand axes and the development of intelligence; therefore, it is convenient to stop and analyze the validity of this relation.

It has been mentioned, in Sections 1 and 2 of this chapter, that in the last 2 or 3 million years the great development of intelligence during the evolution of the human lineage was the result of the very special case of verbal communication actions sanctioned by sexual selection. And if, in addition, that great development of intelligence is related to the use of the hand axe, then, the use of this tool had some influence in supporting those actions approved by sexual selection. I will try to demonstrate that it is so, and also that the use of the hand axe greatly influenced the development of food-sharing, the development of spoken language, and with it, influenced the tradition of informal gatherings, which in turn greatly influenced the great development of our artistic aptitudes, etc.

In considering this important matter, let us ask: What was the use given to the hand axe in graincollection?

Let us imagine a tribe of hominids of 2 or 3 million years ago, migrating and graincollecting somewhere in a savanna of Europe-Asia. (Here I remind the reader that one of the reasons for which I assume that the greater part of hominid evolution, starting about 14 million years ago, happened in the savannas of Europe-Asia, is that the gramineous seeds that are currently our main source of food are aboriginally from those regions, and they must have been the main source of nourishment for our graincollector ancestors during all of their evolution.) In our mind's eye we see mothers carrying their infants on the infants' throne. Some of them carrying a grown-up infant but still as dependent on them for their nourishment as for their transportation. This grown-up infant demands from his mother not only her breast milk, but also the seeds she eats; his mother feeds him those seeds, sometimes pre-chewed by her, and sometimes the way she collects and threshes them. However, during the time of the year when the grasses that grow their seeds in spikes, such as wheat, barley, etc., are ripe, and since a greater effort is needed to thresh them using her small grainthresher than the effort normally made when scraping and threshing oats or other gramineous seeds that do not grow in spikes, she does what seems a very logical and normal action: with that small tool she cuts the spikes along with part of the stem, and makes a bundle of them. Once she has made a big bundle of spikes, she stops, sits on the ground, maybe by the shadow of one of the few trees of the savanna, and threshes all the spikes rubbing them with the palm of her right hand on a bigger stone than her normal grainthresher—a stone that she has chosen with appropriate size and shape for that job. Holding this stone tool with her left hand, she lets the seeds and the chaff fall to the ground from as high as her arms and hands allow. In this way, then, the wind separates seeds from chaff—in other words, *she threshes and winnows the seeds*. A small heap of clean seeds is formed on the ground, which mother and child share.

But this action generates other actions: other mothers in the same position, with grown-up infants, imitate and keep her company. And that imitation doesn't end here: other mothers, still with young infants, see a good opportunity for resting, and with their small grainthresher they cut a bunch of spikes to share with other mothers and their infants. And the males and juveniles and all of the tribe also imitate and follow them and stop in order to share their food. In this way another activity is found for the adult male: with the bigger stone tools they thresh and winnow the spikes that the mothers and other members of the tribe have cut.

Since threshing and winnowing seeds for a whole tribe is hard work, this is done by several males at a time: each one chooses a big enough stone with a suitable shape for threshing spikes (not intended for cutting those spikes as done with the smaller grainthreshers) and devote their time to threshing and winnowing spikes. In this way, without setting out to do so, and without this being their main goal, each male attracts a good number of females to him. Even though the whole tribe is gathered together in one place, small groups are formed surrounding each adult male who is threshing spikes, sharing food, *and talking with those surrounding him* (see plate 4).

When the food-sharing, resting, napping, talking, playing, singing, and dancing meeting is over and the migration must continue, the males who threshed the spikes must decide between the possibility of finding in the next meeting place a suitable stone for the exclusive use of threshing spikes, or *carrying in their hands the stone* they now have, and avoiding the risk of not finding another one later on. The safest thing to do is to carry the one they already have, even if this one is not very light, since finding a stone suitable for that purpose is not always easy.

After thousands of years, this tradition, most probably, dictated graincollectors to give those bigger stones *not* the appropriate shape and size for threshing spikes, since many shapes of stone, even some quite big ones, are suitable for this, *but the optimum shape and size best suited for easily transporting it, day after day, in the palm of the hand* during the migration, and during the time of the year in which the grasses that grow their seeds in spikes are in season. The graincollectors tried to find stones that were small and comfortable enough without having the stone tool lose its main function of efficiently threshing spikes, without the carriers of the stones hurting their hands, without hindering the natural oscillation of the arms when walking, without obstructing blood circulation in the palm of the hand, and, in general, fulfilling the requirements of comfort; that is, still being able to place their hands without having to flex fingers, hand or arm beyond their natural way of hanging and flexion (see Illustration 5). It was a complete, successful, and precise adaptation. The most suitably shaped stone tool for that purpose was, *naturally*, an almond shape, and the size would have been that of an extended hand. For this transportation, when taking it by the rounded part of the almond towards the ground (see Illustration 6), the shape of this tool is almost perfect—difficult to improve even with current techniques. This is logical, since this hand axe was used and culturally improved, little by little, by an artificial cultural system *similar* to the natural biological system of cumulative selection, over a period of 2, 3, or 4 million years. To repeat: *the almond shape of the hand axe was best because our ancestors tried to achieve ease of hand carrying during migratory travel, and not because they tried to achieve the optimal shape for its use.*

Leakey and Lewin (1978: 89, 90) state:

Around 1.5 million years ago an interesting phenomenon occurred at Olduvai: a second stone-tool culture arrived and began a long coexistence with the indigenous Developed Oldowan tool kit. The new technology, known as Acheulian, is best known for its so-called hand axes: these are carefully fashioned teardrop-shaped implements for which, embarrassingly, no one can think of a good use. Some of them are so heavy as almost to defy any possible practical use for them at all; while others *you can hold comfortably in the palm of your hand* and they may well have been put to the use for which their name implies. Perhaps they were simply the way a stone-tool knapper demonstrated his skill: a kind of prehistoric trade-mark! (Italics mine)

Some of the remaining small flakes, when manufacturing hand axes, functioned very well as grainthreshers, and the core served exclusively as a large spikethresher. Maybe the manufacture of hand axes helped improve grainthreshers, since the ones used at the beginning of graincollection were completely natural stones. Or most probably the reverse was true: the technique used to improve the small stone grainthreshers was later on used to manufacture hand axes.

At this point, I'll make a break to highlight two things: one to support the statement that intelligence was never used by our ancestors to thrive; and the other to support the statement that our ancestors used

Plate 4   Graincollectors in the savanna harvesting wheat, in one of their several daily resting-foodsharing-talking gatherings. A male adult is threshing spikes with a hand axe while several females bring spikes to him.

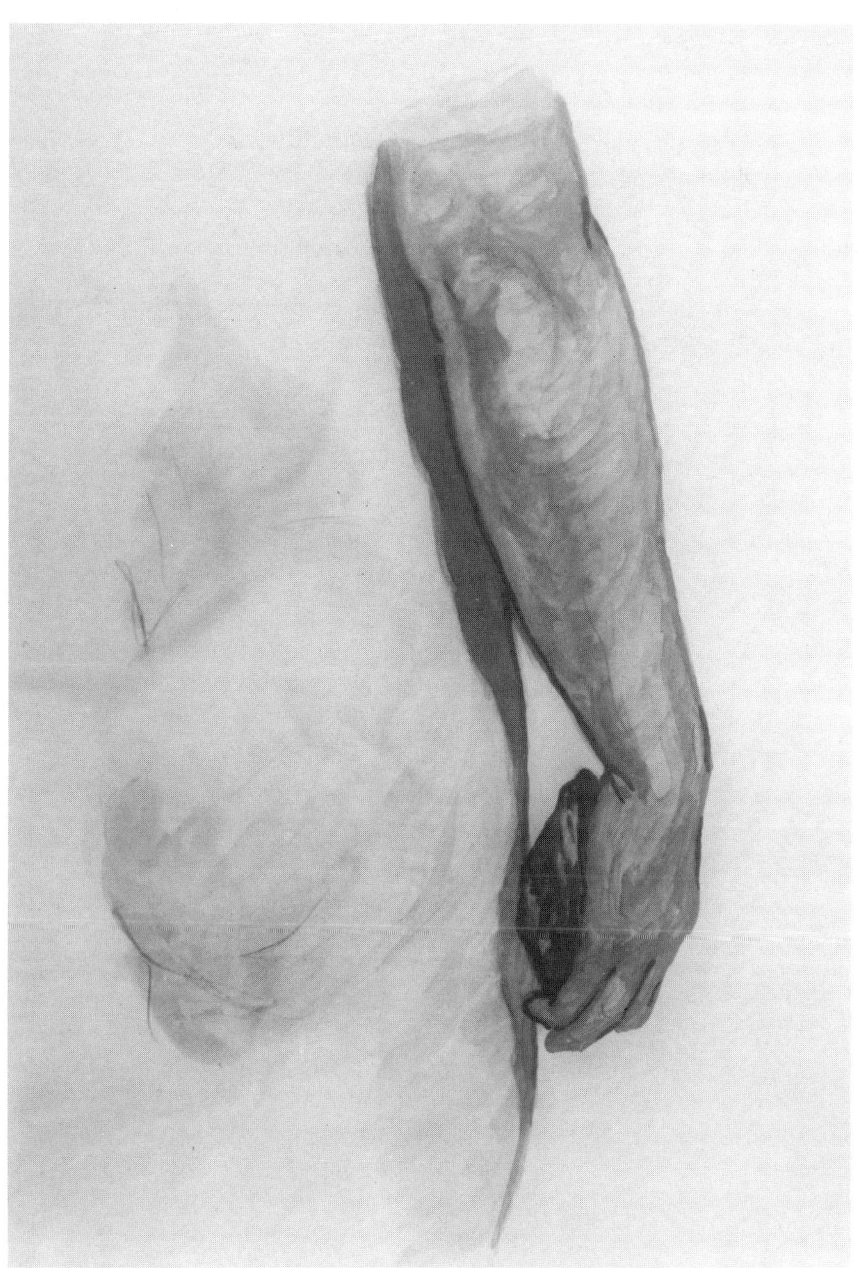

Illustration 5

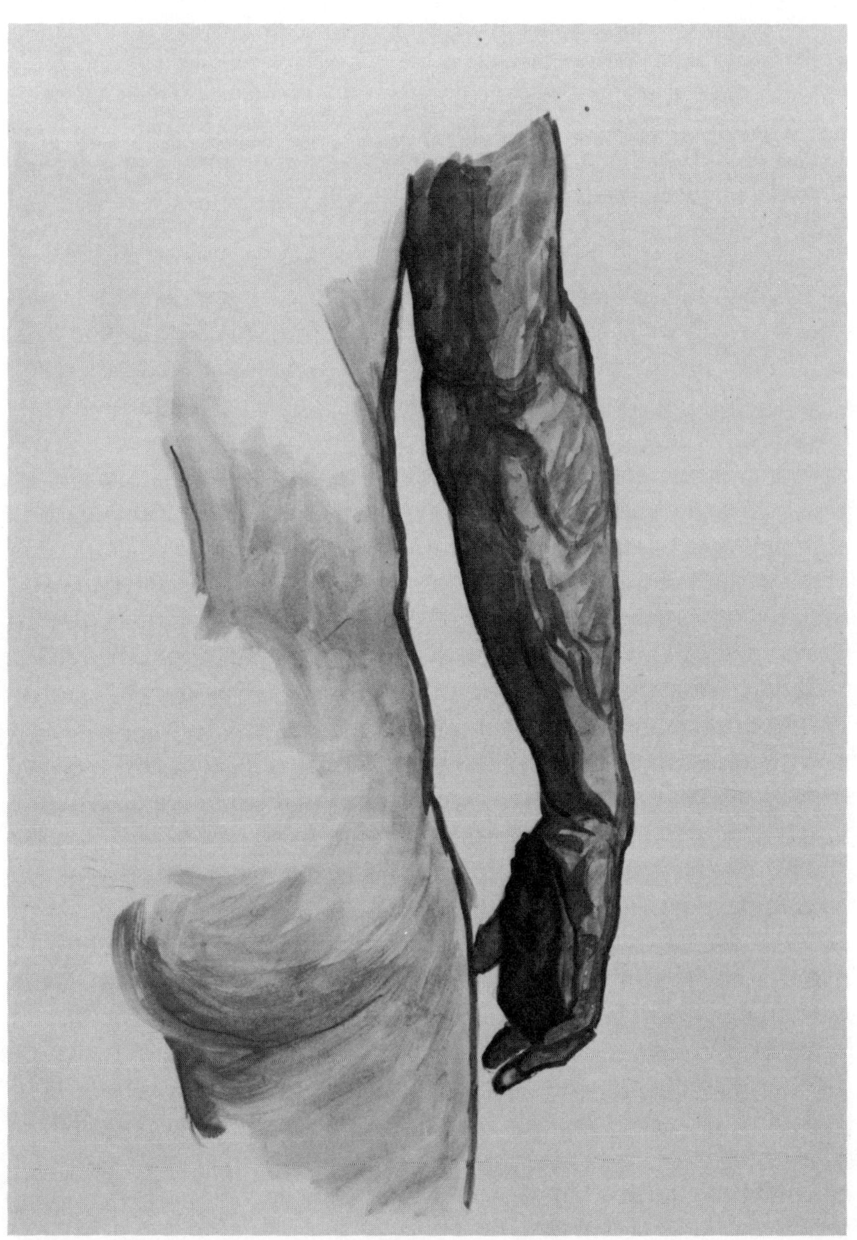

Illustration 6

weapons for hunting only during the last 50 thousand years; *both supports are based on the fact that the hand axes are large spikethreshers.*

Clark (1976: 45) states:

> One of the most striking things, however, about the broad cultural pattern of the Middle Pleistocene is its general "sameness" within the limits imposed by the stone industries. The overall similarity in pattern between the Acheulian and Developed Oldowan cultural assemblages wherever they are situated calls for a common level of behavior . . . Handaxes from Europe, South Africa, or peninsular India are all basically similar tools, and this is also true for the rest of the heavy-duty and the light-duty elements.

During the entire period in which the development of the brain in hominid evolution was so fast and sizable, stone tools remained the same (Wynn, 1988), and served for the same use. An already perfect hand axe, in its almond shape, remained the same from 1.5 million years ago until 150 thousand years ago (or maybe until 50 thousand years ago, the start of the last great glaciation). This shows that intelligence didn't develop due to our ancestors' way of surviving; because if intelligence had developed for that reason, tools would at that time have been diverse and with very different uses or applications. Thus, we would have to assume that the development of intelligence would influence the use of several types of tools in many different contexts.

However, the general sameness of tools throughout this long period of time has proved that other factors were the cause of the great development of the brain and intelligence, and not survival or subsistence reasons. If our ancestors had been hunter-scavenger-gatherers at the time of the great development of their brain and intelligence, they would have developed tool division according to function because, in this niche and context, for animals like humans who lack natural characters for hunting and scavenging, different kind of weapons and tools are absolutely necessary. Different shapes would have become available because many of the flakes released when the hand axes were manufactured could have been used as blades, *and they could have been improved if there had been a need for hunting and butchering.* It is not logical to think that our ancestors, at that time, didn't understand their needs, and that the improvement and division of tools, according to use, could not be achieved earlier than Würm's Glaciation: they didn't improve them previously because it wasn't needed. We can't believe they were at that time incapable of manufacturing blades and spear points if they had had the need to hunt. The Neolithic started recently as a result of Würm's Glaciation by which our ancestors were forced into manufacturing weapons for hunting, because it caused the disappearance of many of the savannas of Europe-Asia, thus, the disappearance of graincollection, and *not because it was only then that our ancestors became intelligent enough to manufacture weapon-tools with proper points and sharp edges.*

An accepted fact by anthropologists and archeologists is the very gradual development and evolution of the stone tools used by our ancestors in the Palaeolithic, due to the 3 or 4 million years that elapsed in the transition from the Oldowan Industry to the Developed Oldowan, and later to the Acheulian Industry. The Acheulian Industry develops in 1.5 million years. Is it not strange then, that in the very short period of the last 30 or 40 thousand years, the types of tools changed radically? It's obvious that something pushed man towards that rapid and radical change: that was the last great Pleistocene glaciation, which turned our ancestors into hunters. That is why they stopped manufacturing tools for graincollecting and instead manufactured weapons.

One of the main differences in the tools of these periods is that the tools in the last 30 or 40 thousand years are, in general, much smaller and with points and sharp edges. Another great difference is that the tools of the Paleolithic are made of rough materials. Semenov (1976) establishes that the quality of tools (weapons) depends on the properties of the material they are made from. However, it seems that the tool manufacturers of the Paleolithic didn't choose raw materials expecting to obtain from them points and sharp edges of good quality. The materials from which these tools are made were quite diverse. Form wasn't rigorous either; more rigorous shapes can be found in the Acheulians' tools, but not in the materials used for their manufacture, since the materials used were of very different textures. Semenov (1976: 36) states:

Commonly, in countries where during palaeolithic and mesolithic times man had had to make his tools out of poor-quality stone, in neolithic times tools appear of technically superior rocks, and also in greater quantity.

It is not probable that the hominid tool-users of the Paleolithic, after 10 or 12 million years of using and manufacturing tools wouldn't choose *good* raw materials because they didn't have the proper " . . . skills of sawing and grinding . . . " needed to work with " . . . hard actinolithic rocks (nephrite, jadeite, serpentine) . . . " as Semenov believes (1976: 36). It is more probable that those *good* raw materials were not the best suited for the goal they sought, or because those goals could be obtained with materials easier to work with; i.e., since they were not hunter-gatherers or scavenger-gatherers, they were not interested in fine and sharp cutting edges that could be better achieved with other materials.

We must notice that, in general, signs of wear are not seen in the hand axes because all the tool body is used in order to thresh spikes, and not only the edges; besides, hand axes don't really have cutting edges. The light marks that could remain in the body when threshing gramineous spikes can be easily confused with marks left by natural stubs (such as animal steps or kicks) after the tool was lost or abandoned on the ground or at the bottom of an ancient lake or puddle and exposed to the elements (natural erosion).

The fact that signs of wear are not evident on hand axes could be another proof that they were used in graincollection, and very probably used to thresh gramineous spikes in the manner already described.

To return to our main topic of this section: In the presence of good weather conditions and after the house sparrow *(Passer domesticus)* has fully satisfied its hunger, generally just after midday, flocks of house sparrows gather on the trees where males and females devote their time to groom themselves and prattle—behavior instinctive in them.

Few natural human activities provide more pleasure than gathering in groups to share food and talk. The most satisfying and more common human gatherings always were and still are those in which food is shared—an instinct in us. During the last 50 thousand years this instinct has *not* been completely satisfied in humans, since it was traditional that all the tribe gathered to share food and talk several times during the day, every day. However, at present it still remains the main reason of all human gatherings. It is more important than sport or play gatherings, or those intended to share our artistic accomplishments, or gatherings for grooming and talk, as the house sparrows do. This tradition that is ingrained in humans originated in the resting-foodsharing-talking gatherings that our graincollector ancestors had every day during the Upper Pliocene and Pleistocene.

Now, humans will start to understand how we should, in a simple but intense way, enjoy our life, as we observe the simple but intense way in which animals enjoy their life.

5. On the Origin of Language

Jonas and Jonas (1976a: 525) state:

. . . it is of some interest that vocalizations are among the bonding mechanisms of some other mammalian species. After a ewe, for instance, has separated her newborn lamb from its membrane and licked it dry, she begins to "talk" to it in a very specific way, to which it responds.

Hewes (1974: 1) states:

Although there is a sizeable literature on the general topic of the functions of language, there has not been much written about how language might have served its earliest users . . . Geoffrey Sampson (1972) observes that it is by no means clear why possession of language should be adaptive for a species, and further that it is hopelessly circular to explain the utility of language by describing its function in terms which have meaning only in a theory of language. The same weakness applies to formulations in logical terms, since logic was originally a formalization of the content of natural language.

A developed intelligence and spoken language are particularly human characters. This is the reason why many researchers of human speech linked it to the development of intelligence.

There are many theories regarding the origin of spoken language. The one proposed by Jonas and Jonas (1975) seems to be the most logical and probable from the point of view of graincollection and transportation on the infants' throne. Their article (1975: 630) ends as follows:

It is our contention that the first context in which protolanguage proved adaptive was in the attachment behavior between the hominid mother and her infant, and that our human powers of speech and our languages developed from this matrix.

A year later, Jonas and Jonas (1976b: 748) state:

It was not directly on the infant's babbling that we focused, however, but on the tendency of the adult female to respond to it, reinforcing mother-infant bonding, and selection for her ability to modify call sounds, such as those indicating warning or recalling from a distance, until identifiable vocalizations were associated with an increasing number of specific meanings.

The Jonases rightfully assume that the protolanguage of vocal sounds which developed as a result of the mother-infant bond, were not the first sounds that our ancestors were capable of emitting, since many animal species, and particularly primate species, emit vocal sounds in different situations and contexts; instead, those vocal sounds previously acquired were the biological preadaptation, which, later on in its evolution, and as a result of the mother-infant bond, they could develop into a true language of vocal sounds.

From the time of its publication, this theory, although subjected to many criticisms, was very well accepted. This suggestion of Jonas and Jonas didn't have at that time the solid support that the graincollection theory can now offer, since they assume that the protolanguage originated in a hunting-gathering context.

To assume that the protolanguage originates in a graincollecting context gives several conclusive supports: First: in the Upper Pliocene, at the beginning of the hominid great and rapid brain development, our ancestors already had 10 or 12 million years of living as graincollectors. Life for them within the ecological niche of graincollection had always been calm, with an abundance of spare time that could have been used for socializing, and very suitable for activities which support the development of intelligence, such as satisfaction of their natural animal curiosity, playing, singing, etc.; therefore, even before the great brain development, they already possessed a somewhat developed intelligence. Second: they had also been free of predators for those 10 or 12 million years due to the fact that they were able to use tools, wield branches, throw stones, etc. In this way, the graincollector mother could very confidently walk through the savanna carrying her grown-up infant without danger of being attacked by predators. If their capability of throwing stones and wielding branches hadn't been well developed and rooted in the graincollectors' behavior since the Middle Miocene, this mother-infant bond would not have been capable of extending for so many years of the infant's life; even less with the hindrance that transporting a grown-up infant represents within the graincollecting life-style. Third: due to the fact that the infant, when traveling either sitting or standing on the infants' throne, was always close to his mother's body, the distance between them was minimal. Fourth, and most important: *When traveling on the infants' throne, neither infant nor mother could see each other's arms or face for a great part of the day.* Gestures could not have had a great influence in their communication, and the only influences were the infant's movements that the mother perceived through her body, *the sounds emitted by the infant when babbling, and the mother's answering with vocal sounds to that babbling.* Therefore, Jonas and Jonas are right: infant babbling in their first years of life (mainly when asking for food), the answer to that babbling, and the bonding among mother and infant *for so many years,* facilitates the development of those first sounds into real and differentiated words with true meanings, which were decisive for the origin of a protolanguage within the graincollecting context; that is, in an environment and circumstances totally suitable for its appearance. Velo (1976: 525) states:

> I am at odds with the Jonases on the circumstances promoting the use of a protolanguage. I do not see any situation demanding the use of a language more than one connected with immediate survival. I can see no other activities more immediately connected, at the earliest hominid level, with individual and group survival than hunting and fighting. . . . *Had the hominids lived in an ideal situation in which they were spared the crudities of the daily struggle for life, then perhaps the deeply emotional aspects of the mother-baby relationship would have sufficed for the emergence, in the long run, of some sort of language.* (Italics mine)

This situation suggested by Velo (1976) is precisely graincollection, since we must remember that graincollection had to be in fact "an ideal situation" in order to allow a graincollector mother to carry for so many years the heavy load that was her offspring, and to allow her, at the same time, to graincollect seeds for the nourishment of both herself and her infant, without having to depend on a male.

If to this behavior and to this mother-infant bond we add the tradition graincollectors had (which appeared in the Upper Pliocene) of meeting several times during the day for resting-foodsharing-talking, where singing in groups must have been a normal habit, we notice a set of actions that must have *necessarily* originated a spoken language.

The abovementioned supports the idea that spoken language originated as another way of enjoying life and not as an aid for survival.

I want to emphasize a logical and very important hypothesis made by Richman (1976), which strengthens the idea that the resting-food-sharing-talking meetings of our graincollector ancestors were decisive in the origin of spoken language; maybe as much as the mother-infant bond was. Richman points out that early hominid males, when entering puberty and changing tribe, were subject to a selective pressure that might have forced them to use vocalizations, the way it happens among the *Theropithecus gelada*. I will quote Richman (1976) in this connection, since what he says is very important and useful in the presentation of the theory of graincollection. Richman (1976: 523) states:

By concentrating on only one human personal bond, however, they [Jonas and Jonas (1975)] underestimate the significance of intimate personal bonds of all types as the general social condition under which language evolved. I should like to present what might be called a hypothesis of human speech growing out of grooming and personal bonds.

I have been struck by the importance of the formation of intimate personal bonds in the social organization of some *Papio* and *Theropithecus* groups. A new perspective on *Papio* social groups has recently been presented by the work of Shirley Strum in Gilgil, Kenya (Moss 1975, Strum 1975). (William Malmi, who studied the Gilgil troop before Strum, has confirmed to me the correctness of her findings.) In this work, the formation and maintenance of intimate personal bonds, "friendships," takes on crucial significance. What is striking to me is that the formation of these bonds in a *Papio* group, for example, in the situation of an outside male trying to enter a new group by forming "friendships" with several resident females, involves persistent attempts by the male to stay close to a female and groom her, but little or no vocalization. In contrast, the formation of such bonds in a *Theropithecus* group involves much the same gestural, proximity, and grooming behavior, but also a tremendous amount of mutual vocalization (cf.

Kummer 1971 on pair-forming in geladas). It is my hypothesis that the great range of vowel-like, consonant-like, and other types of vocal sounds that geladas now produce arose during the course of gelada social evolution precisely under the exigencies of this situation—the formation of personal bonds using a tremendous amount of mutual vocalization. It seems that the present gelada social organization, involving the use of a great range of vocal sounds in the context of the formation and maintenance of intimate personal bonds, is a good model for an early stage of the social use of vocal sounds in early hominid groups. The early hominid mother-child bond suggested by the Jonases could be included in this general model.

To support Richman's hypothesis, we must remember and take into consideration that the use of the grainthresher gave hominid graincollectors a great amount of spare time, which earlier, while being seed-eaters without tools, had to be devoted for a great part of the day to foraging, the way it is currently done by the gelada baboons who feed from gramineous seeds. Kawai and Iwamoto (1979: 265) state:

One of the most characteristic activities of gelada baboons . . . is the extremely frequent feeding behavior. Of their overall daytime activities, males spent 78.2% and females 81.6% on feeding, on average. The time spent on feeding and moving alone represented almost 90% of the total activity. Gelada baboons thus appear to devote most of their day to foraging behaviour.

Washburn and Ciochon (1974: 778) state:

. . . vervets *(Cercopithecus aethiops)* spend several hours per day in obtaining food for a 12-to-15-pound body. Gibbons spend some 85–90% of waking time hanging and feeding (Ellefson 1968). . . . Rhesus monkeys not only eat seeds, but may spend many hours of the day doing so (Dolhinow, personal communication). *Eating seeds is an exceedingly time-consuming process* . . . (Italics mine)

Since the beginning of graincollection, and before the use of the hand axe, early hominids must have had plenty of spare time for socializing, precisely because they used a tool to obtain food; later on, after the invention of the hand axe, their spare time could have increased. This tool gave them, in addition, the chance of meeting together, sharing food, and conversing. Consequently, the resting-foodsharing-talking meetings of the graincollectors of the Upper Pliocene and Pleistocene must have been very common, because they could, in a short period of time, cut a sizable number of spikes with their grainthresher, and then meet and share those seeds by using the hand axe as an exclusive and efficient spikethresher.

Speech highly improved at these informal gatherings for conversation, and even more when sexual selection favored those members of the opposite sex who expressed themselves better. Therefore, speech was the selective pressure that developed intelligence even further, and it wasn't a developed intelligence that originated speech. Pollack (1967: 92) states:

Man's involvement in language behavior is so pervasive that some theorists have suggested that the human brain not only made language behavior possible, but its evolution was fashioned by language.

Mayr (1979: 634, 635) states:

The assumption that rather small-brained hominids were experienced tool users and manufacturers raises at once the question of the nature of that (tremendous) selection pressure which caused an increase of brain size during the mid-Pleistocene at an unprecedented rate (Haldane 1949b). Average cranial capacity rose from 1000 to 1400 cm^3 in less than 1 million years . . . *It seems likely that the ability to make tools contributed far less to this selection pressure than did the need for an efficient system of communication, that is, speech.* (Italics mine)

Ruse (1988: 17) states:

Articulate, spoken language is certainly not a necessary condition for any kind of intelligence whatsoever (although perhaps intelligence presupposes at least some ability to communicate). However, human intelligence as we know it is very much bound up with our language abilities. Indeed, today many philosophers would say that language-use is the very essence of rationality and intelligence (Black, 1968).

Jerison (1988a: 10) states:

Intelligence evolved, I have argued, as an aspect of the evolution of encephalization. The "excess" capacity represented by encephalization is used primarily for the construction of reality—of the representation of a world that is the reality of each species. Human reality, according to this view, is deeply associated with human language. It is reasonable to extend this implication to the specialized correlates of encephalization in other species, and to suggest that their adaptations may be as unusual as language.

Chomsky (1967, 1972), says that humans, when speaking, perform a totally new intelligent act in each sentence that's said, in each phrase that's pronounced. We learn one or several languages already existing, but every sentence that is said in any language is completely different from the ones heard or said before. Then, in order to talk, humans must be very intelligent. *Speech generated a great development of intelligence since everything when spoken is new.* The previously constructed sentences that we use when speaking are very few. *We are generating totally new intelligent acts every time we say even the smallest imaginable sentence.* Chomsky (1967: 76) states:

> . . . normal linguistic behavior, one's normal behavior, as speaker or reader or hearer, is quite generally with novel utterances, with utterances that have no physical or formal similarity to any of the utterances that have ever been produced in the past experience of the hearer or, for that matter, in the history of the language, as far as anyone knows.
>
> If you want to convince yourself of the truth of this remark, the easiest way to do so is to take an arbitrary sentence and wait until you hear it, or read the *New York Times* until you find it; or take the first sentence in the first book in the Library of Congress and keep reading until you find a repetition of it; or any other such test you wish to try . . . Normal use of language has this property of unboundedness.

Spoken language didn't originate from the need hominids of the Upper Pliocene and Pleistocene had to thrive in the niche of graincollection and in the ecosystem of migratory grazers, but from the need they, as all animals, have of enjoying life: Mother and child *played* with spoken language; that spoken language was improved and increased in the graincollectors' resting-foodsharing-talking meetings—activity where speaking was also a game. If it later acquired survival value and was sanctioned by sexual selection, it was only a coincidence that it didn't influence the graincollectors' way of thriving, nor the original biological balance of all their ecosystem. The hominids of the Pleistocene didn't need to talk in order to survive as graincollectors, since their ancestors had survived in that same way, and without speech, for 10 or 12 million years. But now they had to understand and be able to speak well in order to be well informed of all the "news," and, of course, to participate in conversations; it was a very interesting game. Jerison (1973: 427) states: "We need language to tell a story much more than to give directions for an action." *But mainly, they had to speak well to be accepted as consort partners by the members of the opposite sex.*

The sounds language of dolphins has great similarities with the humans' spoken language. Lilly (1975) has fully proven that dolphins are capable of imitating human voice, and believes, in addition, that someday we will be able to talk to dolphins in English.

Even though Lilly has not proven that the language of dolphins has the same function as human speech, their qualities of great intelligence, enormous brain, and perfect hearing make us think that this is possible. We may not as yet have understood the dolphins' language due to four main reasons: First, because their language hasn't been studied exhaustively. Second, as already mentioned, because we still haven't started to understand why animals want life. Third, due to the fact that sound-based language can have a rapid evolution following *unexpected paths* (as we'll see in more detail later on in this section). Therefore, if dolphins have a sounds language for communicating among themselves, this language is, most certainly, *totally foreign* to us. Fourth, because we are looking for two nonexistent things: the survival value of dolphins' language, and their intelligence.

Jerison (1973), in his studies regarding the evolution of the brain and intelligence in animals, compares the weight of brain relative to body weight among several animals. But he takes Karl Lashley's proposition, mentioned at the beginning of Section 1 of this chapter, as a support when comparing these weights among animals of different sizes, and says that intelligence can be measured by obtaining E.Q. (encephalization quotient). (According to Jerison, E.Q. is the ratio of an animal's actual brain size to its *expected* brain size; and the expected brain size is the brain size relative to body size for an average living mammal.) He later deduces a way of finding what he calls N_c (number of excess neurons).

The idea was to specify how much neural tissue is available for the job of creating perceptual worlds, that is, for "intelligence", not to say where the neurons are. (Jerison, 1975: 416)

Jerison (1973: 351) had earlier stated:

The enormous expansion of the neocortex in living whales is the most interesting of the adaptations, since relative to the brain as a whole the bottlenose dolphin, for one, exceeds even man in this regard.

Jerison finds that the only animals with a sounds language—humans and dolphins—also are the only ones who have a greater E.Q. Jerison (1988a: 2) states:

Man, dolphin, and killer whale *(Homo, Tursiops, Orcinus)* are approximately equal in encephalization, despite their evolutionary separation by more than 60 million years of history and by their niches in terrestrial versus marine adaptive zones.

Booth (1988), based on studies made by several primatologists and undergraduate students on bottlenosed dolphins, points out the great similarity of the dolphins' social system with that of the chimpanzees of the Gombe Stream Reserve studied by Jane Goodall. What is striking is not only the similarity of the dolphins' social system with that of the chimpanzees as indicated by Booth, but the similarity of the dolphins' social system with that of the graincollector humans; one remarkable similarity is the long time infant dolphins spend by their mothers' side. Booth (1988: 1274) states:

Mothers and offspring [dolphins] form some of the tightest bonds in the community, remaining together until the calf is weaned between the ages 3 and 4 years.
Indeed, like chimpanzees, sons and daughters may often closely associate with their mothers years after weaning.

The graincollector mother and her dependant infant spend several hours a day without looking at each other's face or hands, making gestural communication difficult. Calf dolphins and mothers can't communicate fine details with gestures and postures, making it more possible for the appearance of a sounds language among them, since dolphins mainly use sounds as a biosonar medium similar to the one of bats; that is, as some kind of radar that enables them to *"see"* all around them. This character was the preadaptation for the evolutionary acquisition of the sounds language they now possess. Their great brain development probably emerged when they were able to use sounds similar to those of their biosonar for fine communication among them; in this way they acquired a language, maybe as perfect as humans' sounds language.

It also calls my attention to another similarity with human behavior: the importance of dolphins' play behavior and the care given to it by their mothers. Booth (1988: 1274) states:

> Female dolphins with calves are extremely cooperative. The mothers will often form "playpens" around youngsters and allow them to interact within the protective enclave. Episodes of "baby-sitting" are also common, where one female will watch another's calf while the mother is occupied elsewhere. In many cases, Wells [biologist Randy Wells] says that the cooperating females are related.

Dolphins are also similar to humans in their mating system (Booth says that this similarity is with chimpanzees) since the mating system of graincollectors, as we'll see in Chapter V, Section 1, was based on promiscuity like the chimpanzees' currently is, for monogamy, the nuclear family, and long-term bonds between husband and wife appear, *as a foreign social system*, after Würm's Glaciation. Booth (1988: 1274) states:

> The mating system for dolphins, like chimpanzees, is a promiscuous one. Males and females do not form long-term bonds. Females may mate with a number of different males. . . . Says Wells [biologist Randy Wells]: "The early development of sexual behavior, many years before sexual maturity, suggests that sex is quite important in the lives of these animals."

Dolphins are gregarious aquatic mammals, almost always traveling and migrating as a pod, very similar to the migratory grazers graincollectors; and, as with graincollectors, their sounds language used for social interactions and protection against predators is very important. We notice that the evolutionary result in dolphins is similar to that of humans: a large brain, developed intelligence, and sounds language.

A large E.Q.—that is, a large brain in relation to body mass, as well as an extensive sounds language, as humans and dolphins have—is very rare in animals. These two characters together in one animal species is an extraordinary occurrence indicating that both are unavoidably interdependent. What was assumed by Charles Darwin and by many researchers from that time up to our days has been proven: that speech is the cause for the great brain and intelligence development in humans; and I believe now we can add: and in dolphins.

Now let's consider what Jerison (1973: 351) stated:

> The evidence from paleoneurology adds a dimension of time to findings such as these because, as far as one can judge from endocasts and estimates of body size, this may have been an ancient adaptation that has characterized the cetaceans during the past 15 or 20 m.y., at least. The evolution of the human brain is a phenomenon of the past few million years. . . .

Dolphins do not use tools with their mouths, nor have hands similar to those of humans. Neither their intelligence nor their sounds language has given them an extraordinary advantage that could have caused an adaptive radiation in 15 or 20 million years since the start of the great development of their brain and intelligence. All of this indicates that neither great intelligence nor sounds language have survival value in dolphins, the same way they don't have it in humans. If, in addition, we take under consideration that the dolphins' social system is similar to that of human graincollectors, and that their sexual life is very important "many years before sexual maturity" (Booth, 1988: 1274), then it is valid *to suspect* that the improvement of their sounds language and their great brain and intelligence development were caused by the pressure of sexual selection: *they had "to speak well" to be accepted as consort partners by the members of the opposite sex.*

What seems most important is the many similar circumstances and results in the appearance of a sounds language among dolphins and the appearance of human speech; and, above all, their similar great brain development.

As we have seen, speech, typical of and particular to humans, gives the false appearance that it didn't develop from systems of communication shared with some other mammals or, more particularly, shared with some other primates, since its characteristics are unique because the circumstances around which it appeared were unique and quite special. But even though it *seems* that it didn't evolve from more primitive systems of communication shared with other primates, we'll see right away that in fact it did evolve from these systems of communication. This indicates that this phenomenon could occur again in the evolution of other animal species and would present in them many strange and new peculiarities and properties. As a matter of fact, dolphins have a *very special and strange* sounds language. It, too, may give the wrong impression that it is not the result of the evolution of a *"more primitive"* sounds system of communication shared with other mammal species, because it is the result of a great number of *very special* circumstances. Chomsky (1972: 66, 67) states:

> Anyone concerned with the study of human nature and human capacities must somehow come to grips with the fact that all normal humans acquire language, whereas acquisition of even its barest rudiments is quite beyond the capacities of an otherwise intelligent ape—a fact that was emphasized, quite correctly, in Cartesian philosophy. It is widely thought that the extensive modern studies of animal communication challenge this classical view; and it is almost universally taken for granted that there exists a problem of explaining the "evolution" of human language from systems of animal communication. However, a careful look at recent studies of animal communication seems to me to provide little support for these assumptions. Rather, these studies simply bring out even more clearly the extent to which human language appears to be a unique phenomenon, without significant analogue in the animal world. If this is so, it is quite senseless to raise the problem of explaining the evolution of human language from more primitive systems of communication that appear at lower levels of intellectual capacity.

Three years later (Chomsky, 1975a: 10, 11), he seems to contradict what he had stated:

> But human cognitive systems, when seriously investigated, prove to be no less marvelous and intricate than the physical structures that develop in the life of the organism. Why, then, should we not study the

acquisition of a cognitive structure such as language more or less as we study some complex bodily organ?

At first glance, the proposal may seem absurd, if only because of the great variety of human languages. But a closer consideration dispels these doubts. . . . The idea of regarding the growth of language as analogous to the development of a bodily organ is thus quite natural and plausible.

We are aware that all of our organs have evolved from older structures which we genetically share with phylogenetically close or somewhat distant species, depending on the organ under consideration. It may be because of that that Chomsky now considers spoken language to be predetermined by genetic factors that we can share with other species.

The sources of confusion to serious students of the origin of human language are: On the one hand, it exhibits sudden and great *evolutionary* changes that make us think that " . . . there is no striking similarity between animal communication systems and human language" (Chomsky, 1967: 73). On the other hand, there is the fact that any human infant can perfectly learn any language, since all humans have the *genetic bases* to do so, and we are already born knowing how to use the grammar of any language *without having to learn it* (Chomsky, 1967, 1972, 1975a, 1975b).

The great number of particular circumstances that caused the appearance of spoken language make this character a very particular phenomenon, and have given it qualities which make some linguists think that spoken language in humans *appeared isolated; that is, without sharing the genetic bases with those species phylogenetically close to us.* This is, of course, a mistake: at another level, these bases are genetically shared with those species, but the fact that some linguists consider it such an exceptional character should give us pause.

Let's see why those linguists are making such a mistake: In cases where human populations spoke only one language, and later separated into several populations that throughout many millennia were cut off from one another, it was found that each population independently developed a language completely different from the original one as well as from those currently spoken by sister populations. Even though all new languages have a structure derived from the original language, members of those different populations do not understand those of others: each population followed *very different paths* in the evolution of their spoken language. This happens because spoken language can follow, and in fact follows in its evolution, very different paths from the previous ones, *since, when we speak, all our utterances are always new* (Chomsky, 1967). This also happens because *there isn't any need for, or any way of thriving with, spoken language*; there are no rules or laws *for that game.* It was born as play, and it's still that—a certain way of enjoying life. And even though *presently* we use language as an implement for thriving, and therefore we subject it to *rules* designed to impede its free evolution, our graincollector ancestors never used spoken language in order to thrive: they allowed it to evolve freely. This is the reason that, presently, human language is so different from the communication systems of other animal species, *as well as different from the first sounds language that our ancestors formerly had.* Then, we can't expect to perceive in the living African pongids, whose respective lineages are separated from ours by 3 or 4 million years, a conclusive indication that our common ancestors had a primitive system of communication by means of vocal sounds from which our present human language derives, when we are witnessing that in only 20 thousand or fewer years of separation, the languages of two human populations between whom communication was cut off are totally different. In addition, the culture of graincollection was lost 3 or 4 million years ago during the evolution of all apes' lineages; that is, a long time ago they lost that appropriate environment for the development of a true spoken language.

Even though human speech has characteristics that make it very special in each population—and completely different to all other systems of animal communication—*it necessarily had to evolve from a communication system shared with other animal species.* Lieberman (1975: 5) observes:

> Evolution proceeds in small steps, and the only reason that human language appears to be so disjoint from animal communication systems is that the hominids who possessed "intermediate" languages are all dead.

Steele (1989: 422) states:

Deacon (1988b) speculates that the highly encephalized human brain is a product of selection for expanded prefrontal cortex, which is implicated in language production and comprehension, and has demonstrated (Deacon, 1988a) that the prefrontal cortical areas known to be involved in human auditory processing and in speech production have homologues in non-human primates, as indicated by his own experimental work on macaque monkeys; thus the basic neural circuitry of human language capabilities represents no major species-specific structural innovation (refuting both Chomsky's invocation of a human "language organ" and some palaeoanthropologists' invocations of hominid neuroanatomical reorganization).

I wish to mention only one example, which should suffice to demonstrate that our spoken language must have had, at the beginning, the same genetic bases as those now present in many other primates, and particularly in baboons, and which we still share with them; and it should also suffice to demonstrate that *all animal species have, more or less, the same way of having fun and enjoying life*, be this at informal gatherings for conversation, the way humans enjoy life or, in general, any comparable actions having nothing to do with thriving or other utilitarian objectives.

Richman (1978) in his article entitled "The Synchronization of Voices by Gelada Monkeys" (remember that these baboons, *Theropithecus gelada*, are natural *seed eaters* as humans are, and that they also have daily social meetings for the enjoyment of life, even though they do not share food in those meetings the way humans do), says that these monkeys, in the course of their social interactions, produce a great quantity and variety of vocal sounds. He indicates that this great quantity and variety of sounds is amazing compared with the repertoire that phylogenetically close species, such as *Papio*, have in similar social circumstances. Furthermore, Richman says that during a variety of social interactions, it very frequently happens that while one baboon produces a string of sounds with a definite tempo and rhythm, a second baboon tries to produce sounds very closely synchronous to the tempo and rhythm of the first baboon's string of sounds, and he adds:

Many times these attempts at synchronizing vocal outputs are so successful that for one particular sound of a string the onset of the second monkey's sound will be within 20 msec of the onset of the first monkey's sound. This onset time difference is significant in that it is so small that it rules out the interpretation that the second monkey is *responding directly* to the onset of the other's sound with his own sound to produce the synchronous effect. The reaction time necessary to do this is relatively so large—of the order of 150 msec—that the monkey could not physiologically be doing this. Rather, I will argue here that the second monkey is responding not directly to the onset of the first monkey's sound but to the onset of the *previous* sound in the string of the first monkey and that this task requires some sort of internal time mechanism that can "figure out" the rhythm and tempo of the first monkey's vocal output. Such precise control of the timing of vocal output that this synchronization task requires has not been reported previously for non-human primates. Neither has the synchronization of voices been reported for non-human primates—though, of course, humans show great abilities in synchronizing vocal and other outputs when singing, dancing, or playing music together. Also, the production of the suprasegmental aspects of human speech requires precise temporal control of the rhythms of speech involving quite complicated internal temporal mechanisms. It would be significant in this regard if a non-human primate showed some evidence of precise temporal control of its own vocal output and an ability to figure out the tempo and rhythm of other voices. This would show that geladas at least have abilities in controlling the rhythmical and temporal outputs of their voices that are analogous to the abilities humans use in the rhythmical aspects of human speech, just as there is evidence that geladas can produce vocal distinctive features that are analogous to those used in human speech (Richman, 1976). (Richman, 1978: 569, 570. Italics author's)

Let us remember that not only linguistic researchers, but laymen as well, are aware that all human languages are mainly rhythm and tempo; human languages are chanting like the *dual singing* of the gelada baboons, and like the singing of the gibbons. Darwin, in *The Descent of Man*, mentions the singing of the gibbons to indicate a character from which human speech possibly originated. Wescott (1974: vi), in the preface, says that Otto Jaspersen also suggested, in 1894, "that chanting preceded talking" in humans.

This, and all of the foregoing, compels us to think that once human speech originated, starting from communication systems shared with other animal species, and since the human communication system has no relation with our way of thriving, our ancestors were capable of allowing their sounds language rapidly to evolve through completely *unexpected* paths: play, singing, and diversion are not forced to follow some kind of rule or law; they are simply based on the existing physical and mental abilities of animals, and follow the path that the enjoyment of life and not the need for survival determines. Humans, at present, do not understand how animals enjoy their lives, because we haven't researched these subjects; as well, humans are currently living in an environment that alienates us from nature and from the possibility of understanding the way animals enjoy life in nature. This is the reason why some linguists view our speech *"so particular and exclusive to humans."*

The great number of strange coincidences occurring at the same time in the course of the evolution of the human lineage include the following: mastering an easy way of obtaining food, lack of predators, traveling in the infants' throne, the inability of mother and child, in this situation, to see each other's face or hands for many hours every day throughout the infant's extended childhood, noises and babbling expressed by infants to attract their mother's attention, the mother's response to this babbling, gatherings for rest-foodsharing-talking, sexual selection favorable for those best endowed with speech, etc. All of these factors made us very intelligent and talkative animals; and, in this character, very different from the rest of the animals, but *by no means should we believe that our greater intelligence makes us basically different or superior to them, nor can we brag of having earned this character with great will and effort, or because we are "the culmination of animal evolution," or because we are made "in God's image."*

All of this was due to good luck; or maybe to bad luck. It may have been bad luck that, in the last 50 thousand years, we humans made use of our intelligence to thrive and, therefore, we do not enjoy our lives anymore as we *know* our graincollector ancestors did, because, if they had not *fully* enjoyed life, intelligence would have not developed in such a fast and great way; they used their intelligence *only* to enjoy life, and they always enjoyed it, *even before their great brain development,* the way all animals who are within their natural ecological niche and ecosystem do.

If we take a look at the imbalance we have created in the last 50 thousand years in all the ecosystems of the world, and the high price we are paying for this abuse, since we are *working* instead of enjoying life and increasing our intelligence at the same time; and with that work we are *impoverishing* many other living beings throughout the whole planet, impoverishing other humans and ourselves, and at the same time, we impoverish our minds. If we think about the great damage we have brought down upon so many animal and plant species since commencing to use our intelligence to thrive, we should ask ourselves: Was it good or bad luck, having the capability of speech and being so intelligent? Haven't we greatly misused that intelligence? Haven't we greatly abused such a perfect communication system?

Body Language

Reexamining the previous sentence, is it correct to refer to ours as *"such a perfect communication system"*? Wouldn't the opposite (such an *imperfect*) be more accurate?

Our ancestors didn't have a spoken language during the main part of their evolution. From the time that life appeared on this planet, until some 2 or 3 million years ago, our ancestors didn't have a verbal system of communicating; therefore, humans, as all other animals, are perfectly *adapted* to instinctively understand body language rather than spoken language. As a matter of fact, two people that do not understand each other, because they speak different languages, are able to understand their body language, despite the fact that the current habit of wearing clothes somewhat distorts the corporal signs we emit.

Even though body language is sometimes used in play, it didn't adaptively appear as play, but rather appeared out of a vital need to survive. On the other hand, spoken language did in fact appear as play, and is now, and always will be, play.

Spoken language has taken away *part* of our capability of completely understanding body language. However, all humans understand body language and express it instinctively; body language is our only universal *language.*

We should take under consideration the fact that most of the times when we want to express something verbally, we say something at least somewhat removed, because we have trouble expressing it precisely. Furthermore, the listener might give our words a different meaning or interpretation from the one we had intended to give to our words, even if we assume we expressed it correctly from the start. With spoken language, we can deliberately lie, and we do. Therefore, we can conclude that spoken language is for playing, since in playing we can and should lie and confuse, as well as also tell truths; if we didn't, it would not be play. This is another reason why spoken language has no survival value. Body language does have survival value because it evolved due to the natural expression of life: our ancestors expressed all their emotions because they couldn't or didn't want to cover them. Only predator animals, when acting as such, and those animals when hiding from predators, or animals when bluffing to avoid fighting, want to cover their emotions—and even they are not always successful. Humans, when speaking, can attempt to conceal their true emotions, but their body language always tells the truth. Therefore, body language, *and some sounds whether vocal or corporal*, represent a universal communication system among all animals. It makes all animals of an ecosystem aware of all what is happening in their surroundings, what other members of that ecosystem want, do, and what it means to them. Human body language is mixed with that of other animal species of their natural ecosystem and with their few vocal and corporal sounds. Body language makes it possible for all animal members of an ecosystem to communicate and understand each other to the degree that is required of or useful to them.

If we understand the body language of other animal species of our ecosystem, we might be better able to understand that of our group partners. It could be that the body language and some vocal sounds that our distant ancestors used, formed the groundwork for a spoken language that later on turned into a language formed almost exclusively of vocal sounds, even though human speech is *always and inevitably* linked to body language.

If spoken language had survival value, as body language does, all humans would understand each other in one and the same language, the way we express and understand ourselves with only one body language. Body language, like our instincts, unites all humans; it makes us feel and know we are one community.

Spoken language, for the last 50 thousand years, has been keeping us apart and making us feel different. This feeling of estrangement didn't exist before the start of the last great Pleistocene glaciation, despite each graincollector population probably speaking its own language, because their perpetual migrating character would have unified those languages at the periodic encounters they had with other graincollector populations. Another possibility is that all members of each of those populations spoke all those languages, which probably were not very numerous or different. Those annual or semiannual encounters and meetings among different graincollector populations, lasting for several days or months, allowed all linguistic novelties to spread among them, specially among the infants and juveniles. Graincollectors also possessed a complete body language used for better understanding and expressing themselves, since their body was naked. These periodic tribal encounters gave, in addition, the opportunity for those males who had reached puberty, to change tribe, and in this way accelerated the unification of languages.

The true separation of languages, the true confusion, the true Tower of Babel occurred when human graincollectors turned *territorial* hunter-gatherers during Würm's Glaciation. The estrangement of languages became even more severe when they turned into sedentary farmers. This separation of languages was caused by the lack of contact among populations, as well as by the invention of clothes originally used to protect themselves from the cold at the beginning of the last great glaciation, by the invention of private property that appeared at that time, derived from the territorial character of hunter-gatherers, and by the invention of religions, politics, and war (our ancestors were already armed then).

We may conclude that all the actions and reactions that have a well-defined survival value *are not* the ones that originated what is known as animal intelligence since, if they had originated it, they would have created a spiraling increase of intelligence. The reason they haven't generated such a spiral is because those actions and reactions are limited and balanced by natural selection at a very low level of intelligence. However, when intelligence has greatly increased, as in the case of humans and dolphins, it has led to a rapidly spiraling increase throughout their evolution because those actions and reactions, not damaging to anyone, later gave origin to a special case of sexual selection, through which it acquired survival value.

We can conclude that *when intelligence is used by an animal to thrive* (to obtain a material benefit), *it is then damaging to that same individual, to all the members of the population, to all the members of the ecosystem, and maybe even to all the inhabitants of the planet in which that individual lives;* and it is then rejected by natural selection.

We can conclude that all animals not only struggle for survival and for maximizing lifetime reproductive output, as has been believed up to now, but *they also are impelled to enjoy life with their loved ones.* They also struggle every moment of their short lives to be considered someone within their natural group; to belong to that group, and to know that the group belongs to them, since the greater pain for any animal is to feel alone. We must consider the happiness and joy all animals, or maybe *all living beings,* feel when living within their natural ecological niche, among their loved ones.

We can conclude that intelligence represents the way that each animal species has of enjoying life. It would not, however, be true to say that more intelligent animals enjoy life more, but rather that their way of enjoying life is more complex. The less intelligent animals have simpler pleasures, but equally satisfying.

When humans acquire a better understanding of the abovementioned, we will start to understand the behavior of other living beings, as well as ourselves.

It can be concluded also that tool using, spoken language, great intelligence, and all the characters derived from them—artistic sense and the like—*all* of these human characters have appeared during the evolution of our lineage derived and supported in the altruistic devotion that the human graincollector mother used to give to an only child for 7 or 8 years. A tacit and authentic acknowledgment that humans give to that altruistic quality of mothers, to that altruistic quality of all women, is evident in the following facts:

When our ancestors learned to name beings and things, they called the Woman who gave them life, Mother; they called the Earth they walked on and gave them food, Mother; they called the Ocean, Mother; they called Nature, Mother; and they called God, Mother.

Chapter V
The Tribe; Explanation of Goals;
the Oral Tradition and Genesis

> What I find most unforgettable about Convoluta is this: sometimes it happens that a marine biologist, wishing to study some related problem, will transfer a whole colony of the worms into the laboratory, there to establish them in an aquarium, where there are no tides. But twice each day Convoluta rises out of the sand on the bottom of the aquarium, into the light of the sun. And twice each day it sinks again into the sand. Without a brain, or what we would call a memory, or even any very clear perception, Convoluta continues to live out its life in this alien place, remembering, in every fiber of its small green body, the tidal rhythm of the distant sea.
> —Rachel L. Carson, *The Sea Around Us*. New York: Oxford, 1951

In 1953 I read Rachel Carson's book, *The Sea Around Us*, with great pleasure. The above quoted paragraph moved me deeply by its beauty and strength; also by a certain mood of pain the author gave to it.

As an extrapolation of Rachel L. Carson's theme, let me state that what I find most remarkable about humans is this: more than 50 thousand years ago, at the start of the latest great glaciation, Würm's Glaciation, humans lost their natural ecological niche; that is, they lost their natural profession, their natural way of subsistence, their natural habitat, their natural social system; they lost everything. Since then, nothing has been recovered, for the ecosystem and habitat of the savanna where their ancestors lived as graincollectors for more than 14 million years was so severely disturbed and changed, and for such a long time, that presently they scarcely remember, through very old oral tradition, what their mission is among living beings. Like a dream, like an unreality, like a legend they remember their life in that paradise. With a great brain and a great memory, but without a very clear perception of what happened and what's happening, each human, since the time of conception throughout all his life keeps trying to accomplish, in this present alien environment, the activities and functions accomplished by his ancestors in their habitual environment; remembering in every gene, in every fibre of his naked body, the life's cadence, and the rhythm of the perpetual migrations in the distant savanna.

1. The Graincollector Tribe; the Nuclear Family; Parenthesis for an Unmentionable Theme

Currently, the basic social systems of most human societies are the nuclear family (mother, father, and their children), the extended family (a group of close relatives along either the father's or mother's line, usually not along both), as well as the unimale polygynous harem (a marriage from which a man has two or more wives and their children at the same time). The extended family is derived from the nuclear family and is commonly found in many societies in the world. The unimale polygynous harem is also derived from the nuclear family, and it is also commonly found in many societies; its origin is due to the low status women presently have in all nuclear families in the world.

The acceptance of the nuclear family is reinforced throughout the world both through religious precepts and secular laws. However, an important point that I want to demonstrate in this chapter is that the nuclear family is not instinctive or natural in humans, but is an *abnormal* social system that has appeared since the start of the last great glaciation:

If, from the material already covered, we are convinced that we still are graincollectors, all of our characters are those of graincollectors, and because of this our instincts require us to live within the same social system in which our ancestors lived, then all I have to demonstrate is that our graincollector ancestors didn't have the nuclear family as the basis of their social system.

I'll start from the basis that our ancestors remained graincollectors for 14 million years and that they were still graincollectors some 50 thousand years ago. The graincollector mother devoted herself exclusively to the care and rearing of only one infant from the time of conception up until the age of 7 or 8 years old when he was weaned. This can be deduced from the way seeds were collected by our ancestors in the long-grass savannas, from the migratory character of graincollectors in those long-grass savannas, from the primate inheritance of the mother of always carrying her dependent infant on her back and the infant's extended maternal dependency, from their great intelligence and spoken language which could only be developed, through evolution, due to the character of mother-infant of being *always* together during that extended maternal dependency; and can also be deduced from many other characters that humans possess. It also can be inferred from the many years of care and celibacy the infants of wild pongids receive from their mother.

From conception up until the time when her infant was weaned—a period of about eight to nine years—the graincollector mother didn't go into estrus or have sexual intercourse, since she wouldn't have been capable of migrating in the long-grass savanna carrying more than one dependent infant, nor would she have been able to feed them. Furthermore, graincollector mothers, despite having to feed themselves and their infant during extended maternal dependency, were completely independent of males for their subsistence. Therefore, one male would be unable to keep a harem due to the rare periods of receptivity of females. Such a harem would have to be formed by numerous females; and one male would be unable to defend such a large number from predators, to look after so many females and their infants. This would only be possible if several males of different tribes were to form alliances to defend groups of related females, like the savanna baboons do. *These facts eliminate the nuclear family (as well as its derivatives, the extended family and the unimale polygynous harem) as a possible basis of the social system of the graincollectors. We are then compelled to think on some kind of multimale polygynous (promiscuous) tribe as the basis of their social system.*

We can deduce the origin of the current nuclear family. We know that all grazer ungulate species that live in herds in the savanna, when times of drought, extended cold weather, or other factors make the normally available food or water scarce, disperse into smaller groups. If the bad conditions continue, those groups disperse into even smaller groups.

If, in a relatively short time everything returns to normal, the herds rejoin. If the bad conditions do not improve, the result could be extinction, or those groups would be very decimated and diminished when rejoined. Würm's Glaciation was a *sudden and extended* phenomenon that, while causing natural conditions to deteriorate, also brought about maximum dispersion and decimation to graincollector populations and tribes. Only those very small human groups who hunted and formed nuclear families survived, since the woman with her dependant infant could not, under these circumstances, go out hunting or live independently the way she always did while being a graincollector; she now depended on a male for her subsistence. Kinzey (1987: xiii, xiv) states:

> . . . [the nuclear family] appear[s] to occur only among industrial societies or in gatherer-hunter groups where, for ecological reasons usually related to a need for mobility, foraging in large groups would be counterproductive.

Since the arrival of Würm's Glaciation our ancestors took to living in caves, in natural rock shelters, or dwellings built out of wood, stone, bone, or skin in order to protect themselves from the intense cold; and it is in those places where the mother could stay and look after her children while the father went out hunting. It is, in short, the beginning of the commonly called cavemen age. The nuclear family is at that time a useful social system, but unimaginable within graincollection. We haven't at present abandoned the social system of nuclear families, since we still haven't returned to graincollection and because our current way of life is still similar to that of the hunters of the cavemen age. While the father goes out *working and making a living*, similar to going out to hunt, a woman, with several dependent children, is totally dependent on her husband for their subsistence. But living in a nuclear family is not natural nor instinctive in humans.

It is very probable that once our ancestors were definitively established as graincollectors some 14 million years ago, they didn't suffer significant social changes up until 50 thousand years ago, since during that long period of time they remained graincollectors, and due to this, the social elements didn't change much. Even though they suffered many vicissitudes, such as droughts, cold weather, and even several glaciations that could have thrown them out of their natural ecological niche, they were, however, able to return to their graincollector existence. The social dynamic, the reproduction dynamic, the way of bringing up infants, and the way of subsistence were basically unchanged throughout that long period of time. In addition, as mentioned in Sections 1 and 2 of Chapter IV, we have reasons to suspect that the advanced intelligence, acquired by our ancestors in the last 2 or 3 million years, didn't influence any basic changes in their social system.

The foregoing indicates that humans are still perfectly adapted to the graincollectors' way of life and society, and that *the current nuclear family is abnormal because it is not inherent of our natural and instinctive social system.*

Therefore, we take particular interest in knowing as much as possible about the natural social system of graincollectors, inasmuch as that is our natural and instinctive social system.

For this purpose, when taking the studies of Dunbar and Dunbar (1975) on the social dynamic of gelada baboons as evidence and support, and from the material covered in Part One of this book, we can deduce that our ancestors' populations, tribes and, in general, the whole social system *before graincollection* (as part-time seed-eaters) were *in every aspect* very similar to those of the living gelada baboons. The gelada baboons' natural habitat, food, structure of their reproductive units, maternal dependency, way of bringing up their infants, daily migrations in the same reduced geographical areas, etc., are more or less similar to the ones we must assume for protohominid part-time seed-eaters. Even after they turned graincollectors, their diet, habitat, etc., remained very similar to their previous one. Hominids must have kept more or less the same social system, although with some small changes due, mainly, to their new migratory pattern that now took in wide geographical areas, and to the adaptive huge increase in the infants' maternal dependency, among others less important.

Dunbar and Dunbar (1975: 1) say:

The gelada baboon *(Theropithecus gelada)* of the Ethiopian highlands represents a relict population of a formerly widespread genus [Jolly, 1972]. In the Pleistocene, representatives of this genus occurred throughout the savanna plains of eastern and southern Africa. Today, the only extant species, *T. gelada,* occupies a retreat habitat on the inaccessible gorges which dissect the Ethiopian Amhara Plateau [Tappen, 1960]. Jolly's [1972] reconstruction of the genus' palaeo-ecology suggests that it evolved in a treeless grassland *niche* along the shores of shallow lakes and rivers. Here it seems to have been the predominant non-human primate, and Jolly [1972] suggests that the extinction of all the species except *T. gelada* was probably due to a combination of hominid hunting pressure and the extensive changes in the eco-system caused by hominid activity. Except for *T. gelada*, the other species of the genus were large in size, and their disappearance from the African scene some 50,000 years BP parallels the simultaneous extinction of many large plains species [Cooke, 1963].

As the last surviving member of a once successful genus, the gelada baboons are of considerable interest from an evolutionary point of view. . . .The species has also figured prominently in theoretical discussions of the evolution and adaptive significance of primate social systems.

As we can see, living gelada baboons have remained exclusively in places almost unreachable by humans, and not in open savannas as happened in the Pleistocene; therefore, the study of their social system can only give us an idea of the graincollectors' social system. In this way, it is an acceptable aid in the formulation of reasonable speculations, but the study of their social system, as well as that of the savanna baboons, the olive, yellow and chacma, *won't* yield precise information regarding our ancestors' social system, since none of them can be the same as that of the graincollectors. Nevertheless, we must take them under consideration in order to have an idea of several possibilities and options.

Let's take a look at the opinion of Washburn (1978) against considering other animals' biology, particularly that of other primates, as a method for deducing human biology. Washburn (1978: 71) states:

Human behavior is so varied and complex that little can be predicted from studying the biology we share with other primates.

According to Washburn (1978), there are many researchers who have promoted the idea that by studying other animals' behavior, especially that of primates, we can better understand human behavior. Many sociologists and sociobiologists have tried to find " . . . 'general laws of the evolution and biology of social behavior,' which may then be applied to human beings." (Washburn, 1978: 70). He then adds:

Obviously, we studied animal behavior to find both possible similarities and possible differences. As time has passed it is the differences that seem more important, especially when considering social behavior. Human evolution produced a unique kind of creature. The point I would like to stress is that a meaningful study of the complexities of human behavior must begin with human beings, *not* with other animals. (Washburn, 1978: 70. Italics author's)

In his article, Washburn says that all those researchers use evolution theory to make questionable comparisons of human and animal behavior; and that many of them base themselves in genetics when making comparisons, simply because the behavior has a biological basis, even though we know it is impossible to infer that special genes account for human behavior. Washburn demonstrates that we *cannot* predict human behavior by studying the biology we share with other animals.

I wish to emphasize the following: When studying the behavior, social systems, and in general the biology of many animals, that of other animals can be predicted with a slight chance of error. Why, when dealing with humans, are our predictions so frequently wrong? Washburn has already answered that, but I want to give a different answer based on what we've seen up to now in this book: *because the human animal is the only one that currently uses its intelligence to thrive—the only one that goes beyond the biological norms. For the last 50 thousand years, the abnormal is normal among humans*, an unfortunate fact.

Present human behavior is so abnormal in nature, that researchers, when trying to predict it from studying the biology we share with other animals, are doing something similar to trying to predict the behavior of mentally unhealthy people by studying the behavior of mentally healthy people. This is not possible. In the same way, it is not possible to predict the behavior of animals who *are out* of their ecological niche, by studying the biology of animals who *are in* their ecological niche. The behavior that animals display within their natural ecological niche is predictable, but not that of animals out of their niche, and even less of animals that, in addition, use their intelligence to avoid extinction.

Later on I will demonstrate that using our intelligence to thrive, because we are living out of our natural ecological niche, is the reason for all of our social malfunctions and the insanity dominant in all human societies, but for now, I just want to emphasize the following:

Human present behavior can't be predicted based on those studies, *but we can predict with reasonable certainty the behavior of our graincollector ancestors*, because graincollectors, like all other animals, did not use their intelligence in order to "overpower nature" as humans are currently doing—instead, they used their natural instincts only to take from nature whatever belonged to them, according to their animal essence.

But this prediction, however, is not going to be easy to formulate, since, despite the fact that graincollectors are part of a natural migratory grazing ecosystem and have some general biological similarities with baboons, particularly with *Theropithecus gelada*, they also have differences.

Another aid to formulating this prediction is to look for, among those we've called "primitive people," a tribal social system that we suspect has some similarities with that of our graincollector ancestors. The !Kung people (Kalahari Desert hunter-gatherers of South Africa) have noteworthy similarities, since they are greatly dependent on gathering and very little on hunting; and because infants travel with their mothers who use a sling (kaross) for carrying them. This is a manner of infant transportation similar to the one graincollector mothers accomplished by the infants' throne. Furthermore, infants are weaned between three and eight years of age (Draper, 1976; Konner, 1976; Shostak, 1976), similar to graincollector infants who were normally weaned between ages seven and eight. !Kung people were also affected by Würm's Glaciation, since they also marry, live in nuclear families, and their children are psychically damaged when their mothers have more than one dependent infant at the same time—the same way all children are hurt in all the nuclear families, in all the extended families, and in all the unimale polygynous harems of the whole world. Let us look at what Shostak (1976: 251) says about a !Kung woman who relates her childhood:

Long ago my mother gave birth to my younger brother Kumsa. I wanted the milk she had in her breasts and when she nursed him, my eyes

watched as the milk spilled out. I cried all night, cried and cried, and
then dawn broke.

Some mornings I just stayed around and my tears fell and I cried and
refused food. That was because I saw him nursing, I saw with my eyes
the milk spilling out. I thought it was mine.

Once, when my mother was with him and they were lying down
asleep, I took him away from her and put him down on the other side
of the hut. Then I lay down beside her. While she slept, I squeezed some
milk and started to nurse and nursed and nursed and nursed. Maybe she
thought it was him. When she woke and saw me, she said, "Where . . .
tell me . . . tell me where did you put Kumsa? Where is he?"

I told her he was lying down inside the hut. She grabbed me and
shoved me. I landed far away from her; I lay there and cried. She took
Kumsa, put him down beside her, and insulted me by cursing my
genitals. . . . I stayed there crying and crying, and then I was quiet. I got
up and just sat, and when my father came home, she told him:

"Do you see what kind of mind your daughter has? Hit her! Hit her,
don't just look at her. She almost killed Kumsa. This little baby, this little
thing here, she took from my side and dropped him somewhere else. I
was lying here holding him and was sleeping. She came and took him
away, then left him, and lay down where he had been and nursed me.
Now, hit her!"

I said, "You're lying! Me . . . daddy, I didn't nurse. I refuse her milk
and didn't take him away from her."

He said, "If I hear of this again, I'll hit you. Now, don't ever do that
again!" . . . We slept. When dawn broke my father and my older brother
went and I ran behind. I knew that if I stayed in the village, mother would
stringe her milk and wouldn't let me nurse. But when my older brother
saw me, he pushed me away and told me to go back to the village,
because the sun was too hot, and he said it would kill me.

In addition, !Kung people form patrilocal as well as matrilocal,
territorial, exogamous bands (Lee, 1976). However, we know that
"Groups of related females are the core of most mammalian societies
as well as most primate societies." (Jolly, 1985: 138) That is, most
mammal species instinctively form matrilocal, matricentric and exogamous groups or bands; then, we may think that *territorial property*
is the probable cause that made hunter-gatherer societies become
patrilocal societies. Lee (1976: 75) states:

This patrilocal, *territorial*, exogamous band or "horde," as Radcliffe-Brown called it, has proven to be a remarkably persistent construct in the study of hunting and gathering peoples. (Italics mine)

From what we are witnessing in all the world, the people we think have a similar social system to our ancestors' have not escaped the effects of the last great glaciation; nevertheless, besides the similarity of infant transportation to that of the infants' throne, !Kung people still have several other traditions that other people in the world have lost completely, as we will see. Regarding !Kung people, Draper (1976: 215) states:

The long birth spacing (average 3.8 years) means that most mothers of 2- to 3-years-olds are not occupied with another infant and can still devote much of their attention to the knee child (Howell n.d.).
Most children are nursed for at least 3 years and sometimes longer if the mother does not become pregnant.

Konner (1972: 295) states:

The frequency of nursing and freedom of access to the breast from birth to weaning are very high. The first instance of the use of the mother as a base for exploration occurs when, by the second month, the infant stares at interesting sights while relaxed by suckling. At 5 months he may vocalize continually while nursing and from time to time be answered by his mother. By 8 or 9 months he begins to fondle the free breast while nursing, and though this behaviour is persistent and not entirely gentle, most women in no way discourage it. *It continues until weaning, which, if the mother does not conceive again, may be as late as 6 or 8 years.* Nursing is an experience engaging the whole body, associated with extension-flexion movements in the legs and pelvis, moving skin-to-skin contact with the mother, sometimes dramatic state changes, the pleasure of suckling and the assuagement of hunger. As the infant passes through the second year, it gradually becomes the one reason for approaching the mother's body for which the approach is never refused. Finally, all attachments of any kind between Zhun/twa [!Kung] *adults* involve continual giving and receiving of food. Perhaps feeding is an unimportant aspect of attachment in England, or even in Uganda, but here it emphatically is not. (Italics mine)

Birth spacing is much closer in most of the world's human societies than it is in !Kung people, and even though the time between sibling births has sometimes been greater: achieved through unnatural methods like contraceptives, abortions, infanticides, etc. (infanticide is also practiced occasionally by !Kung people [Konner, 1972]), the exclusive attention of the mother to only one child is not respected (it isn't respected among !Kung people either), since the mother isn't all day, and every day, by the side of her dependent infant as was true of graincollector mothers. Besides, in the human societies of the whole world, infants are nursed at the most until they reach one year of age, in comparison to the 7 or 8 years graincollector mothers nursed, or to the 3 to 8 years !Kung mothers nurse.

An infant instinctively expects that long period of care and attention; currently, the lack of this long period of care and attention is psychically damaging to all human infants. This unnatural life is also damaging psychically to the mothers, who, forced by the sexual demands of the husband (sexual demands that graincollector mothers were not subjected to), are compelled to resort to abortions, infanticides, and contraception.

In addition, !Kung women with children keep more of their subsistence independence, since it is they who gather the greater part of the food consumed in those tribes (Yellen and Lee, 1976; Lee, 1968), in contrast with women in most human societies, in which this dependency on males, which they aren't instinctively used to, hurts husband-wife relationships by giving the woman a completely inferior status in the nuclear family, in the extended family, and in the unimale harem.

Based on this, it becomes evident that observing the current social systems of human groups won't be of much help; however, observing the social systems of some baboons will help us to deduce the social system of graincollectors. The solution to this problem is very important for humans, since it deals with finding our own natural social system. However, since it is not easy to solve, we might make mistakes and misinterpretations while attempting to do it. But we should keep in mind the following as we progress: Any social system we are capable of projecting or synthesizing through speculations based in the social systems of baboons, with hopes of this being the true social system of graincollectors, and of being adopted by some human groups who would want to return to graincollection, would bring about improvements in human mental health, as well as for the ecological balance of the whole planet, as compared to the status quo: the nuclear family, extended family, or unimale harem. The current social systems in which we have been living for the past 50 thousand years are damaging to our mental health, while the projected one is not, since it would be in better agreement with our natural instincts. Furthermore, if a group of humans attempted to return to graincollection and adopted the projected social system, *they could later on allow their natural instincts to take them, step by step, to their true natural social system*, which, most probably, wouldn't be too different if in the projected system we take under consideration all, or almost all, of the instinctive human social characters that must be satisfied.

When speculating on such a scenario we could consider, among many other characters of graincollectors, the following, which I believe to be very important:

Due to their migratory character, graincollectors do not take territories as *property*, the way hunter-gatherers do; therefore, they most probably have a matrilocal, matricentric and exogamous social system, the way it is in nearly all mammal species, and particularly in most primate species, except chimpanzees, because they are *territorial* (Goodall, 1986: 528), and this character is, most probably, the reason why their social system is patrilocal.

In one same graincollector population, different tribes must have been formed by females originating and residing in their respective original tribe, and males originating from other tribes of this same population or from other populations, due to their natural instinct of avoiding incest. (All living beings who reproduce sexually naturally try to avoid incest.) This implies that males, when reaching puberty, leave forever their original tribe and may be accepted in any tribe other than their original tribe. It implies as well that females develop an opposition or instinctive rejection towards native females of other tribes, even though they may all originate from the same population; implying also the natural and instinctive sexual rejection towards males of their own tribe, and male rejection of same-tribe females.

Because females remain celibate for 8 or 9 years before entering their rare period of receptivity, a male would seek only the friendship of graincollector females, so that later on they could choose him as consort. Therefore, a strong group cohesion must be present among females, besides the fact of being relatives (which makes them more

200

similar), the way it happens in the olive baboon troops studied by Strum (1987) and by Smuts (1985), and the gelada baboon troops studied by Dunbar and Dunbar (1975).

The strong feminine tribal union, the total independence of grain-collector mothers for subsistence, their nursing condition, as well as the tribe's matrilocality and matricentrality, makes the female status honorable and respectable, and, of course, far superior to the one presently granted to women in the unimale harems, extended families, or nuclear families in today's world. *Graincollector females "own the tribe,"* so to speak, since "Hundreds of field studies have revealed that among nearly all social primates, females form the cores of groups; they remain during maturity and become the group's bearers of tradition and repositories of collective knowledge." (Ghiglieri, 1987: 70)

In such a strong feminine tribal union, and furthermore, as a result of the prolonged celibacy of nursing mothers, a male cannot form one harem with only nursing females; besides he would have to look out for and protect many females and their infants. The formation of nuclear families isn't possible either.

The likely scenario, then, would be as follows: *Forming alliances, several adult males in one tribe would have to sexually share all the adult females of that tribe when those females are in estrus;* and it is probable that they wouldn't allow the access of males from other tribes, even if they belong to the same population.

With those large female groups, many adult males cohabit, and have, among other natural missions, the mission to protect females and infants from predator attacks, since they are the *fathers* of all the infants born in the tribe, and the *husbands* of all adult females.

But do all these speculations coincide with what *seem to be* the true social instincts we humans have?

We could relate many instinctive behaviors that *currently* appear and are evident in humans, with the corresponding instincts that *had to be* natural instinctive behaviors of our graincollector ancestors. Of course, this can be subject to wrong interpretations and mistakes, since, on the one hand, we do not know exactly what the social behavior of our graincollector ancestors was; and on the other hand, the greater part of our true natural instincts are repressed and do not appear because we are not living within our natural ecological niche, nor within our natural social system.

Therefore, this is a difficult task for sociologists, sociobiologists, psychologists, and all scientists who study any of the varied aspects of human behavior. In order to relate behaviors, these scientists must research thoroughly and consult with scientists of many different areas, such as anthropology, human evolution, biology, etc., before reaching a supportable and acceptable conclusion. Among many other issues involving human social instincts, they would have to study and discuss the following:

(a) Are humans instinctively sexually promiscuous?

(b) Do females presently try to live closer to their original family (to their parents) than males?

(c) Do sisters form stronger family ties with each other than those formed between brothers?

(d) Do males and females that are not related, but who grew up together in communities, like the kibbutz children (that could be similar to growing together in one tribe) attract each other sexually?

(e) Whether or not the so-called Oedipus and Electra complexes (whose origin has at present been wrongly explained) are due only to the instinct the human infant has. The boy or girl expects the *total and absolute* attention of his or her mother during some 8 years and, due to not receiving it, the infant male is jealous of his father who has taken his mother away from him, and the infant female blames her mother for giving attention to her father instead of giving it to her. Therefore, the infant male, as well as the infant female, try to attract the mother's attention in any way.

All these are very complicated subjects which cannot be resolved easily and rapidly. Nevertheless, let us examine superficially only the human sexual character.

Our natural instincts, whether we are men or women, impel us to have sexual intercourse with several partners. Because of the existence of this instinct—in order to reinforce unity in the nuclear family—there originated the religious commandment that, *Thou shalt not commit adultery.* The existence of these instincts are also presently recognized by secular law and are judged as *faults to morality*, just as it is also considered a fault to morality in going out naked, or bathing naked in the beach, because, as a convenience to the nuclear family, rules of law have been mandated, and religious commandments written against *our bad instincts*, as they have been called in several religions.

The reason why those actions are viewed as "bad instincts" is because we have gotten used, *over 50 thousand years, to judging as immoral our own natural instincts.* Here lies the incompetence and arrogance of *our* intelligent reasoning.

In a scientific article written by a field researcher, when referring to the promiscuous behavior of chimpanzees, she says that every time a female goes into estrus, many males have sexual access to that female; *and she designates this as an "orgy."* But the meaning of orgy is excessive indulgence, vice. Therefore, that scientist *is judging as immoral an animal instinct that is a natural law.* If that is the natural way the chimpanzees, in the course of their evolution, have adaptively developed for their reproduction, why is it designated as excessive indulgence and vice? Does that scientist think she can intelligently judge nature's laws as good or bad? By the same token, all humans think themselves capable of judging intelligently our own natural instincts or the natural instincts of animals. Why, instead, isn't our intelligence used to judge as a fault of morality and law those human *intelligent actions (not instinctive actions) that truly go against natural laws*—for example, the fact that the father and guide of the nuclear family is the one who sleeps with the mother, and not their infant for whom the *natural* way of sleeping is by his mother's side? *As a result, the infant, who instinctively expects to receive his mother's total attention, is psychically traumatized, and, due to this, presents abnormal behaviors and deviations in his adult life.*

Why isn't it a violation of morality and law that, due to this, *the mother conceives prematurely, losing her breast milk which, for a period of 7 or 8 years, belongs to that infant?* Why isn't it a violation of morality and law that a two-year-old infant (and even younger) is removed from his mother's side, where he belongs, due to the early arrival of a sibling, which, within the natural graincollecting life, would have been delayed 6 or 7 more years? Why is this new baby also emotionally hurt from early birth when he fails to receive from his mother all the *exclusive* care his nature requires? Why do we accept the abandonment of a woman and her many children by her husband; or, when not abandoned, being forced to have more children? Why do men, by sexual demands, force women into abortion, contraception, and even infanticide? Why isn't it a violation of morality that those mothers, already responsible for several children, still deliver more children, but with pain for it? Why isn't it a violation of morality and law that couples in nuclear families, *due to the nonexistence of natural instincts to form such families*, do not promote the strength of that unity, and, instead, destroy it through divorce? The children are left either with their mother or father, and when either member of the couple remarries, those children feel like strangers in their new home, when their instincts require them to live not only within a complete and well-formed nuclear family, but within *a whole tribe* in which they have a special place; where they are loved and respected; where they feel they are somebody and belong to all the tribe and all the tribe belongs to them.

Why isn't a violation of morality that, while the father and mother work, the child is left throughout the day in a day-care center away from his mother, and being able to be with his parents for only a few hours a week? Between living at the day-care center and sleeping away from his mother, his life goes by in a state of complete abandonment, when his instincts require his mother to be *always* by his side, and that a whole tribe of *close relatives* will look after him, nurture him, pamper him, and, above all, understand him. It is well-known how much a child enjoys playing in front of *his people*; being in contact with all his loved ones—*his tribe*. It is well-known that it is not instinctive in children to live only with other children and a nurse. In this way, since all of these instincts remain unsatisfied, those infants remain psychically traumatized for life, feeling they do not belong to a society, and that a society does not belong to them. *These are the main causes of all of our current social problems—the confusion, terror, and social collapse that presently prevail in the world.*

Let us now deal with a subject that scientists, by strong custom, never mention.

Scientists have always separated science from innate belief in God; science is detached from the social reality in which human beings live, since 90% to 95% of the inhabitants of the planet believe in God, and are aware of the instinctive *wonder* we have before God and His Creation. Science has to look for and rely on what can be proved; if not, it *wouldn't be science.*

But in truth, science cannot be isolated from social reality, since *there's only one truth*, so that there can't be a "*scientific interpretation*" and a "*religious interpretation*" of that one truth. We can't allow scientific tyranny to isolate us from our natural and instinctive *wonder* before God. In the same way we can't allow religious tyranny to take advantage of that instinctive *wonder* and keep us from seeing scientific reality.

All people on earth display a deep belief in God. That innate awe has always been revealed by searching deep down in their *old* oral tradition and rejecting all superstition, magic, or witchery acquired during the cavemen age in which we are even now living; and rejecting also what is only modern myth and religion. From their *old* oral tradition we know all people in the world believe in one God, one Creator of the universe.

What I've just said regarding our innate wonder before God opposes Darwin's conclusion, since in *The Descent of Man*, he states that believing in God is *not* instinctive nor innate in humans; he says (1871: 394, 395, Vol. II):

> The belief in God has often been advanced as not only the greatest, but the most complete of all the distinctions between man and the lower animals. It is however impossible, as we have seen, to maintain that this belief is innate or instinctive in man. On the other hand a belief in all-pervading spiritual agencies seems to be universal; and apparently follows from a considerable advance in the reasoning powers of man, and from still greater advance in his faculties of imagination, curiosity and wonder. I am aware that the assumed instinctive belief in God has been used by many persons as an argument for His existence. But this is a rash argument, as we should thus be compelled to believe in the existence of many cruel and malignant spirits, possessing only a little more power than man; for the belief in them is far more general than of a beneficent Deity. The idea of a universal and beneficent Creator of the universe does not seem to arise in the mind of man, until he has been elevated by long-continued culture.

However, in the previous paragraph (1871: 394, Vol. II) Darwin had said:

> The moral nature of man has reached the highest standard as yet attained, partly through the advancement of the reasoning powers and consequently of a just public opinion, but especially through the sympathies being rendered more tender and widely diffused through the effects of habit, example, instruction, and reflection. It is not improbable that virtuous tendencies may through long practice be inherited. With the more civilised races, the conviction of the existence of an all-seeing Deity has had a potent influence on the advancement

of morality. Ultimately man no longer accepts the praise or blame of his fellows as his chief guide, though few escape this influence, but his habitual convictions controlled by reason afford him the safest rule. His conscience then becomes his supreme judge and monitor. *Nevertheless the first foundation or origin of the moral sense lies in the social instincts, including sympathy; and these instincts no doubt were primarily gained, as in the case of the lower animals, through natural selection.* (Italics mine)

In Darwin's time, it wasn't known that culture and intelligence in humans had nothing to do with their innate and instinctive goodness. It wasn't known that, through intelligence, morality could not be acquired. It wasn't known either that what we've called *civilization* is in fact the withdrawal from our natural ecological niche; that such civilization is the greatest moral, social, and intellectual loss that we've suffered in the whole course of hominid evolution.

Due to the foregoing, we realize that Darwin didn't *consciously* know that our belief in God is instinctive, since that belief could not have appeared in that corrupted civilization, nor in " . . . the more civilised races . . . " as he says. On the contrary: in those more civilized races and in that "civilization," beliefs in evil gods, as well as beliefs in " . . . the existence of many cruel and malignant spirits, possessing only a little more power than man . . . " (Darwin, 1871: 395, Vol. II) originated. Those beliefs in evil gods originated due to a lack of natural enjoyment of life, which our ancestors previously had within graincollection. Also, all the existent religions in the world originated during this cavemen age. *Religions originate only when there's a struggle to avoid extinction*; they emerged during and due to our present wrong living, since those beliefs cannot appear when everything in our life is perfectly satisfactory and normal, when all of our natural instincts are satisfied, and when we do not have to execute actions against our natural instincts.

Darwin knew that absolutely all current religions were *intelligently invented* by civilized humans; but failed to take into consideration its being one of the greatest misfortunes that have occurred in our time, since they have only brought about antagonisms and wars. In the many centuries of their existence, religions have not achieved any positive or beneficial result for humans. We are at present as immoral, vicious, and abominable (or even more so) than our ancestors of 2 or 3 thousand years ago.

However, Darwin had a deep wonder before God. *He knew, even if unconsciously, that our belief in God is instinctive.* He defended his innate wonder before God with all his strength. In *The Descent of Man* (1871: 395, 396, Vol. II), he states:

I am aware that the conclusions arrived at in this work will be denounced by some as highly irreligious, but he who thus denounces them is bound to shew why it is more irreligious to explain the origin of man as a distinct species by descent from some lower form, through the laws of variation and natural selection, than to explain the birth of the individual through the laws of ordinary reproduction. The birth both of the species and of the individual are equally parts of that grand sequence of events, *which our minds refuse to accept as the result of blind chance.* The understanding revolts at such a conclusion, whether or not we are able to believe that every slight variation of structure,—the union of each pair in marriage,—the dissemination of each seed,—and other such events, *have all been ordained for some special purpose.* (Italics mine)

In the final part of *The Origin of Species* (Darwin, 1860: 243), he had said:

Authors of the highest eminence seem to be fully satisfied with the view that each species has been independently created. To my mind it accords better with *what we know of the laws impressed on matter by the Creator,* that the production and extinction of the past and present inhabitants of the world should have been due to secondary causes, like those determining the birth and death of the individual. *When I view all beings not as special creations, but as the lineal descendants of some few beings which lived long before the first bed of the Cambrian system was deposited, they seem to me to become ennobled.* . . .There is grandeur in this view of life, with its several powers, *having been originally breathed by the Creator into a few forms or into one*; and that, whilst this planet has gone cycling on according to the fixed law of gravity, from so simple a beginning endless forms most beautiful and most wonderful have been, and are being evolved. (Italics mine)

Darwin thought that "the first foundation or origin of the moral sense lies in the social instincts, including sympathy; and these instincts no doubt were primarily gained, as in the case of the lower animals, through natural selection." (Darwin, 1871: 394, Vol. II) From this we see that, deep inside him, Darwin knew that human morality is instinctive, and that morality lies in the obedience to nature's laws. Maybe, he *didn't express* his thought that animal instincts are Laws of God since in his time he didn't have all the scientific support we presently have, and had against him the power that religious leaders had at that time, but I am sure that a man of his genius didn't fail to think that, because when he expresses his wonder at and belief in God, he admits that the universe's complexity could only have a divine origin; therefore, he surely thought that biological evolution, through variation and natural selection, is a Law of God, for he says, " . . . the laws impressed on matter by the Creator . . . " (Darwin, 1860: 243)

Therefore, Darwin knew and presumed, but expressed it in a very moderate and modest way, that all our human virtues were acquired by our ancestors when they exclusively followed their natural instincts.

As done in the past by Darwin, scientists presently moderate, hold, and restrain their expressions when dealing with their instinctive belief in God, despite the fact that expressing wonder before the universe's complexity is not antiscientific. Pugh (1977: 448) says:

> If we were to lose our reverence for cosmic mysteries of human existence we would damage some of our most important human values.

Darwin restrained himself from any immoderately strong expression, and due to his restraint, that man, who was a deep believer in God, was called atheist for admitting a scientific truth and for seeing in God a power greater than that seen in Him by religious people. To this day, many researchers, who have studied and analyzed the way in which Darwin came to be mentally prepared to develop his Theory of Variation and Natural Selection, consider that between October 1836 and January 1839, much of his faith in God was lost. This shouldn't surprise us: Darwin himself believed that his wonder before God wasn't instinctive, but a product of the human civilization he was immersed in.

Out of respect to religious beliefs and to religious leaders, or from an inability to explain it with facts, scientists do not mention their innate and innermost belief in God, since it is not possible that a scientist, who likely has a *better idea* of the mysteries of Creation, would not deep inside him, feel wonder and see God the way Darwin did. Nor is it possible that a religious person who studies and *understands* biology, would fail to realize that biological evolution is one more natural law among all the laws of God.

In my youth I was an atheist, or more accurately, *I thought* I was an atheist; in time I realized that my basic expressions showed the opposite. That's why I think that Darwin also *thought* his wonder before God *wasn't* instinctive, since we see that his basic expressions show the opposite: The expression of greatest wonder and awe before God, of a great devotion, certitude, and reverence pronounced by a scientist. This is an irrefutable truth, which will probably be, in the near future, the expression that will "consciously" join all human beings in God's certitude, as it "unconsciously" already joins all living beings, expressed in the following words by that genius: "To my mind it accords better with *what we know of the laws impressed on matter by the Creator . . .* " (Darwin, 1860: 243)

How beautiful it is that the matter on Earth, due to an event that had great probabilities of not happening, gave birth to living beings! How beautiful that those living beings can feel loneliness, love, sadness, pain, joy, wonder!

It has been three years now without rain. The herd of camels has had nothing to eat except some hard and dry twigs. There have been threats of rain every day for the last week, but they didn't materialize. The sky is again gray and cloudy. At last, in the desert, a rainstorm! All camels jump and run in joy, they play, romp, and cavort with joy as they feel raindrops on their bodies, breathe the humidity, and look at the thirsty sand getting wet. Is their joy guided only by the laws that rule the physical phenomena of matter? What a beautiful event has occurred on our planet!

A colt is born. The delivering mare licks and protects him. He's only a few hours old; most of the horses—stallions, colts, fillies, and mares of the herd, get close to him surprised in meeting the new member. The delivering mare raises her head while the colt finds support on her and looks at his surroundings amazed. All the members of the herd, gathered together, keep looking at him also in surprise; they haven't stopped observing him for quite a while. . . . Could this be the equine way of congratulating the mother and welcoming the newborn? Could this be the equine way of showing maternal pride? I do not know what drives horses to do these things. . . . Are they driven only by the laws that rule the physical phenomena of matter? If they are driven by those laws, how beautiful that they have that power! If they aren't guided by them, then, by what power are they being driven? What magical eventuality happens on Earth!

Animals, mainly cubs, play and investigate without a material purpose. What drives a scientist to try to explain the natural phenomena but his animal curiosity? How are we going to interpret that animal curiosity? Is it another animal instinct? Is he guided only by the laws that rule the physical phenomena of matter? What a beautiful eventuality! How beautiful that in this planet something so wonderful happens!

How beautiful that all these acts are ruled by the same natural and universal laws that rule the physical phenomena of matter!

All the Laws of The Universe have the same exquisite style The Creator gave them. They allow us to recognize only one Author.

Everything is changing in the universe. On our planet, wind, snow, and water rapidly erode the surface of the earth; falling meteorites are pieces of planets or stars, or are intergalactic matter that didn't integrate. Earthquakes and volcanism transform the face of the earth. All the universe transforms, from the smallest particle of matter to the largest celestial body. Weather changes on our planet; the environment changes, and due to the changing environment everywhere, living beings obey; populations, through several generations, follow God's Laws—the natural laws that allow them, and force them, to adapt to that changing environment; otherwise they would perish. Therefore, to deny biological evolution is to deny these laws. And to deny these laws is to deny this power in the laws of God.

I no longer wish to hold back my intimate certitude and wonder. I will express my certitude, not in a god whom somebody could derogatorily call Darwin's or Spinoza's, but in Whom *all living beings* instinctively trust; Who shows His exquisite style in all His laws; Who is also Darwin's and Spinoza's: God.

It is *not* we humans, who, in our respective artificial religions, will "create" or "invent" *convenient* laws and make them look like the laws of God. And it is not humans who will choose, among the true laws of God, those which *we think* are good and those which are not. As Darwin stated, God made and impressed them in each particle of matter when He created all the universe. God impresses those laws in each of the cells of all living beings. *Our natural instincts are part of those laws.* God doesn't need religions and religious leaders to make us know His laws. We do not have to learn His laws: we are born with them impressed in each molecule, in each cell, in each fiber of our body. *His laws cannot be written or spoken because they are ineffable.*

To avoid, during this last great glaciation, the extinction thrust upon us according to nature's laws, the corrupt habit of judging the laws of God was born in humans: this corrupt habit is the origin and basis of all our current religions, the origin of ethics and the origin of positive law. Nature's laws, being the laws of God, are simply to be obeyed by us, as done by all other living beings—not to be judged by our intelligence because, according to nature's laws, the function of our intelligence is to enjoy life, to enjoy God's creation, not to judge His laws. Furthermore, by having impressed in our cells the laws of God, we are not born with bad instincts. *All our instincts are good.* The apparently bad instincts that we see in humans are unhealthy behaviors that emerge from our failure to fulfill our *true* natural instincts, in a habitat and within a social environment that are not natural in us. Morally unacceptable behaviors are caused because we force ourselves to perform actions that are neither natural nor desirable to us; and are also the result of the psychical traumas we suffered during our childhood by not having the exclusive and complete attention of our mother for many years; that is, they are the result of a sickness and are not our true natural instincts. *If we lived within our natural ecological niche of graincollection, we would see all of our natural instincts emerging and fitting perfectly in that ecological and social environment*; furthermore, unhealthy behaviors wouldn't emerge from us. Therefore, I repeat: *humans do not have bad instincts.* What is wrong and produces perverse behaviors in us is the current antinatural social system that we have designed through our intelligence to avoid extinction since the start of the last great Pleistocene glaciation. What is wrong is that, due to the lack of the prolonged celibacy of women in the current nuclear family, the global human population has increased enormously in the last millennia—to the extent that it is producing a complete imbalance in all the ecosystems of the planet. The appearance of territorial property in the hunter-gatherer groups, in addition, brought about the creation of the private property system in the agricultural, herding, and industrial societies that descend from them, and is the cause of the wars, terrorism, drug addiction, alcoholism, confusion, social collapse, etc., that presently affect all human societies.

On the other hand, the apparently bad instincts that *we think* animals possess are a result of the lack of understanding we have of their behavior, because we still haven't started to understand our own behavior, and because humans have forced many animal species to live out of their own natural ecological niches and ecosystems. We have forced them to behave in an unhealthy way. Something very similar to what is happening to us since the start of the last great glaciation now happens to them, but in truth their natural instincts are not bad. *Never again should we think that a living being that has emerged from the matter in which God impressed His laws, has bad instincts.* It is the *religious pride* that developed in humans during this abnormal cavemen age that has made us erroneously think that bad instincts can exist in humans and in other animals, or that animals shouldn't behave in certain ways. It is the *religious pride* that has made us believe that we know good and evil, and that we can be more compassionate than God; that we can discern in some animals bad instincts that God failed to notice or that He mistakenly gave us; or that He doesn't know nature which He Himself created.

The existence of "the Devil" who incites in humans our "natural bad instincts" is even believed in some religions throughout the world; or that "Satan," with similar powers to those of God, provokes evil in us. *According to religious leaders, this is what makes humans follow their religions, since "we must moderate our bad instincts through religion."*

We can appreciate here that all religious people, or rather, all humans, haven't realized that the only evil we suffer from is the fact that we live out of our natural ecological niche, beyond the laws of nature; beyond the universal laws, which are the only laws of God. *We do not realize that, as a result of not having bad instincts, we do not need any religion to moderate them.* What we urgently need is to return to our natural ecological niche, to graincollection, to heal ourselves from the sickness we are suffering, so everything will then be normal and our healthy natural instincts will completely emerge in each one of us.

Some people will say that Würm's Glaciation pushed humans into unnatural behaviors, and since this glaciation was an act of God, therefore our current wrong behaviors resulted from an act of God and, in this way, humans are free of guilt. We cannot look at it this way: the extinction of the greatest part of the species during the whole course of biological evolution in our planet has been, and is, the natural norm. All those animal species, including our ancestors and the relatives of our ancestors, have always accepted extinction, or life, when each had to happen according to nature's laws. *The extinction of the greatest part of the graincollector populations during the whole course of hominid evolution has been the natural norm.* But the use of intelligence to thrive, and therefore to avoid extinction, goes against nature's laws. All animals, including our ancestors, have *always* survived, thriving with their natural instincts and not by using their intelligence, since, applying intelligence for survival purposes damages *all* living beings. The disobedience of *some* human populations when they manufactured weapons to hunt and when they used their intelligence to thrive, is the cause of the current deterioration of all the ecosystems in our planet, and of the *disappearance* (not extinction) of the few graincollector populations that could have survived as such during the last great glaciation, if they hadn't been subjugated by the armed groups that did not want to face extinction, as God ordered. Those disobedient groups were our ancestors—and ourselves, their descendants. But there is still some good in us: we also descend from the graincollectors that were subjugated by the armed disobedient groups.

2. Explanation of Objectives

I will give an explanation of the objectives presented in the Preface, so the reader will know, in addition, why I am following this path.

Presently our world is, in *all* aspects we may want to imagine or consider, severely damaged by our human actions—so much so that we must *do something to repair it* if we believe we have within our reach a future, a light, a path that might be the right one. I should stop here, leaving the reader to draw his own conclusions and judgments and propose his own solutions, whether or not he is convinced of our graincollector past. But the fact remains that there are many serious social problems in the world, and due to this, in this book I want to propose the *start* of the path towards a solution. I hope this proposition is valid in the reader's eyes.

What is our true objective when trying to find out, with more or less precision, the natural social system of our graincollector ancestors? The objective we are after determines the way we can focus our research. We may choose very different paths if our objective is to satisfy a simple scientific curiosity or make a small contribution to the advancement of science, but since the objective we seek is to show our present human reality, and offer a path that will change that reality, artificial now, into a reality within the nature's laws, then, the first step must be this: To bring this matter to the attention of *all scientists*, so that, after serious research, *and upon their acceptance of graincollection as our true nature*, have them undertake the task of finding a way for all human beings to return, first, to a social system similar to our natural social system; and, little by little, start diminishing human population—that women restrict themselves to deliver one child during all their life, until the world's human population is small enough such that we may all live within nature, taking from it what is ours according to our animal essence, in this case, taking from it what exclusively belongs to graincollectors. Second, there must be the return of all humans to an absolutely natural graincollecting way of life, even though for the weather conditions that would allow humans to live naked, *and since the last great glaciation is not completely over*, we can only count on a few natural savannas in the Old World, which was, and is, our only home as graincollectors. In this way we will restore the ecological balance in the whole planet and we will again respect the laws of God without judging them through the intervention of our intelligence. We must remember, after all, that *our ancestors were able to survive as graincollectors during all the glaciations of the Pleistocene*, except for the last one during which, by using their intelligence to thrive, they turned hunters.

Will some scientists be interested? Will they at least consider what I am now offering as a start to a solution? Will they see it appropriate but unattainable? Will they pronounce that humans should follow the path we are in, since our intelligence in the future will solve all of our current problems? Will the religious leaders of the whole world oppose it, since this idea is not convenient to their selfish interests, because they presently have dominion and power over many human beings? If the idea is rejected because scientific reality contradicts our graincollector past, I'll agree with its rejection, *but if our reality is that we are suffering the nuclear family and suffering all the present artificially made societies,* just because we haven't found our true nature, and only because such alien societies are our ill-fated inheritance from the last great glaciation, if the truth is that presently everything in the world is deteriorating because our natural instincts demand something we can't reach in this unnatural social system, and because we are taking from nature what is not meant for us, then, all humans must struggle for a return to graincollection and leave behind the cavemen age in which we are still living.

I believe this idea will be considered; I believe that a return to nature will happen very soon. Therefore, as a second step, we must direct all our efforts toward the objective that all the people in the world, especially the young ones, see a light, a goal to follow, a feasible world in which everything is in harmony with nature; but I want them to follow this goal after being convinced, *through scientific reasoning,* that graincollection is our true nature, not by impulses analogous to religious fanaticisms that have divided our societies in the last 50 thousand years.

My objective is that all humans will find and follow *the truth,* alone, for there's only one truth. My objective is that all humans find and follow God's certitude. God's certitude is also only one. *To have God's certitude is to feel intimately the instinctive confidence that makes us obey His laws, nature's laws, without judging by our intelligence.* God's certitude, as many other natural instincts in us, does not presently flourish in humans because we do live neither within our natural niche, nor our natural social system. My objective is to make it flourish completely in all of us, as well as to make flourish in all of us all of our other natural instincts. It is also my objective that the youth will stop thinking of *"my religion,"* of *"my faith."* Faith and religion separate humans from all other animals, and from all other living beings—and, as if they were our nationality, as if they were our own language, also divide humans. *God's certitude joins us, and joins us with all living beings and with all God's creation.*

I want all humans to respect animals the way our graincollector ancestors respected them; to stop treating them in a cruel and despicable way, since *animals are our siblings.* The human animal, within nature, is neither prey nor predator of any animal, but is instead their guide in the grazer's migrations. Therefore, I want humans to obey this natural duty, as well as never to torture them any more to obtain material benefits from their meat, milk, eggs, etc., or to use them for our enjoyment without concern for their suffering, and without concern of the right God gives them to fulfill their life and to enjoy it within their natural ecological niche. *All animals are the children of God. The creation is only one. . . .*

Within Nature, within our natural ecological niche, humans are as good, noble, and kind, as are all other animals. God didn't make us in a different way: All the Laws of The Universe have the same exquisite style the Creator gave them.

I know I will achieve my objectives.

3. The Oral Tradition and Genesis

The *recollection* of life in a *paradise* is general among the oral tradition of *all* people on Earth. Man's rebelliousness against God's mandate, and therefore the expulsion from that paradise, is part of the old oral, and later on written, tradition of *all* of the world's ethnic groups, even though expressed differently in each ethnic group. That tradition was kept by the people to which the first author and compilers of what was later on known as Genesis, belonged to.

I will try to demonstrate that this lost paradise which all humans "remember" is in fact graincollection, and that the first three chapters of Genesis are a very old tradition of people that could only have been graincollectors, and who had never been hunter-gatherers, agricul- turists, or shepherds. The contents of The Holy Scriptures including the fourth chapter of Genesis and on, are chronicle, history, or very modern tradition of people who were definitely agriculturists and shepherds and had all the faults and social sicknesses of people who had already been thrown out of their natural niche for a long period of time; therefore, I am only going to consider the *old* oral tradition which was written, 50 thousand years later, in the first three chapters of Genesis.

First, I will mention a belief that seems to be common among many researchers of anthropology, psychology, sociology, etc.:

I recently read in the magazine of science and technology for the general reader, *Discover*, in its December 1988 issue, an article by Jared Diamond entitled: "The Golden Age That Never Was," subtitled, "Man has never lived in harmony with nature. Our ancestors were no less rapacious than we are—just less powerful."

Diamond starts as follows: "Environmentalists sickened by the damage that industrial societies are wreaking on the world often look to the past as a golden age." Later, he continues: "The nostalgia for a lost golden age extends beyond the environmentalist view; it's part of a larger, historical tendency to see the past as golden in many other respects."

Diamond says that this tendency is present in humans because our ancestors, by not living in harmony with nature, have always exhausted the flora and fauna of their own habitat to the point that in the recent past they have had to abandon small or large cities in search for new places, or their cultures and civilizations have disintegrated. According to him, as our ancestors faced emigration and witnessed the destruction caused to their own habitat, they became attached to the belief that in the past, life was lived in harmony with nature; and this is the reason why later on they live with the nostalgia of a lost paradise and the belief that the past was always better.

Diamond points out that to the degree in which humans have had more and better technology, they have destroyed their habitat faster and have caused the extinction of many animal species, and he adds that our ancestors have "always" been destroyers and "rapacious," as we currently are, "just less powerful."

Diamond gives several examples of lost human civilizations which disappeared because they exhausted their habitat. This, he deduces, is the reason why all humans grieve for the Garden of Eden, or "The Golden Age," as he calls it. Since humans become more "rapacious" and more destructive, elder people always remember and talk of a much better past than what they are presently living; and adds that it has *always* been like that in the whole course of human evolution.

Therefore, according to Diamond (and maybe to many other scientists who share this belief), The Garden of Eden, so much awaited and missed by all humans, never existed; and, in addition, our ancestors never lived in harmony with nature.

If we analyze the last 50 thousand years, that is, from the start of the last great Pleistocene glaciation up to the present time, we see that what Diamond says is absolutely true: by using our intelligence, not our instincts, to thrive, humans have been steadily and increasingly destroying all the habitats and ecosystems in which we thrive, *because we are not a natural part of those ecosystems.*

The start of the last great glaciation pushed humans to manufacture weapons and to hunt; since then, we have only destroyed ecosystems in our struggle to avoid extinction. When referring to this part of our evolution, the idea of Diamond, that "man has never lived in harmony with nature," is true, *but only during this period of time*, since it isn't logical to believe that our ancestors were able to survive the last 14 million years (or, more accurately, since the beginning of life on this planet), if they hadn't *always lived in harmony with nature*.

Diamond makes this statement based on the belief that we descend from hunter-gatherers, since he sees, and rightly so, that within that niche and context, and due to the natural characters we possess, our ancestors would have never been integrated with nature.

We must take under consideration, too, that humans, like all other animals, *instinctively* expect to enjoy life. We presently cannot enjoy our life because we've been living in an unnatural manner for 50 thousand years. This lack of satisfaction of our natural instincts within this current alien environment, and the execution of acts contrary to our instincts, makes us grieve for a better life.

If, as Diamond states, hunter-gatherers are *always* destroyers of the habitat and environment in which they live, then this is further evidence that our ancestors were never hunter-gatherers before the start of the last great glaciation—evidence, too, that agriculturists and shepherds were and are destroyers of the habitat and environment in which they live, and that using our intelligence to thrive is detrimental for ourselves, and for the other beings of the world.

A simple analysis of Genesis 1, 2 and 3 reveals evidence of our recent graincollector past.

Genesis 1 shows that, previous to the last great glaciation, our ancestors already had an idea of biological evolution and of the evolution of the universe.

Let's observe that the first thing our ancestors thought to have life on Earth was grass and herb yielding seed, which is the main source of nourishment of graincollectors. In the words of Genesis 1:11:

> And God said: 'Let the earth put forth grass, herb yielding seed, and fruit-tree bearing fruit after its kind, wherein is the seed thereof, upon the earth.' And it was so.[*]

[*] All Holy Scriptures quotations of this section are from The Jewish Publication Society of America edition, Philadelphia, copyright 1917, 1945, and 1955.

In Genesis 1:26–30, God creates man and woman, and gives them dominion over animals and over the earth; *but to humans, for their nourishment, only gives herb yielding seed, and fruit-tree bearing fruit.* Genesis 1:29 says:

> And God said: 'Behold, I have given you every herb yielding seed, which is upon the face of all the earth, and every tree, in which is the fruit of a tree yielding seed—to you it shall be for food.'

A great difference is found in Genesis 1:30, since God gives animals "every green herb" for their nourishment; but seeds are not mentioned. We must remember that the ungulates that follow humans in the grazers' migrations apparently ate only green herbs, since the seeds of grasses have already been collected by humans.

It would be illogical to believe that if our ancestors had *always* been omnivorous hunter-gatherers, they would have had an oral tradition in which God gave them *only* seeds and tree fruits for their nourishment. Furthermore, making *seeds* so important for human nourishment *is not* in accordance with a hunting-gathering tradition. Nevertheless, an agriculture tradition that could also fit in this context would be too modern (being approximately within the last 10 thousand years) to be part of the *old oral tradition*, since we see that agriculture and shepherding traditions, recorded in The Holy Scriptures from Chapter 4 of Genesis, came into being subsequent to God's punishment of man and man's expulsion from the Garden of Eden—that is, subsequent to the start of Würm's Glaciation when our ancestors already covered their bodies with garments of skins to protect themselves from the elements.

When God orders man "to have dominion" over animals, and "subdue" the earth, this tradition likely refers to *guiding the animals, and to taking the food that earth gives them maternally*, since in the grazers' migrations, humans always went ahead, guiding the animals. Let's remember that we humans frequently designate the Earth "Mother," the way our ancestors did according to very old oral traditions that were universal in all people of the world and exist to this day. We therefore owe respect and veneration to Mother Earth, and we can't assume the old tradition literally meant to "subdue it." Most probably there is an incorrect interpretation of those old oral traditions, or an incorrect translation of the original texts of Genesis, since by the time they were put in writing, and later translated, our ancestors had definitely become shepherds and agriculturists and could have accepted that erroneous interpretation or translation. This maternal giving to, and guiding of, animals, is most probably what the old oral tradition means, and not that man could dominate and subdue earth and animals.

In the second chapter of Genesis, life in the Garden of Eden is described, and here we learn about the old tradition that humans must *not* know good and evil. The strongly stated order was to obey the Laws of God *without judging them*, as stated in Genesis 2:16–17:

> And the LORD God commanded the man, saying: 'Of every tree of the garden thou mayest freely eat; but of the tree of the knowledge of good and evil, thou shalt not eat of it; for in the day that thou eatest thereof thou shalt surely die.'

Thus, our graincollector ancestors already knew that humans could use their intelligence with survival as their objective, but it was extremely wrong to do, being against God's will and against nature's Laws. *They realized that creating an imbalance in their ecosystem and habitat could be fatal*, since the old tradition says: " . . . for in the day that thou eatest thereof thou shalt surely die."

Further evidence that this is a graincollectors' tradition, and that it predates the last great Pleistocene glaciation, is seen in Genesis 2: 24–25:

> Therefore shall a man leave his father and his mother, and shall cleave unto his wife, and they shall be one flesh. And they were both naked, the man and his wife, and were not ashamed.

From what we have read in Genesis 2:24, graincollectors, like most mammals and particularly primates, formed matrilocal and matricentric exogamous groups, and we know that graincollectors didn't have any territory, nor recognize property; but this *isn't* a characteristic of human hunter-gatherers. Lee (1976: 75) states:

> This patrilocal, territorial, exogamous band or "horde," as Radcliffe-Brown called it, has proven to be a remarkably persistent construct in the study of hunting and gathering peoples.

It isn't a required characteristic of agriculturist and shepherd peoples either; even at present, there are many societies of this type in the world.

Graincollectors, due to their ability to wield branches and to throw stones, did not have predators; however, they were in great danger of disturbing or even stepping on a snake when they walked in the long-grass grasslands. The snake is the most feared animal by any human who walks in the savanna. Most probably, that is why many stories and legends are to be found, based on actions of snakes against humans. In Genesis 3, the snake is said to be guilty of causing our expulsion from the Garden of Eden. It is the snake that advises the woman to eat of the tree of the knowledge of good and evil. To quote Genesis 3:2–5:

> And the woman said unto the serpent: 'Of the fruit of the trees of the garden we may eat; but of the fruit of the tree which is in the midst of the garden, God hath said: Ye shall not eat of it, neither shall ye touch it, lest ye die.' And the serpent said unto the woman: 'Ye shall not surely die; for God doth know that in the day ye eat thereof, then your eyes shall be opened, and ye shall be as God, knowing good and evil.'

The graincollectors' precept of respecting the laws of God without judging them is confirmed; they never tried to know good and evil, since the reason for our expulsion from the Garden of Eden, according to the old tradition, was the belief that we were capable of judging such laws like gods. Our ancestors thought the serpent was the woman's instigator, and woman the man's.

Genesis 3:21 states that God made for man and woman garments of skins, and clothed them. This tradition indicates a period at the height of the glaciation. We can imagine, then, what happened to our ancestors at the arrival of the intense and *sudden* cold, since the change in weather might have been total and severe for the first hundred years after the arrival of the glaciation. First, however, I would like to warn the reader of the following:

In trying to demonstrate our recent graincollector past, the evidences presented up to now, based on the old oral tradition as recorded in the first three chapters of Genesis are, on their own, weak; however, they can be taken as complementary evidence that gains strength when added to other irrefutable evidence. Genesis 3:16, however, provides some strong evidence:

> Unto the woman He said: 'I will greatly multiply thy pain and thy travail; in pain thou shalt bring forth children; and thy desire shall be to thy husband, and he shall rule over thee.'

This could have only been said and thought by a graincollector based on his own reality, in his own life, and can only be understood thinking like a graincollector. No hunter-gatherer, agriculturist, or shepherd could have had the imagination to think about or express this concept. That is why present-day humans, having forgotten our grain-collector past, have been unable to understand or interpret it with the precise meaning with which it was expressed by our ex-graincollector ancestors of 50 thousand years ago, as we will see.

Let us first consider the prevalent interpretation that is given to that verse. We are told that it partly explains the mystery of human suffering and death—that, presently, women deliver children who have a bigger head, and they consequently suffer more during delivery. But didn't they suffer the same before? During human evolution the great brain expansion started 2 or 3 million years ago. The evolutionary adaptation of the woman to deliver children with a bigger head is total. Maybe presently, with a lack of natural life—lack of daily walks, peaceful life, etc., delivery is more difficult, since we see that women who live closer to nature, despite being hunter-gatherers, like the !Kung women, when they are about to deliver, walk to a place away from the village or the meeting center of the tribe, deliver their child, and in a few hours walk back with their child in arms. Konner (1972: 287) states:

> Zhun/twa [!Kung] women are remarkable for the equanimity and independence with which they approach pregnancy and childbirth. There is no medical supervision of pregnancy or delivery, and there are no midwives or other expert native persons traditionally concerned with birth. A woman is very much on her own. When the first uterine contractions begin, she simply leaves the village alone or with one or more other women. The delivery is completed in the bush a short distance away. If the infant lives, she returns with it to the village.
>
> She may resume her normal activities at once, or rest for a few days, depending on her inclination and condition. There is no ritual lying-in period before or after delivery.

A mare delivers her colt, and few hours later the colt runs, jumps, and escapes predators; that is, the colt must already have his brain, muscles, bones, etc., sufficiently developed in order to have these capacities. Women deliver children that cannot walk or transport themselves for a long time. Females of precocial mammal species must suffer more when delivering; however they are *all* adapted to their natural way of reproduction. But all mammal females experience some kind of suffering at delivery.

Our graincollector ancestors knew this very well, since for more than 14 million years they migrated ahead of, but close to the equines, and, in addition, they knew the life of many other animals; therefore, our ex-graincollector ancestors of 50 thousand years ago never thought that women were going to experience more suffering at delivery, despite having become hunter-gatherers since, as we've already seen, present-day !Kung women, with a way of life that includes exercise, especially walking, and even though they live out of humans' natural ecological niche, deliver their children with the same ease and speed as a mare.

Let us now consider what happened to the graincollectors when the intense cold weather arrived and stayed for so long.

When grasses and their seeds were scarce, the populations and tribes first dispersed, and then dissolved into smaller groups. The minimum group would be a woman with her child, and a man; that is how the *unnatural* nuclear family was formed—pushed to it by the glaciation.

Now, the nourishment of that woman and her infant depended on what a man was able to provide. According to nature's laws, it is at this point that all humans unable to survive as graincollectors should have either perished, or emigrated to warmer savannas to survive in an instinctive and natural way, as their ancestors did in several previous great glaciations of the Pleistocene. But this time it didn't happen that way. Under these conditions the mother suffered when her child wanted to be nursed and she was unable to produce any more breast milk.

When our ancestors were graincollectors, women, and not men, were the core of the tribe; it was women who knew the routes through which their tribe traveled in the annual grazer migrations, because they had been born in those tribes and it was they who, in addition, passed on traditions to their descendants. At that time women were the ones who *legislated, oriented, and guided the tribe*, and used to advise men as to what should be done in strange or dangerous circumstances. Therefore, under the strange and dangerous circumstances that the glaciation brought about, the woman was the one who *suggested* to man that he use his intelligence to thrive, i.e., to manufacture weapons and hunt animals in order for the family to have something to eat. However, according to the graincollectors' age-old precepts, we shouldn't consider ourselves to be like gods and decide whether these actions are good or bad, but, instead, should obey our instincts, and not make use of our intelligence. Hunting is not instinctive in humans; it is an intelligent act carried out with intelligently manufactured weapons. That day our ancestors ate the fruit of the tree of the knowledge of good and evil. That day they opened their eyes and saw as gods do. That day they were expelled from the Garden of Eden, since from that day up to the present we humans have *always* acted against the laws of God. That is the way our ancestors felt for the last 50 thousand years: we know it through our oral tradition. That's how it has been recorded in Genesis.

I will now continue with what I consider most important to demonstrate—God's punishment to women; the punishment that only a graincollector can express and only someone who thinks like a graincollector can understand:

(a) A woman, while still a graincollector, was totally independent in her actions and subsistence, and the tribe *belonged* to her, to her sisters, to her female cousins, to her mother, to her aunts, to her daughters and nieces; to people very close to her. Now she was alone and subjected to the will of a man.

(b) Previously, a graincollector mother devoted all her time and attention, for many years, to one child, and nature would time the arrival of another infant 7 or 8 years later. *Now, the man on whom she was dependant wouldn't allow her to remain celibate for all that time; she would be forced into having children more frequently.*

The oral tradition, recorded in Genesis, tells us that the ex-grain-collectors of 50 thousand years ago blame the woman for having advised man to use his intelligence against nature's laws, *but as a punishment from God she had received the multiplication of deliveries, not the multiplication of her pain and travail; and instead of receiving her children with the happiness she did before, she received them with sorrow and pain at not being able to care for and nurse several children at the same time.*

In modern societies, in order to escape from that punishment, humans resort to corrupt actions like abortion and contraceptives; even, at times, to infanticide. In most hunter-gatherer societies, since the time they were unnaturally formed 50 thousand years ago, people resorted and resort to infanticide. This wouldn't be a *normal practice* among today's humans if our ancestors had *always* been hunter-gatherers, since, within this niche and way of life, woman would have already been adapted to depend on a man for her subsistence, and therefore, to having many children. Our way of reproduction and rearing children would, in that case, be very different from that of graincollectors. If these corrupt actions are done currently, despite the horror, sorrow, pain, and disgust these practices give us, it is because *it isn't natural for women to give birth so frequently*. Konner (1972: 287) comments regarding !Kung women as follows:

> The second method [of population control], which many Zhun/twasi [!Kung] report to have been practised commonly until recent years, is *infanticide*. This was accomplished by burial of the infant within seconds after birth, probably before it breathed. Infants reported to have been abandoned in this way include *those born too soon after a sibling* (provided the latter was still alive), one of a pair of twins, and certain instances of malpresentation and malformation, such as breech birth, or agenesis of limbs or ears. (Italics mine)

The multiplication of deliveries; that is, the reduction in interbirth interval, and subservience to the husband's will, is the true meaning of this tradition, since, in any other way, these two actions wouldn't be linked together and recorded in the same verse. *These two actions which, in reality, are automatically linked to the rough, sad, and overwhelming change for women, from a tribal graincollector's life, to life in the nuclear family, when linked in one verse, because this is how it was dictated by our oral tradition, can only have this meaning and not another, since multiplying labor pains and travail is not linked to the fact of being dependent to the husband's will, but multiplying deliveries is.* Furthermore, if these two punishments had been mentioned in different verses, we could think their meaning might be different.

We realize this can't be a tradition of natural hunter-gatherers, since for hunter-gatherer women, multiplicity of deliveries wouldn't be a punishment, since they were already overwhelmed by them and they would be adapted to live that way. Also, being subjected to their husband's will wouldn't be a punishment, since they were already subjected to it. The same could be said of the agriculturist or shepherd women. Only the change from graincollection to hunting-gathering, and later on to agriculture and shepherding, brings about such a *degrading* change for women.

The best proof that neither hunter-gatherers, agriculturists, nor shepherds could think of, imagine, or express what was recorded in that verse, or were even able to understand or interpret it correctly, is what I already mentioned, and would like to repeat: Since the time our ancestors abandoned graincollection, that old oral tradition, later on recorded in Genesis 3:16, has never been correctly understood, and moreover it was incorrectly expressed when it was recorded, *since we do not think that women used to space their pregnancies and deliveries so far apart, nor that their subsistence was independent of a man or men.*

Such hard and sad changes for women, which make them totally dependent on a man, haven't been and will never be assimilated, since their natural instincts demand their independence. Furthermore, their instincts make them want to take charge of *the legislation, control, and guidance of their tribe.*

We are presently witnessing that women do not accept being dependent on men. Women are currently instinctively seeking the independence their ancestral mothers always enjoyed before and during graincollection. This fact is also an evidence of our recent graincollector past, since if our ancestors had been hunter-gatherers for million of years, as assumed in the currently accepted theories that deal with our origin, women would be excellently adapted to and used to that dependency. In addition, the mother's method of rearing children in that context *wouldn't* have permitted *only one* child to be dependent on her for so many years; human evolution and behavior would surely have been completely different: sedentary, rearing of *several* children in dens, living sites, etc.

For those animal species that in their natural life, due to the great number of predators they have, due to the risks and dangers to which they are exposed, or due to difficulty in obtaining food (living in environments in which food supply is very uncertain), their chances of reaching reproductive age are low. Adaptively, they compensate for those great obstacles by their females giving birth more often and having larger litters (species subject to r-selection). In contrast, the chances of reaching reproductive age are higher for those animals without predators and for whom obtaining food is easier (living as they do in stable environments). In their case, females adaptively compensate for their comparatively easy life by spacing birth intervals and delivering only one infant (species subject to K-selection). Auto-regulation of births (interbirth interval) and number of infants born (size of litters) are natural laws for all living animal species since, in the first case, *if they didn't reproduce quickly and abundantly*, that species would become extinct; and in the second case, *if they reproduce fast and abundantly*, that species would also become extinct due to the resulting scarcity of their natural food.

The simple and easy life of graincollectors is evidence that the graincollector mother would space pregnancies and births adaptively, and would give birth to only one child in each delivery. If graincollectors had reproduced at the same rate as hunter-gatherers, agriculturists, and shepherds have in the last 50 thousand years, they would have caused their own extinction. Therefore, the huge spacing between births in graincollector females is a natural law, and not a speculation without support. Then, the curse for woman recorded in Genesis 3:16 is the multiplication of births, not the multiplication of pain and travail.

Another curse that according to oral tradition was going to be fullfilled, and that our graincollector ancestors predicted due to their vast knowledge of natural life, is that recorded in Genesis 3:17–19 and 23:

> And unto Adam He said: 'Because thou hast hearkened unto the voice of thy wife, and hast eaten of the tree, of which I commanded thee, saying: Thou shalt not eat of it; cursed is the ground for thy sake; in toil shalt thou eat of it all the days of thy life. Thorns also and thistles shall it bring forth to thee; and thou shalt eat the herb of the field. In the sweat of thy face shalt thou eat bread, till thou return unto the ground; for out of it wast thou taken; for dust thou art, and unto dust shalt thou return.'
> . . . Therefore the LORD God sent him forth from the garden of Eden, to till the ground from whence he was taken.

Right after our ancestors lost graincollection, they realized the damage they were doing to their ecosystem, and in general to all living beings in the planet, since their oral tradition says: " . . . cursed is the ground for thy sake . . . "

The oral tradition says that, before God's punishment, our ancestors didn't have *to work* in order to obtain their food. If they had been hunter-gatherers they would have *always worked*, since hunting, for humans, is very difficult; even more so without weapons, since it wasn't until the arrival of the last great glaciation that our ancestors were armed; and even those weapons, if compared with the modern weapons and poisons that !Kung people currently use to hunt, were very inefficient; and !Kung people *work very hard* in order to obtain a prey, *because hunting is unnatural in humans, since they rapidly deplete the animal prey population. For humans hunting is more difficult than working the land; if this were not so, the Neolithic hunters would have remained hunters, and agriculture would never have emerged.* Therefore, the curse of having to work the land and sweat in order to obtain food wouldn't have been a curse to a hunter-gatherer, but a blessing, a benefit. *The only natural way for humans to live without working is graincollection.* This type of life is the one our ancestors longed for during Würm's Glaciation, and it's the one we presently long for: *our instincts require of us to enjoy life, and, without any great effort, take the seeds that nature, through the laws of biological evolution, placed exactly at the height of our hands.*

The tradition regarding the punishment of having to work the land for survival was subsequent to the loss of graincollection, since agriculture is a very recent activity; it started 10 thousand years ago at the most; therefore, the original tradition must have been what was stated in Genesis 3:18:

Thorns also and thistles shall it bring forth to thee; and thou shalt eat the herb of the field.

The old oral tradition states that our ancestors *remembered* a simple and easy way of life and that they didn't have to hunt; even less without weapons. As already stated, hunting, for humans, is a more difficult activity than agriculture; therefore, the original oral tradition, recorded in Genesis, already indicated that since the beginning of the last great glaciation "working" for survival didn't exist in their past, and now "working" was required for survival.

Furthermore, I repeat, our ancestors of 50 thousand years ago were perfectly aware of the mistake of using their intelligence against nature's laws, against the laws of God, since Genesis 3:22 states:

And the LORD God said: 'Behold, the man is become as one of us, to know good and evil; and now, lest he put forth his hand, and take also of the tree of life, and eat, and live for ever.'

Our ancestors were aware of these mistakes 50 thousand years ago. Presently, we still don't begin to understand them, since living against Nature's Laws for so many millennia has brought about in us a lack of understanding that going against nature is going against ourselves and against all living beings.

And the curse was and continues to be fullfilled, just as it was foreseen by our graincollector ancestors: We don't enjoy life anymore the way God intended us to; we work, and with our work we destroy the life God created in this planet, instead of enjoying it as part of Nature: " . . . cursed is the ground for thy sake . . . "

Nothing that could pertain to a hunting-gatherer past has been recorded in the first three chapters of Genesis, but there are many instances of an *exclusive* graincollector's past. At the most, what could appear to be some kind of hunter-gatherer past, is the clothing of Adam and Eve with animal skins; but this appears after God's punishment, that is, at the height of the glaciation. It is not until they are expelled from the Garden of Eden that God covers them with animal skins, since Genesis 3:21 says:

And the LORD God made for Adam and for his wife garments of skins, and clothed them.

That is: they are out of the Garden of Eden, at the height of the glaciation, and have already killed animals and dressed themselves with their skins. The oral tradition states that it was God who clothed them like that.

We must take under consideration that, in order to keep an ex-graincollector's tradition *intact* for 50 thousand years or more, in people that during those 50 thousand years must have mixed with many other people, that tradition would have had to be also common among all the other people, since, if every different human population or ethnic group had had different traditions, then these traditions would have been lost in many confusing legends. That is why I have pointed out that the tradition of a lost paradise and God's punishment to man is one that is common in all people of the world. It is very significant that an ex-graincollector's tradition was kept, without any confusion, for such a long period of time; and that it not only refers to that lost paradise and punishment, but that it also includes other actions and circumstances that *do not* fit with the tradition of hunter-gatherers, agriculturists, or shepherds.

The first author who wrote what was later called Genesis *necessarily* had to record, first, their old oral tradition, since it was at that time the tradition accepted by his people. *First, and above all, that author had to make his narrative congruent with the basic, accepted, and worshipped oral tradition of the people to which he belonged—* more so since he was dealing with their origin. Therefore, *what was first recorded in Genesis is absolutely and necessarily old oral tradition* and not chronicle, history, or modern tradition.

Another reason that helped maintain intact, during the last 50 thousand years, the ex-graincollector's tradition of a lost paradise, is that during that time of chaos and destruction of habitats and ecosystems, in truth *all past time was better*, and we grieve for that "Golden Age," as Diamond (1988) says. Life before the last great glaciation was always calm and delightful; life within graincollection was *always* enjoyed, as our genetically based aptitudes for art, dance, sports, play, informal gatherings, etc., show. Before the last great glaciation the tradition of a better past could not have existed, since humans of those times were an integral part of their migratory grazing ecosystem; they were part of nature; all times were always good and delightful and never boring. Our developed intelligence and large brain also show that our ancestors always enjoyed their life, and always led a calm and relaxing life-style.

Nevertheless, we shouldn't be surprised at how this tradition was kept untouched for so many years: a worshipped and loved oral tradition can remain untouched through generations, more so if that past is instinctively grieved for, since humans instinctively expect to enjoy life, and not have to endure the kind of *miserable* life we live at present.

Most probably, the old oral traditions of the last 50 thousand years didn't have, at that time, a religious meaning, which did not come about until they were recorded in writing, since, at the time they were written (already very modern times), the damage done to nature by humans was already great. We had already caused the extinction of many animal species, destroyed many natural habitats, etc.; and, as recorded in the rest of the Holy Scriptures, the social confusion caused by so many millennia of living out of our natural ecological niche and natural tribal society was such, that *the intervention of our intelligence* was needed in order *to try* to repair the confusion and unnatural living. Therefore, *religions*, as well as *positive law*, emerged: they intend for us to follow laws that will guide humans towards "goodness." But those laws are not in agreement with nature's laws. Those laws are not in agreement with our natural instincts. Therefore, they never were and they will never be effective despite the fact that positive law is based on what we've called "natural law"; that is: is based on the small extent to which natural instincts have flourished *at present* in each of us— since, living in this unnatural society, within this alien environment, most of our natural instincts have remained repressed. This is also the origin of *ethics*, which is only the *artificial* formalization of what *we think* are moral values, since we have forgotten, or haven't yet understood, that the true moral values and true moral laws, as all natural laws, are instinctive in animals; they are God's laws which are impressed in each one of our cells; but, in order for these laws to flourish in animals, these must be living in their natural ecological niche and able to follow only their natural instincts. Humans are able to follow their natural instincts only by living as graincollectors. *With ethics, religions, and positive law, when trying to solve the current wrongdoings of humans, we are accepting and repeating that which was the cause of our expulsion from the Garden of Eden. We believe ourselves to be made in God's image; we adopt the role of gods: we believe that because we are intelligent, we are animals who distinguish good and evil.*

Among the purposes of following a religion, is this: to find God; however, the natural and *conscious* encounter of God emerged a long time ago in each and every one of our graincollector ancestors, *due to their very developed intelligence, to their understanding of nature*, and to their lack of understanding of many natural phenomena they saw (and that we still presently see) as being unexplainable, had they not admitted the intervention of The Creator. As we see in the first three chapters of Genesis, this made our ancestors question the origin of all living beings, the origin of the world and the universe.

Our ancestors were submerged in all the natural phenomena, and realized that a small imbalance in their natural ecosystem, brought about by intelligent actions, could be disastrous (as we also see in the first three chapters of Genesis). At the onset of the intense cold they changed their way of life, removing themselves from their natural ecological niche. In addition, they resorted to intelligent and unnatural activities for their survival, and realized they deserved God's punishment, as they state in the oral tradition. This proves that God wasn't found by our ancestors through religions; instead, they consciously found Him long before the invention of such religions. *They found Him through their wonder before His creation.*

In this way, the ex-graincollectors' wonder before God was *consciously* developed, since their graincollector ancestors already had a deep wonder before God and His creation, as expressed in Genesis 1, 2, and 3.

We now realize the great intelligence, wisdom, and basic knowledge our graincollector ancestors had—above all, their great wonder before the universe and nature, *since it is only that wonder that leads to the natural and conscious encounter of God.*

Our ancestors had God's Certitude: *they instinctively obeyed* nature's laws without judging them. That obedience was their fundamental precept, since by living within nature they knew that nature's laws were the *only* Laws of God. If graincollectors had accepted other laws, these would have been part of their old oral tradition and would have been mentioned in Genesis before the actions of modern agriculturists or shepherds, the way all their old traditions are mentioned. If the first author and later the compilers of Genesis didn't mention them, it is because such laws didn't exist, because never in all of their evolution did our graincollector ancestors have the *need* for laws other than *the authentic ones,* for they always lived within their natural ecological niche. Only those humans who have lived out of their natural niche for thousand of years, and want to try to artificially repair their unnatural way of living, must *invent* other laws which are not the natural laws, which are not the Laws of God. It is for this then, that religions, ethics, and positive law have had some use.

The first three chapters of Genesis have made us realize that, from the last great glaciation to the present, there has been in humans a process of regression of the basic knowledge and understanding of nature, and maybe even of intelligence too, due to lack of contact with nature. Not even in the modern times of Jesus, Buddha or Muhammad, nor even a century ago, would somebody have suspected the great damage humans were doing to nature. However, our ex-graincollector ancestors of 50 thousand years ago did know it. Despite our long-standing knowledge that many civilizations and ancient cultures have disappeared due to the ecological imbalance they created, we are making a very serious mistake in not taking into account their failures and using their experience to control and moderate our own performance and, in this way, try to avoid new failures. Those civilizations still had other places to which they could emigrate; we do not have another world to go to, since it's absurd to believe, as some scientists do, in the possibility of living on other planets of the Solar System, or in those of other solar systems in our galaxy. This is not only precluded by the impossibility for humans to travel there, but their discomforts would far exceed those of the earth's poles or deserts. There aren't any more Americas to conquer; there aren't any more conquests of the West.

Today, humans do not understand nature any more: this has been the cause of our present chaos and ruin, and the present ruin of all other living beings in this planet. The governments of some industrial societies of the whole world have *just started* to realize the great damage we have done to all the ecosystems on earth.

The fundamental importance of the oral tradition recorded in the first three chapters of Genesis is rooted in its indication that it is only by having God's Certitude—*by living within Nature's Laws, and without judging them*—that humans can come back to The Garden of Eden. The only possible Garden of Eden for humans is that within which all of our anatomical, physiological, and behavioral characters *perfectly fit,* and where all our natural instincts are satisfied, and furthermore, where we do not have to resort either to contrived actions or laws that are not instinctive in us:

Graincollection is the remembered and awaited human Garden of Eden.

Chapter VI
Conclusions

In our planet, in our unique world, the brief wink of over 50 thousand years of madness and confusion will soon be over. It could be for the better: that human beings, repentant of the abuse of their animal curiosity transformed into intelligence, will rejoin wild life, like the one led by their graincollector ancestors. Or it could be for the worse: the self-destruction of those arrogant and cruel semi-gods who in their tragedy are dragging along innocent beings. But be it with or without humans, and despite the extinction of thousands of species in this disastrous stage, in the near future, in this presently exhausted planet, animal instincts—always firm, always complete—will triumph over intelligence—always perplexed, always insufficient—and life will take again its usual pleasant course.

> For them [the Arctic Wolves], the pups are the center of the universe, communally fed, reared, and defended.
> L. David Mech, in *National Geographic*, May 1987, p. 567

Our Children Are the Center of the Universe.

1. Only One Way

The Original Sin Was Pride

Our ex-graincollector ancestors of 50 thousand years ago considered themselves gods, and thought they knew good and evil. Therefore, they believed they had the right to use their intelligence in order to hunt and kill animals. This judgment went against the natural and universal laws, against the laws of God.

The Current Sin Is Pride

Humans believe God created and gave us the soul which He didn't give to animals; therefore, we feel we deserve more than all other living beings on this planet, and that we can do as we please with them—even subdue, torture, and kill them for our benefit or enjoyment. Humans believe we have the right to make animals' *only life*, given by God to each and every one of them so they can enjoy His creation, one of suffering, torture, and loneliness. We believe animals are mere stupid brutes that have to obey nature's laws due to their limited intelligence, and that "we are cultural persons" who, with our intelligence, science, and technology, can conquer and transform nature, and thus *free* ourselves from natural laws in order to create our own environment. We believe that our intelligence is similar to God's, since "we have been created in His image and after His likeness." We believe that with this intelligence we can judge His universal and natural laws. We believe we have the capability of pronouncing positive, moral, and ethical laws. We believe ourselves to be gods who know good and evil.

Will humans continue to think that, as recorded in Genesis 1, God let us have dominion over all the earth; that science and technology can disturb with impunity the natural life of any living being or disturb our own; and that disobeying nature's laws, the laws of God, is allowed, since God created the world exclusively for the intelligent humans?

Will humans continue to apply their intelligence for the development of medical sciences, torturing animals in scientific investigations to depravedly extend our lives, and, in order to balance the resulting human overpopulation, practice abortions, use contraceptives, and commit infanticides to delay the free arrival of infants who have the natural right to birth, and whose births *must be again controlled by nature*? Will we, as individuals, feel terror and hate instead of natural fear toward death and, as a species, towards extinction, when one of these specific events, determined by nature's laws, must happen? Will we continue extending our lives only from the fear of death and not from the desire and capability of enjoying our life?

Will religious leaders, *knowing now* the prejudice and damage they are causing to all people, continue proselytizing, and thus ruining the life of all members of their communities? Will they impede our return to the natural laws, to the laws of God?

Will humans continue, owing to religious leaders' Pride, calling God "Father," even though our graincollector ancestors always called Her "Mother"?

No, those things won't be happening any more, because humans will soon return to their natural ecological niche.

The Beginning of the Path Back to Graincollection

We cannot know for certain if, as recorded in Genesis, woman is guilty for the expulsion of humans from the Garden of Eden, or man for following her suggestions. But we know that the return to that paradise will surely be led and guided by women—groups formed by mothers, daughters, female cousins, aunts, nieces, etc. They will be groups of women related to each other, or groups of women who do not have blood relationships, but because they grew up together, and as a result of that deep friendship or *instinctive tribal tie* that amounts to a kinship tie, will create tribes whose objective will be our return to graincollection. We can rest assured that, just as our ancestral mothers *believed*, more than 50 thousand years ago, they were benefiting their children and therefore caused our expulsion from The Garden of Eden; in that same way present mothers, repentant of that sin committed by our ancestral mothers, and *knowing they will benefit their children*, will soon guide our return toward that life. Men, without having kinship ties to any woman in a tribe, will attempt to be admitted in that tribe. Women will, gently and lovingly, guide the graincollector tribes again.

How will humanity leave this present cavemen age chaos: the nuclear family, territorial and private property, positive law, ethics, and moral laws, etc., all created by humans? How will humans leave the division and separation of the world into nations? How will we leave politics, religions, wars, and the absolute command of men? How will humans stop using their intelligence in order to take advantages that, within the universal order, do not belong to us? I don't know for sure how, but the truth is that we'll leave it all to the *women who will do it for their children*. They will recover the power and great status they *always* had in the graincollector's society. Men will soon realize the power of women. Soon, women will legislate and guide their tribes again, and all humans will soon be living again within the universal order.

A society, similar to the *original* kibbutzim social arrangement that Israel had in their first years when it was founded would be quite acceptable *as a beginning of our return* to graincollection, because that type of society has *certain similarities* with what *must have been* the natural social system of our graincollector ancestors. But now, in order to reach graincollection, the social system of those kibbutzim must undergo the following *main* changes:

(a) In the original kibbutzim society, each kibbutz was formed without taking into consideration whether the founding members were related or not. In a present-day adaptation, *the founding men of a kibbutz should not be related to any of the women in that same kibbutz.* Also, an attempt should be made *to ensure that all women in a kibbutz are closely related to each other (mothers, daughters, nieces, aunts, cousins, etc.).* In the event that all women are not *closely* related, those more or less closely related would then be accepted. And if this is not possible, an attempt will be made to include women who grew up together—all with the purpose of forming a "tribal tie" as strong as a kinship tie.

(b) In the original kibbutzim society, in each kibbutz, men and women had the freedom to make love with whoever they wished, unbound by any association, marriage, etc. Now, their sexual behavior in addition, should be, and *must be, promiscuous* between the members of the same kibbutz.

(c) In the original kibbutzim society, women lived more or less apart from their children from the time the children were approximately 4 weeks old. Now, they must *always* live (day and night) with them until children are 8 years old. Women must remain celibate during those years of complete dedication to their *only child.* They will try to breastfeed their child the longest possible time, until, little by little, women will reacquire, through several generations, the biological capability of nursing their infant until he reaches 8 years of age, just like our ancestral graincollector mothers did; and until women also adaptively reacquire the infants' throne (steatopygia), biologically useful to accumulate fat reserves for nursing and for easy transportation of their infant once we return to the true graincollecting way of life.

Women with children under 8 years of age will restrict themselves to do only those jobs that will allow them to be always close to, or carrying their child. Children under 8 will never again be away from their mother for long periods of time. Women will spend much of the time with the whole tribe. In this way they will develop their artistic, sporting, etc., capabilities. All of this should be followed until a true graincollecting society is reached, where there will be no more work, and our natural instincts will rule our behavior.

(d) The property system in the original kibbutzim society was communal to all members. Now, *women must be the only owners of all material goods in each kibbutz*, and, as a group, they will inherit all the material goods in their respective tribal organization or kibbutz, for some time only, while a true graincollecting society, where property does not exist, is reached.

(e) In the original kibbutzim society, the men and women could remain in their kibbutz or leave it if they pleased. Now, *men will abandon their original kibbutz when they reach puberty*, taking with them, as their only inheritance, their physical attributes; *and women will remain in their original kibbutz for life.*

Men will show their natural physical attributes and their capability for work when trying to be accepted in other tribe/kibbutz, while a true natural graincollecting society, in which work will no longer be necessary, is reached.

The men admitted in that tribe will obtain the great prize of being husbands to all women in childbearing years, and therefore, fathers to all infants that are born.

(f) In the original kibbutzim society, any activity that would produce income (industrial, agricultural, etc.) could be developed. Now, all kibbutzim must become, little by little, less technical and entirely agricultural entities; exclusively growing cereals and some fruit-bearing trees. Later on, sustenance based only on the consumption of *wild* gramineous seeds and fruit will be possible. Likewise it will later on be possible to return to the perpetual migrations in the savanna, with all the other grazing mammals, the way our ancestors did starting some 14 million years ago.

If this social system is soon established throughout the world, our return to the Garden of Eden is guaranteed, if, in addition, and for some time, women restrain themselves to deliver only one child in all their life; diminishing in this way, little by little, the world's population until a total population capable of living a natural graincollector's life is reached. Then, nature's laws will be the ones to indicate what our obligations, joys, and privileges are, since they will *never* be imposed again by our intelligence.

If this social system, and the beginning of our return to graincollection is not established soon, our self-destruction is guaranteed, since we are currently moving rapidly toward it. Maybe some scientists, technicians, intellectuals, religious leaders, and philosophers will advance this self-destruction by pridefully pronouncing that human intelligence will soon solve all our problems—for the development of science, technology, morals, and ethics is already "quite advanced." Maybe the religious leaders will also help in our self-destruction in another way: by their reluctance to lose the present power and dominion they have over millions of human beings—so they will then divide humans in groups of arrogant fanatics, the way all religions have always done since their invention, because each religious leader, in his own arrogance, believes he knows the "truth" and is the intermediary between God and the *faithful*; or that he is the "possessor of the knowledge and wisdom" of our religious ancestors. *But, before long, women will reject all of men's commands, particularly when seeing the damaged world we are leaving to our children, and will, in this way, prevent our self-destruction.* Women will own the tribes again; they will own and spread tribal traditions, as it always was in the past. Then, we will again respect, love and admire our brother animals, plants, and all of God's Creation.

Our ex-graincollector ancestors (hunters, shepherds, or agriculturists) had the same defects and virtues we now possess. In the same way in which we cannot accept as logical and normal that our descendants would approve, venerate, and worship the laws or religions we could at this time invent, which would be products of our contaminated thoughts, we must not accept the present positive laws and religions we have inherited, which were created in the last 50 thousand years by our ancestors' contaminated thoughts. We should accept, venerate, worship, and respect the natural and universal laws, the laws impressed on matter by the Creator, the same way our graincollector ancestors *always* did. But let's take into consideration the following:

We know that the laws of God are ineffable, and we have inherited them accurately because they are directly impressed in our cells.

Therefore, nothing that has been transmitted orally or through writing is God's Word, moral law or God's commandment. Our ancestors didn't transmit the laws of God to us in this way, but in a direct way where there's no place for judgments, writings, or words: they transmit the Laws of God to us through *their genes*; we inherit them in *our genes*, in each one of our cells. Therefore, there isn't a holy book, there are no holy scriptures, or holy words. Nothing that has been transmitted orally or in writing is sacred or deserves to be worshipped, *even if it is the old tradition of our ancestors*. Only the natural and universal laws of God are sacred, and these are never pronounced, never written, since they are impressed in each molecule, in each atom, in each of the constituent particles of the universe. All living beings, all matter in the universe has the laws of God impressed even in the smallest particle of their being.

Currently, the discrimination, hatred, and arrogance that unfortunately exists in human societies has not developed from those people who presently live as each other's enemies. We've had to live in confusing times in which, from the first mistake and sin committed by our ancestors, a chain of mistakes and sins has followed, generation after generation. Therefore, in our so-called "civilization," we now bear the load of the sum of the mistakes and sins of all our ex-grain-collector ancestors: from the ones committed 50 thousand years ago, to the ones we are currently committing. We have received a corrupted and partially destroyed world as an inheritance. Humans presently cannot blame ourselves, for we all were born in a depraved social environment in which we were taught how to hate, discriminate, and despise; we were even taught how to kill. We didn't learn how to respect nature's laws. We were born in a social environment in which we learned how to despise women, possess material goods, and feel jealousy and greed. We learned to have enemies. We were taught a religion that separates us from our brothers. We learned to manufacture weapons and fight against our brothers.

If we talk with a child from anywhere in the world, be this the child of our "enemy" or our friend, we'll immediately see his or her innocence; we'll see the perfection in God's creation. We were like that: simple and perfect in our childhood. What happened to us later? However, we must not forget that deep inside ourselves that child still exists.

Let's destroy our weapons, forget our current differences and forgive each other. With all humans united in brotherhood let's start planning and *executing* our return to nature, our return to God, since with prayers we won't return to Him. Instead, let God's Certitude flourish in us: The instinctive and absolute obedience to His Natural and Universal Laws, the way all other living beings do. Let's not beg with vain words but with real actions. Let's stop our pride. *That is the true praise, the true prayer to God for the renewal of our days of old.*

References

Altmann, J., 1980, *Baboon Mothers and Infants*, Harvard Univ. Press, Cambridge, Mass.

Asimov, I., 1984, *Asimov's New Guide to Science*, Penguin, N.Y.

Beck, B. B., 1982, "Chimpocentrism: Bias in Cognitive Ethology," *Journal of Human Evolution* 11: 3–17.

Bell, R. H. V., 1971, "A Grazing Ecosystem in the Serengeti," *Scientific American* 225: 86–93.

Bindra, D., 1976, *A Theory of Intelligent Behavior*, John Wiley, N.Y.

Birdsell, J. B., 1975, *Human Evolution: An Introduction to the New Physical Anthropology*, Rand McNally, Chicago.

Blurton-Jones, N., 1972, "Comparative Aspects of Mother-Child Contact," in *Ethological Studies of Child Behavior* (N. Blurton-Jones, ed.), Cambridge Univ. Press, London.

Bonner, J. T., 1980, *The Evolution of Culture in Animals*, Princeton Univ. Press, Princeton, N.J.

Booth, W., 1988, "The Social Lives of Dolphins," *Science* 240: 1273–1274.

Bower, B., 1988, "Retooled Ancestors," *Science News* 133: 344–345.

Bunn, H. T. and Blumenschine, R. J., 1987, "On 'Theoretical Framework and Tests' of Early Hominid Meat and Marrow Acquisition: A Reply to Shipman," *American Anthropologist* 89: 444–448.

Campbell, B. G., 1974, *Human Evolution: An Introduction to Man's Adaptations*, Aldine, Chicago.

Campbell, B. G. and Bernor, R. L., 1976, "The Origin of the Hominidae: Africa or Asia?" *Journal of Human Evolution* 5: 441–454.

Cann, R. L., Stoneking, M., and Wilson, A. C., 1987, "Mitochondrial DNA and Human Evolution," *Nature* 325: 31–36.

Caro, T. M., 1987, "Human Breasts: Unsupported Hypotheses Reviewed," *Human Evolution* 2: 271–282.

Caro, T. M., 1988, "Adaptive Significance of Play: Are We Getting Closer?" *Trends in Ecology and Evolution* 3: 50–54.

Carson, R. L., 1951, *The Sea Around Us*, Oxford Univ. Press, N.Y.

Chomsky, N., 1967, "The General Properties of Language," in *Brain Mechanisms Underlying Speech and Language* (C. H. Millikan, chairman and F. L. Darley, ed.), Grune and Stratton, N.Y.

Chomsky, N., 1972, *Language and Mind*, Harcourt Brace Jovanovich, N.Y.

Chomsky, N., 1975a, *Reflections on Language*, Pantheon, N.Y.

Chomsky, N., 1975b, *The Logical Structure of Linguistic Theory*, Plenum, N.Y.

Ciochon, R. L., 1983, "Hominoid Cladistics and the Ancestry of Modern Apes and Humans, A Summary Statement," in *New Interpretations of Ape and Human Ancestry* (R. L. Ciochon and R. S. Corruccini, eds.), Plenum, N.Y.

Clark, J. D., 1976, "African Origins of Man the Toolmaker," in *Human Origins* (G. L. Isaac and E. R. McCown, eds.), W. A. Benjamin, Menlo Park, Calif.

Clutton-Brock, T. H. and Harvey, P. H., 1977, "Primate Ecology and Social Organization," *Journal of Zoology*, London, 183: 1–39.

Curio, E., 1973, "Darwin's Finches," in *Grzimek Animal Life Encyclopedia*, Vol. 9: 358–366. (B. Grzimek, ed.), Van Nostrand Reinhold, N.Y.

Darwin, C., 1860, *The Origin of Species*, John Murray, London, 1952; Encyclopaedia Britannica, Inc., Chicago, IL.

Darwin, C., 1871, *The Descent of Man and Selection in Relation to Sex* (Vols. I and II), John Murray, London, 1981; Princeton Univ. Press, Princeton, N.J.

Dawkins, R., 1986, *The Blind Watchmaker*, W. W. Norton, N.Y.

De Bonis, L., 1982, "Comments on Wolpoff M. H.: *Ramapithecus* and Hominid Origins," *Current Anthropology* 23: 501–522.

Devine, J., 1985, "The Versatility of Human Locomotion," *American Anthropologist* 87: 550–570.

DeVore, I. and Washburn, S. L., 1963, "Baboon Ecology and Human Evolution," in *African Ecology and Human Evolution* (F. C. Howell and F. Bourliere, eds.), Viking Fund Publication, N.Y.

Diamond, J., 1988, "The Golden Age That Never Was," *Discover* 9, No. 12: 70–79.

Dobzhansky, T., Ayala, F. J., Stebbins, G. L., and Valentine, J. W., 1977, *Evolution*, W. H. Freeman, San Francisco.

Dobzhansky, T. and Boesiger, E., 1983, *Human Culture: A Moment in Evolution*, Columbia Univ. Press, N.Y.

Draper, P., 1976, "Social and Economic Constraints on Child Life Among the !Kung," in *Kalahari Hunter-Gatherers: Studies of the !Kung San and Their Neighbors* (R. B. Lee and I. DeVore, eds.), Harvard Univ. Press, Cambridge, Mass.

Dunbar, R. I. M., 1976, "Australopithecine Diet Based on a Baboon Analogy," *Journal of Human Evolution* 5: 161–167.

Dunbar, R. I. M. and Dunbar, E. P., 1974, "Ecological Relations and *Niche* Separation Between Sympatric Terrestrial Primates in Ethiopia," *Folia Primatologica,*, 21: 36–60.

Dunbar, R. and Dunbar, P., 1975, *Social Dynamics of Gelada Baboons*, S. Karger, Basel.

Edelstein, S. J., 1987, "An Alternative Paradigm for Hominoid Evolution," *Human Evolution* 2: 169–174.

Eibl-Eibesfeldt, I., 1974, *Etología, Introduccion al Estudio Comparado del Comportamiento*, Ediciones Omega, Barcelona.

Eldredge, N. and Gould, S. J., 1972, "Punctuated Equilibria: An Alternative to Phyletic Gradualism," in *Models in Paleobiology* (T. J. M. Schopf, ed.), W. H. Freeman, San Francisco.

Fagen, R., 1981, *Animal Play Behavior*, Oxford Univ. Press, N.Y.

Farris, J. S., 1984, "The Logical Basis of Phylogenetic Analysis," in *Conceptual Issues in Evolutionary Biology* (E. Sober, ed.), M.I.T. Press, Cambridge, Mass.

Fischer, W., 1972, "Subfamily: Old World Vultures," in *Grzimek's Animal Life Encyclopedia*, Vol. 7: 391–406 (B. Grzimek, ed.), Van Nostrand Reinhold, N.Y.

Fleagle, J. G. and Simons, E. L., 1978, "Humeral Morphology of the Earliest Apes," *Nature* 276: 705–707.

Frädrich, H., 1972, "Swine and Peccaries," in *Grzimek's Animal Life Encyclopedia*, Vol. 13: 76–108 (B. Grzimek, ed.), Van Nostrand Reinhold, N.Y.

Galdikas, B. M. F., 1979, "Orangutan Adaptation at Tanjung Puting Reserve: Mating and Ecology," in *The Great Apes* (D. A. Hamburg and E. R. McCown, eds.), Benjamin/Cummings, Menlo Park, Calif.

Gause, G. F., 1969 (reprint from the original of 1934), *The Struggle for Existence*, Hafner, N.Y.

Ghiglieri, M., 1987, "War Among the Chimps," *Discover* 8, No. 11, Nov. 1987, pp. 66–76.

Goodall, J., 1986, *The Chimpanzees of Gombe: Patterns of Behavior*, The Belknap Press of Harvard Univ. Press, Cambridge, Mass.

Goodman, M., 1963, "Man's Place in the Phylogeny of Primates as Reflected in Serum Proteins," in *Classification and Human Evolution* (S. L. Washburn, ed.), Aldine, Chicago.

Goodman, M., 1975, "Protein Sequence and Immunological Specificity," in *Phylogeny of the Primates: A Multidisciplinary Approach* (W. P. Luckett and F. S. Szalay, eds.), Plenum, N.Y.

Goodman, M., 1976, "Protein Sequences in Phylogeny," in *Molecular Evolution* (F. J. Ayala, ed.), Sinauer, Sunderland, Mass.

Gould, S. J., 1977, *Ontogeny and Phylogeny*, Harvard Univ. Press, Cambridge, Mass.

Greenfield, L. O., 1980, "A Late Divergence Hypothesis," *American Journal of Physical Anthropology* 52: 351–366.

Greenfield, L. O., 1983, "Toward the Resolution of Discrepancies Between Phenetic and Paleontological Data Bearing on the Question of Human

Origins," in *New Interpretations of Ape and Human Ancestry* (R. L. Ciochon and R. S. Corruccini, eds.), Plenum, N.Y.

Gruber, H. E., 1981, *Darwin on Man: A Psychological Study of Scientific Creativity*, Univ. of Chicago Press, Chicago.

Hannah, A. C. and McGrew, W. C., 1987, "Chimpanzees Using Stones to Crack Open Oil Palm Nuts in Liberia," *Primates* 28: 31–46.

Harvey, P. H. and Partridge, L., 1987, "Murderous Mandibles and Black Holes in Hymenopteran Wasps," *Nature* 326: 128–129.

Herter, K., 1975, "Other Mustelids," in *Grzimek's Animal Life Encyclopedia*, Vol. 12: 60–89 (B. Grzimek, ed.), Van Nostrand Reinhold, N.Y.

Hewes, G. W., 1974, "Language in Early Hominids," in *Language Origins* (R. W. Wescott, ed.), Linstok Press, Silver Spring, Md.

Hodos, W., 1988a, "Comparative Neuroanatomy and the Evolution of Intelligence," in *Intelligence and Evolutionary Biology* (H. J. Jerison and I. Jerison, eds.), Springer-Verlag, Berlin.

Hodos, W., 1988b, "Some Comments on 'Afterthoughts: Anatomy and Intelligence,' " p. 463, in *Intelligence and Evolutionary Biology* (H. J. Jerison and I. Jerison, eds.), Springer-Verlag, Berlin.

Houston, D. C., 1979, "The Adaptations of Scavengers," in *Serengeti, Dynamics of an Ecosystem* (A. R. E. Sinclair and M. Norton-Griffiths, eds.), Univ. of Chicago Press, Chicago.

Iwamoto, T., 1979, "Feeding Ecology," in *Ecological and Sociological Studies of Gelada Baboons* (M. Kawai, ed.), S. Karger, Basel.

Jarman, P. J. and Sinclair, A. R. E., 1979, "Feeding Strategy and the Pattern of Resource Partitioning in Ungulates," in *Serengeti, Dynamics of an Ecosystem* (A. R. E. Sinclair and M. Norton-Griffiths, eds.), Univ. of Chicago Press, Chicago.

Jay, P. C., 1968, "Primate Field Studies and Human Evolution," in *Primates: Studies in Adaptation and Variability* (P. C. Jay, ed.), Holt, Rinehart and Winston, N.Y.

Jerison, H. J., 1973, *Evolution of the Brain and Intelligence*, Academic Press, N.Y.

Jerison, H. J., 1975, "Evolution of the Brain and Intelligence," *Current Anthropology* 16: 403–426.

Jerison, H. J., 1988a, "Evolutionary Biology of Intelligence: The Nature of the Problem," in *Intelligence and Evolutionary Biology* (H. J. Jerison and I. Jerison, eds.), Springer-Verlag, Berlin.

Jerison, H. J., 1988b, "The Evolutionary Biology of Intelligence: Afterthoughts," in *Intelligence and Evolutionary Biology* (H. J. Jerison and I. Jerison, eds.), Springer-Verlag, Berlin.

Johanson, D. C. and Taieb, M., 1976, "Plio-Pleistocene Hominid Discoveries in Hadar, Ethiopia," *Nature* 260: 293–297.

Johnson, L. L., 1978, "A History of Flint-Knapping Experimentation, 1838–1976," *Current Anthropology* 19: 337–372.

Jolly, A., 1985, *The Evolution of Primate Behavior*, Macmillan, N.Y.

Jolly, C. J., 1970, "The Seed-Eaters: A New Model of Hominid Differentiation Based on a Baboon Analogy," *Man* 5: 5–26.

Jonas, D. F. and Jonas, A. D., 1975, "Gender Differences in Mental Function: A Clue to the Origin of Language," *Current Anthropology* 16: 626–630.

Jonas, D. F. and Jonas, A. D., 1976a, "On Gender Differences and the Origin of Language: Reply," *Current Anthropology* 17: 521–526.

Jonas, D. F. and Jonas, A. D., 1976b, "More on Gender Differences and the Origin of Language: Reply," *Current Anthropology* 17: 744–749.

Kay, R. F., 1981, "The Nut-Crackers: A New Theory of the Adaptations of the Ramapithecinae," *American Journal of Physical Anthropology* 55: 141–151.

Kay, R. F. and Simons, E. L., 1983, "A Reassessment of the Relationship Between Later Miocene and Subsequent Hominoidea," in *New Interpretations of Ape and Human Ancestry* (R. L. Ciochon and R. S. Corruccini, eds.), Plenum, N.Y.

Kawai, M. and Iwamoto, T., 1979, "Nomadism and Activities," in *Ecological and Sociological Studies of Gelada Baboons* (M. Kawai, ed.), S. Karger, Basel.

Kinzey, W. G., 1987, "Introduction," in *The Evolution of Human Behavior: Primate Models* (W. G. Kinzey ed.), State Univ. of New York Press, N.Y.

Kleindienst, M. R., 1975, "Discussion and Criticism: On New Perspectives on Ape and Human Evolution," *Current Anthropology* 16: 644–646.

Konner, M. J., 1972, "Aspects of the Developmental Ethology of a Foraging People," in *Ethological Studies of Child Behaviour* (N. Blurton-Jones, ed.), Cambridge Univ. Press, London.

Konner, M. J., 1976, "Maternal Care, Infant Behavior and Development Among the !Kung," in *Kalahari Hunter-Gatherers: Studies of the !Kung San and Their Neighbors* (R. B. Lee and I. DeVore, eds.), Harvard Univ. Press, Cambridge, Mass.

Kortlandt, A., 1974, "New Perspectives on Ape and Human Evolution," *Current Anthropology* 15: 427–448.

Kortlandt, A., 1984, "Comments on Hominid Dietary Selection Before Fire," *Current Anthropology* 25: 158–160.

Kurtén, B., 1972, *Not from the Apes*, Pantheon Books, N.Y.

Kurtén, B., 1988, *On Evolution and Fossil Mammals*, Columbia Univ. Press, N.Y.

Leakey, M. D. and Hay, R. L., 1979, "Pliocene Footprints in the Laetoli Beds at Laetoli, Northern Tanzania," *Nature* 278: 317–323.

Leakey, R. E. F. and Wood, B. A., 1973, "New Evidence of the Genus *Homo* from East Rudolf, Kenya (II)," *American Journal of Physical Anthropology* 39: 355–368.

Leakey, R. E. F. and Lewin, R., 1978, *People of the Lake*, Anchor Press/Doubleday, N.Y.

Lee, R. B., 1968, "What Hunters do for a Living, or How to Make Out on Scarce Resources," in *Man the Hunter* (R. B. Lee and I. DeVore, eds.), Aldine, Chicago.

Lee, R. B., 1976, "!Kung Spatial Organization: An Ecological and Historical Perspective," in *Kalahari Hunter-Gatherers: Studies of the !Kung San and Their Neighbors* (R. B. Lee and I. DeVore, eds.), Harvard Univ. Press, Cambridge, Mass.

Lee, R. B., and DeVore, I. (eds.), 1976, *Kalahari Hunter-Gatherers: Studies of the !Kung San and Their Neighbors*, Harvard Univ. Press, Cambridge, Mass.

Lewin, R., 1982, "How Did Humans Evolve Big Brains?" *Science* 216: 840–841.

Lewin, R., 1987, Research News, "Four Legs Bad, Two Legs Good," *Science* 235: 969–971.

Lewin, R., 1989, *Human Evolution: An Illustrated Introduction*, Blackwell Scientific Publications, Boston.

Lieberman, P., 1975, *On the Origins of Language: An Introduction to the Evolution of Human Speech*, Macmillan, N.Y.

Lilly, J. C., 1975, *Lilly on Dolphins*, Anchor, N.Y.

Lovejoy, C. O., 1981, "The Origin of Man," *Science* 211: 341–350.

Lovejoy, C. O., 1988, "Evolution of Human Walking," *Scientific American* 259, No. 5. (Nov. 1988), pp. 118–125.

Maddock, L., 1979, "The 'Migration' and Grazing Succession," in *Serengeti, Dynamics of an Ecosystem* (A. R. E. Sinclair and M. Norton-Griffiths, eds.), Univ. of Chicago Press, Chicago.

Mann, A. E., 1981, "Diet and Human Evolution," in *Omnivorous Primates* (R. S. O. Harding and G. Teleki, eds.), Columbia Univ. Press, N.Y.

Markl, H., 1977, "The Evolution of Social Behavior in Animals," in *Grzimek's Encyclopedia of Ethology* (B. Grzimek, ed.), Van Nostrand Reinhold, N.Y.

Martin, R. D., 1981, "Relative Brain Size and Basal Metabolic Rate in Terrestrial Vertebrates," *Nature* 293: 57–60.

Mayr, E., 1974, "Behavior Programs and Evolutionary Strategies," *American Scientist* 62: 650–659.

Mayr, E., 1976, *Evolution and the Diversity of Life*, Harvard Univ. Press, Cambridge, Mass.

Mayr, E., 1979, *Animal Species and Evolution*, Harvard Univ. Press, Cambridge, Mass.

McNaughton, S. J., 1976, "Serengeti Migratory Wildebeest: Facilitation of Energy Flow by Grazing," *Science* 191: 92–94.

Milton, K., 1984, "Comments on Hominid Dietary Selection Before Fire," *Current Anthropology* 25: 160–161.

Müller-Schwarze, D., 1978, *Evolution of Play Behavior,* Dowden, Hutchinson and Ross, Stroudsburg, Pa.

Oxnard, C. E., 1975, *Uniqueness and Diversity in Human Evolution,* Univ. of Chicago Press, Chicago.

Oxnard, C. E., 1987, *Fossils, Teeth and Sex,* Univ. of Washington Press, Seattle, Wash.

Paterson, J. D., 1984, "Comments on Hominid Dietary Selection Before Fire," *Current Anthropology* 25: 161.

Patterson, B. and Howells W. W., 1967, "Hominid Humeral Fragment from Early Pleistocene of North–Western Kenya," *Science* 156: 64–66.

Patterson, B., Behrensmeyer, A. K., and Sill, W. D., 1970, "Geology and Fauna of a New Pliocene Locality in North-Western Kenya," *Nature* 226: 918–921.

Pickford, M., 1982, "New Higher Primate Fossils From the Middle Miocene Deposits at Majiwa and Kaloma, Western Kenya," *American Journal of Physical Anthropology* 58: 1–19.

Pollack, I., 1967, "Language as Behavior," in *Brain Mechanisms Underlying Speech and Language* (C. H. Millikan, chairman, F. L. Darley, ed.), Grune and Stratton, N.Y.

Prasad, K. N., 1982, "Was *Ramapithecus* a Tool-user?" *Journal of Human Evolution* 11: 101–104.

Pugh, G. E., 1977, *The Biological Origin of Human Values,* Basic Books, N.Y.

Richman, B., 1976, "On Gender Differences and the Origin of Language," *Current Anthropology* 17: 521–526.

Richman, B., 1978, "The Synchronization of Voices by Gelada Monkeys," *Primates* 19: 569–581.

Ruse, M., 1988, "Intelligence and Natural Selection," in *Intelligence and Evolutionary Biology* (H. J. Jerison and I. Jerison, eds.), Springer-Verlag, Berlin.

Sarich, V. M., 1968, "The Origin of the Hominids: An Immunological Approach," in *Perspectives on Human Evolution, Vol. 1* (S. L. Washburn and P. C. Jay, eds.), Holt, Rinehart and Winston, N.Y.

Sarich, V. M., 1983, "Appendix: Retrospective on Hominoid Macromolecular Systematics," in *New Interpretations of Ape and Human Ancestry* (R. L. Ciochon and R. S. Corruccini, eds.), Plenum, N.Y.

Sarich, V. M. and Wilson, A. C., 1967, "Immunological Time Scale for Hominid Evolution," *Science* 158: 1200–1203.

Schaller, G. B., 1963, *The Mountain Gorilla: Ecology and Behavior*, Univ. of Chicago Press, Chicago.

Schaller, G. B. and Emlen, J. T., 1974, "Observations on the Ecology and Social Behavior of the Mountain Gorilla," in *Man in Adaptation: The Biosocial Background* (Y. A. Cohen, ed.), Aldine, Chicago.

Schultz, A. H., 1969, *The Life of Primates*, Weidenfeld and Nicolson, London.

Semenov, S. A., 1976, *Prehistoric Technology*, Moonraker Press, Bradford-on-Avon, England.

Shipman, P., 1987, Origins. "An Age-Old Question: Why did the Human Lineage Survive?" *Discover* 8, No. 4: 60–64.

Shostak, M., 1976, "A !Kung Woman's Memories of Childhood," in *Kalahari Hunter-Gatherers: Studies of the !Kung San and Their Neighbors* (R. B. Lee and I. DeVore, eds.), Harvard Univ. Press, Cambridge, Mass.

Simons, E. L., 1961, "The Phyletic Position of *Ramapithecus*," *Postilla*, Peabody Museum of Natural History, Yale Univ., 57: 1–19.

Simons, E. L., 1972, *Primate Evolution: An Introduction to Man's Place in Nature*, Macmillan, N.Y.

Simons, E. L., 1976, "The Nature of the Transition in the Dental Mechanism from Pongids to Hominids," *Journal of Human Evolution* 5: 511–528.

Simons, E. L., 1989, "Human Origins," *Science* 245: 1343–1350.

Simpson, G. G., 1953, *The Major Features of Evolution*, Columbia Univ. Press, N.Y.

Sinclair, A. R. E., Leakey, M. D., and Norton-Griffiths, M., 1986, "Migration and Hominid Bipedalism," *Nature* 324: 307–308.

Smith, B. H., 1986, "Dental Development in *Australopithecus* and Early *Homo*," *Nature* 323: 327–330.

Smuts, B. B., 1985, *Sex and Friendship in Baboons*, Aldine De Gruyter, Hawthorne, N.Y.

Spencer, H., 1878, *The Principles of Psychology, Vol. 2.* Appleton, N.Y.

Stahl, A. B., 1984, "Reply on Hominid Dietary Selection Before Fire," *Current Anthropology* 25: 163–168.

Steele, J., 1989, "Hominid Evolution and Primate Social Cognition," *Journal of Human Evolution* 18: 421–423.

Strum, S. C., 1981, "Processes and Products of Change: Baboon Predatory Behavior at Gilgil, Kenya," in *Omnivorous Primates: Gathering and Hunting in Human Evolution* (R. S. O. Harding and G. Teleki, eds.), Columbia Univ. Press, N.Y.

Strum, S. C., 1987, *Almost Human: A Journey into the World of Baboons*, Random House, N.Y.

Susman, R. L., 1988, "Hand of *Paranthropus robustus* from Member 1, Swartkrans: Fossil Evidence for Tool Behavior," *Science* 240: 781–784.

Swartz, M. J. and Jordan, D. K., 1976, *Anthropology, Perspective on Humanity*, John Wiley and Sons, N.Y.

Tattersall, I., 1975, *The Evolutionary Significance of Ramapithecus*, Burgess, Minneapolis, Minn.

Teleki, G., 1974, "Chimpanzee Subsistence Technology: Materials and Skills," *Journal of Human Evolution* 3: 575–594.

Teleki, G., 1981, "The Omnivorous Diet and Eclectic Feeding Habits of Chimpanzees in Gombe National Park, Tanzania," in *Omnivorous Primates: Gathering and Hunting in Human Evolution* (R. S. O. Harding and G. Teleki, eds.), Columbia Univ. Press, N.Y.

Tierney, J., Wright, L., and Springen, K., 1988, "The Search for Adam and Eve," *Newsweek,* Jan. 11, pp. 46–52.

Van Lawick-Goodall, J., 1973, *Mis Amigos los Chimpances,* Editorial Noguer, S.A., Barcelona.

Van Lawick, H., 1986, *Among Predators and Prey*, Sierra Club Books, San Francisco.

Velo, J., 1976, "On Gender Differences and the Origin of Language," *Current Anthropology* 17: 521–526.

Verhaegen, M., 1987, "Origin of Hominid Bipedalism," *Nature* 325: 305–306.

Walker, A. C. and Pickford, M., 1983, "New Postcranial Fossils of *Proconsul africanus* and *Proconsul nyanzae*," in *New Interpretations of Ape and Human Ancestry* (R. L. Ciochon and R. S. Corruccini, eds.), Plenum, N.Y.

Washburn, S. L., 1978, "What We Can't Learn about People from Apes," *Human Nature,* Vol. 1, No. 11, Nov. 1978.

Washburn, S. L. and Lancaster, C. S., 1968, "The Evolution of Hunting," in *Man the Hunter* (R. B. Lee and I. DeVore, eds.), Aldine, Chicago.

Washburn, S. L. and Ciochon, R. L., 1974, "Canine Teeth: Notes on Controversies in the Study of Human Evolution," *American Anthropologist* 76: 765–784.

Wescott, R. W., 1974, "Preface," in *Language Origins* (R. W. Wescott, ed.), Linstok, Silver Spring, Md.

Williams, B. J., 1987, "Rates of Evolution: Is There a Conflict Between Neo-Darwinian Evolutionary Theory and the Fossil Record?" *American Journal of Physical Anthropology* 73: 99–109.

Williams, P. L., 1987, "Reversible Evolution?" *Nature* 328: 21–22.

Wilson, A. C. and Sarich, V. M., 1969, "A Molecular Time Scale for Human Evolution," *Proc. Natl. Acad. Sci. U.S.A.* 63: 1088–1093.

Wolpoff, M. H., 1982, "*Ramapithecus* and Hominid Origins," *Current Anthropology* 23: 501–522.

Wolpoff, M. H., 1983, "*Ramapithecus* and Human Origins: An Anthropologist's Perspective of Changing Interpretations," in *New Inter-*

pretations of Ape and Human Ancestry (R. L. Ciochon and R. S. Corruccini, eds.), Plenum, N.Y.

Wynn, T., 1988, "Tools and the Evolution of Human Intelligence," in *Machiavellian Intelligence* (R. Byrne and A. Whiten, eds.), Clarendon Press, Oxford.

Yellen, J. E. and Lee, R. B., 1976, "The Dobe-/Du/da Environment: Background to a Hunting and Gathering Way of Life," in *Kalahari Hunter-Gatherers: Studies of the !Kung San and Their Neighbors* (R. B. Lee and I. DeVore, eds.), Harvard Univ. Press, Cambridge, Mass.

Zihlman, A. L. and Lowenstein, J. M., 1983, "*Ramapithecus* and *Pan Paniscus*: Significance for Human Origins," in *New Interpretations of Ape and Human Ancestry* (R. L. Ciochon and R. S. Corruccini, eds.), Plenum, N.Y.

Zihlman, A. L., Cronin, J. E., Cramer, D. L., and Sarich, V. M., 1978, "Pygmy Chimpanzee as a Possible Prototype for the Common Ancestor of Humans, Chimpanzees and Gorillas," *Nature* 275: 744–746.

Zuckerkandl, E., 1976, "Programs of Gene Action and Progressive Evolution," in *Molecular Anthropology: Genes and Proteins in the Evolutionary Ascent of the Primates* (M. Goodman and R. E. Tashian, eds.), Plenum, N.Y.

Glossary

ABORIGINAL. The people or organisms native and original to a particular land where they normally live; not introduced from the outside by man. Indigenous.

ACHEULIAN INDUSTRY. Stone tool industry and culture of the Paleolithic, developed in Europe, Asia, and Africa, probably by our ancestors *Homo erectus* during the Lower and Middle Pleistocene (from 1.5 million to 100 thousand years ago, more or less), characterized by the hand axe. (*See also* HAND AXE, PALEOLITHIC, OLDOWAN INDUSTRY, DEVELOPED OLDOWAN INDUSTRY, HOMO ERECTUS.)

ACHEULIAN STONE TOOLS. The stone tools of the Acheulian Industry. (*See also* ACHEULIAN INDUSTRY.)

ADAPT. (1) To change and adjust an individual organism to accommodate to the environmental conditions in which it is living, or to new environmental conditions. (2) To change and adjust a population or species during evolution, through several generations, by improving its means of survival and reproduction in the same or new environmental conditions and requirements. (*See also* POPULATION; EVOLUTIONARY ADAPTATION; EVOLUTION).

ADAPTABILITY. (1) The capacity of a population or species, through several generations, to evolve in such a form that the individuals of such a unit can function, for survival and reproduction, more successfully in their original environment or in a changing environment. (2) The capacity of an organism to adjust to environmental stress or change. (*See also* POPULATION; EVOLUTIONARY ADAPTATION; EVOLUTION.)

ADAPTATION. The process, action and effect of adapting. (*See also* ADAPT; ADAPTABILITY; EVOLUTIONARY ADAPTATION; EVOLUTION.)

ADAPTIVE. (1) Able to adapt. (2) A character showing adaptation. (*See also* ADAPT; CHARACTER; ADAPTABILITY; ADAPTIVE CHARACTER.)

ADAPTIVE CHARACTER. Any character of an organism that enhances its capacity to adjust to its environment (to adapt). (*See also* ADAPT; ADAPTABILITY; CHARACTER.)

ADAPTIVE EVOLUTION. The evolutionary process of modification and adaptation of a population or species, by the pressure of the environmental conditions and requirements (selective pressures), to improve its survival and reproductive efficiency within this environment. (*See also* SELECTIVE PRESSURE; ADAPT; ADAPTABILITY; POPULATION.)

ADAPTIVE RADIATION; RADIATION. The evolution, in a relatively short time, of only one original population or species into several diverse species, each one adapted to living in a different ecological niche or adaptive zone. This is due to the great success obtained through a newly acquired adaptive character. (*See also* EVOLUTION; ECOLOGICAL NICHE; ADAPTIVE ZONE; ADAPTIVE CHARACTER; CHARACTER.)

ADAPTIVE VALUE. The fitness of the totality of the genetic material of an individual organism, compared with that of other individuals of the same population or species, to survive and reproduce in a given environment. (*See also* ADAPT; ADAPTABILITY; ADAPTIVE CHARACTER; POPULATION; FITNESS.)

ADAPTIVE ZONE. (Similar to Ecological niche but more generalized). Way of life, role, and position of a species in a specific ecosystem and environment along with which it evolves. (*See also* ECOLOGICAL NICHE; ECOSYSTEM.)

ADAPTIVELY. In an adaptive form. (*See also* ADAPTIVE; ADAPT; ADAPTABILITY.)

AEGYPTOPITHECUS. A genus of fossil Hominoids members of the Pongidae family. Arboreal quadrupedal apes who lived in the forests of Africa during the Oligocene epoch (about 30 million years ago) and may have been the ancestors of *Dryopithecus*. (*See also* GENUS; FOSSIL; HOMINOIDS; DRYOPITHECUS (Proconsul); PONGID; ARBOREAL; QUADRUPED; APE.)

AFRICAN APES. The gorilla and chimpanzee. (*See also* GORILLA; CHIMPANZEE; APE; PONGID.)

AFRICAN PONGIDS. The gorilla and chimpanzee. (*See also* GORILLA; CHIMPANZEE; APE; PONGID.)

ALTRICIAL. Used of some vertebrate species that characterize by a short period of gestation, large litters, undeveloped offspring that have delayed dependency on the mother before attaining self-maintenance, and have a rapid development. (*See also* VERTEBRATES; PRECOCIAL.)

ANATOMICAL AREA. Any particular region or structure of the body of organisms. (*See also* ANATOMY.)

ANATOMICAL RELATIONSHIPS. Similarity of functional anatomical structures in two or more different species of living or fossil organisms, inferred from comparisons which give an idea of their degree of relativity. (*See also* FOSSIL; ANATOMY; COMPARATIVE ANATOMY.)

ANATOMY. The study of the structures of organisms.

ANIMAL ESSENCE. (1) The normal and characteristic way of life and behavior animals show when they live already optimally fit and adapted, and remain undisturbed within their natural ecological niche. (2) Fundamental nature. (*See also* ADAPT; ADAPTABILITY; ECOLOGICAL NICHE.)

ANTHROPOCENTRISM; ANTHROPOCENTRIC. (1) Considering humans to be the most important creatures of the world. (2) To see all natural phenomenons from a human point of view.

ANTHROPOLOGY. The study of human beings whether physically, behaviorally, socially, etc.

APE. A living chimpanzee, gorilla, orangutan (great apes); or gibbon and siamang (lesser apes). A member of the family Pongidae or Hylobatidae, whether living or fossil. (*See also* PONGID; HYLOBATES; CHIMPANZEE; GORILLA; GIBBON; ORANGUTAN.)

ARBOREALS. Animals that live or are adapted for living in trees. (*See also* ADAPT; ADAPTABILITY; TERRESTRIAL.)

ARCHEOLOGICAL RECORD The remains left by our ancient ancestors. (*See also* ARCHEOLOGY.)

ARCHEOLOGY. The study of the way of life, behavior and culture of our ancestors through the remains left by them.

ARTIFACTS. Objects, usually made of stone, presenting human workmanship.

ASIAN APES. The orangutan, gibbon, and siamang. (*See also* ORANGUTAN; GIBBON; APE.)

ASIAN PONGID. The orangutan. (*See also* ORANGUTAN.)

AUSTRALOPITHECINES. Informal and common name for members of the extinct genus *Australopithecus*. African bipedal tool-using hominids who lived since the Lower Pliocene to the Lower Pleistocene epochs (5 million to 750 thousand years ago, more or less). (*See also* GENUS; AUSTRALOPITHECUS; HOMINIDS; BIPEDALISM.)

AUSTRALOPITHECUS. (Abbreviation: *A.*; informal, AUST.) An extinct genus, comprised of several species, of the family Hominidae (the human family) whose fossil remains have been found in South and East Africa. Bipedal tool-using hominids of the Lower Pliocene to the Lower Pleistocene epochs (5 million to 750 thousand years ago, more or less). (*See also* GENUS; AUSTRALOPITHECINES; HOMINIDS; BIPEDALISM; FOSSIL.)

AUSTRALOPITHECUS AFARENSIS. The earliest australopithecines. They lived in East Africa 5 to 4 million years ago, more or less. About 112 centimeters tall. This species is similar to *Australopithecus africanus. (See also* AUSTRALOPITHECUS, AUSTRALOPITHECUS AFRICANUS.)

AUSTRALOPITHECUS AFRICANUS (Gracile). This species is small in body size, apelike in many characters, and humanlike in dentition and erect posture. They lived in South Africa 2.5 million years ago, more or less. (*See also* AUSTRALOPITHECUS.)

AUSTRALOPITHECUS ROBUSTUS. (Also called *Paranthropus robustus.*) This species is large in body size, with strong molars specialized for feeding on coarse vegetation. They lived in South and East Africa 2 million years ago, more or less. (*See also* AUSTRALOPITHECUS.)

BABOONS. Large monkeys of the Old World. Family Cercopithecidae. They have an elongated muzzle like that of dogs, strong and large canine teeth or tusks, a short tail, and naked ischial callosities (callosities on the buttocks). They live throughout Africa, south of the Sahara Desert. (*See also* CERCOPITHECIDAE; ISCHIAL CALLOSITIES; CANINES.)

BACK MUTATION. A mutation that occurs in a gene so that it reacquires a lost function that was present in an ancestral form. (*See also* MUTATION; FAVORABLE MUTATION; GENE; FUNCTION; EVOLUTIONARY REVERSAL.)

BACTERIA (Singular: BACTERIUM). Microscopic unicellular plants that live in water, soil, organic matter, plants, and the body of animals. They are important to humans because of the fermentation, nitrogen fixation, and many other symbiotic functions they perform in our intestines. Some bacteria cause diseases. They are parasitic in habit. (*See also* FUNCTION; SYMBIOSIS; SYMBIONT.)

BASAL HOMINIDS. The earliest members of the family Hominidae (the human family). (*See also* HOMINIDS; HOMINIDAE.)

BEHAVIOR. The observable natural activities of an animal.

BIOCHEMICAL EVIDENCE (immunological, molecular, etc.). Qualitative and quantitative biochemical differences in the chromosomes of organisms, from which specialized scientists may deduce the phylogenetic relationships and the genetic distance between such organisms; therefore, their evolutionary histories. (*See also* CHROMOSOMES; PHYLOGENETIC RELATIONSHIPS; GENETIC DISTANCE.)

BIOLOGICAL BALANCE OF AN ECOSYSTEM. The natural condition of equilibrium resulting from the natural actions and reactions between the individuals of a community of organisms of different species and between those organisms and the physical environment within which they live. (*See also* ECOSYSTEM.)

BIOLOGY. The study of living organisms and the natural laws that govern their life.

BIOMASS. The mass or weight of a population, or of those organisms considered within a specified unit at a given time. (*See also* POPULATION.)

BIOSONAR. A guidance system that some animals, such as dolphins and bats, use. They produce sounds and utilize the reflection or echo of those sounds to perceive the physical objects around them.

BIPED. Vertebrate animal that naturally walks on the two hind legs. (*See also* VERTEBRATES; BIPEDALISM; QUADRUPED.)

BIPEDALISM. The natural means of locomotion using only the two hind legs in an upright position, characteristic of the hominids. (*See also* HOMINIDS.)

BODY LANGUAGE. The movements, gestures and postures of the body that all animals, including humans, instinctively execute and repeat during the performance of their normal activities. These actions are the cues or signals for other animals of the same or other ecosystems, but mainly to animals of the same species and population of the emitter animal, to instinctively know what is happening in their surroundings and what the emitter needs or is executing or "saying" (mainly if it is an alarm). Sometimes the emitted body language of animals is accompanied by vocal sounds or corporal sounds. (*See also* LANGUAGE; ECOSYSTEM; POPULATION.)

BRACHIATE. To move or progress by brachiation. (*See also* BRACHIATION.)

BRACHIATION. The mode of locomotion that consists of moving rhythmically by means of swinging the forelimbs from one hold to another grasping with one hand, and also propulsively swinging the body to grasp the other hold with the other hand, as in gibbons. (*See also* GIBBON.)

BRACHIATOR. A brachiating animal. (*See also* BRACHIATION.)

CAECUM OR CECUM. The cup-shaped blind pouch, in humans and in many other mammals, that occurs where the large intestine begins and the small intestine opens from one side.

CANIDS. Members of the family Canidae. Carnivorous mammals such as dogs, wolves, foxes, etc. (*See also* HYAENIDS; FELIDS; CARNIVORE.)

CANINES. The four conical, or pointed, and generally large, teeth in the front of the mouth of many mammals. In monkeys and apes the canine teeth are large and generally they project beyond the other teeth; in humans they are reduced and do not project beyond the other teeth. (*See also* APE.)

CARNIVORE; CARNIVOROUS. An animal that eats flesh or animal tissues and depends mainly on meat for subsisting. (*See also* HERBIVORE; INSECTIVORE; OMNIVORE; FOLIVORE; SCAVENGER.)

CATARRHINE. Primates pertaining to the infraorder Catarrhini: monkeys of the Old World, apes and humans. (*See also* PRIMATES; APE.)

CECUM. *See* CAECUM.

CELIBACY. In animals, the instinctive and natural abstention from sexual intercourse when abstention is naturally necessary; generally referring to females.

CELL. A very small microscopic living unit of protoplasm bounded by a membrane. It is the basic living structure of all organisms. All organisms are made of one or several cells.

CELLULOSE. The basic structural part of plants.

CERCOPITHECIDAE. Family in the superfamily Cercopithecoidea. Includes macaques, baboons, etc. (*See also* BABOONS.)

CERCOPITHECINAE. One subfamily of the Cercopithecidae family. (*See also* CERCOPITHECIDAE; BABOONS.)

CERCOPITHECOID. Member of the superfamily Cercopithecoidea; known as Old World monkeys.

CEREBRAL CORTEX. In higher mammals, including humans, the superficial layer or stratum of gray matter of the cerebral hemispheres. Also called neocortex.

CETACEANS. Aquatic mammals of the order Cetacea that live in the ocean, which includes whales, dolphins, porpoises, etc. They are descendants of terrestrial mammals.

CHARACTER. Any inherited trait, structure, or feature of an organism that can also be transmitted to its offspring; but in this case may be modified or altered by mutations. (*See also* MUTATION.)

CHARACTER, DERIVED. See DERIVED CHARACTER.

CHARACTER, PRIMITIVE. See PRIMITIVE CHARACTER.

CHEEK TEETH. In mammals, the molars behind the incisors in both upper and lower jaws.

CHIMPANZEE. The smaller of the living species of African pongids. This ape inhabits rainforests and woodlands and rarely uses an erect posture during locomotion: it uses its arms as forelegs and, with the hand fingers turned inwardly, it supports itself on the knuckles when progressing in a semierect posture (knuckle-walking). It is mainly an herbivore, but sometimes eats flesh. Its hair is sparse. Genus: *Pan,* family: Pongidae, superfamily: Hominoidea. (*See also* APE; PAN; GORILLA; PONGO; HYLOBATES; PONGID; ORANGUTAN; GIBBON; KNUCKLE-WALKING.)

CHROMOSOMES. The small and threadlike structures in the nucleus of the cells of organisms composed of DNA and proteins, and consisting of thousands of genes arranged in linear sequence. They contain the hereditary material of organisms. (*See also* DNA, GENE; CELL.)

CILIATES. Microscopic animals; members of the class Ciliata of Protozoa. They possess cilia (motile hairlike outgrowths) for locomotion and feeding. They live free in fresh and salt water, and also as parasites or symbionts in the intestines of many animals. (*See also* SYMBIOSIS; SYMBIONT.)

CIVILIZATION. The human societies and way of life developed by our ancestors, little by little, more or less since 50 thousand years ago when they lost their natural ecological niche and ecosystem at the beginning of Würm's Glaciation (the Last Glaciation), and within which we are still living at present; characterized by the progressive use of technology for all human activities. (*See also* ECOLOGICAL NICHE; ECOSYSTEM; GLACIATIONS.)

CLADE. A group of organisms consisting of a single, original species and its descendant species.

CLADISTIC. Relating to a clade. (*See also* CLADE.)

CLADOGRAM. A scheme or diagram of an evolutionary tree representing a phylogeny, in which each branch represents a clade. (*See also* CLADE; PHYLOGENY.)

COLON. In vertebrates, the large intestine. (*See also* CAECUM; VERTEBRATES.)

COMPARATIVE ANATOMIST. The scientist specialized in comparative anatomy. (*See also* COMPARATIVE ANATOMY.)

COMPARATIVE ANATOMY. A branch of anatomy that deals with the similarities and differences in the anatomic characters of organisms, mainly for the purpose of achieving uniform descriptions of those organisms or deducing phylogenetic affinities or separations between them. (*See also* ANATOMY; PHYLOGENY; PHYLOGENETIC RELATIONSHIPS.)

COMPETITION. The simultaneous and natural struggle between organisms, especially among individuals of the same species and population, in order to get the natural resources to live and to achieve reproduction; or between populations to occupy the same niche or similar niches in the same ecosystem. (*See also* COMPETITIVE EXCLUSION PRINCIPLE; POPULATION; ECOLOGICAL NICHE; ECOSYSTEM.)

COMPETITIVE EXCLUSION PRINCIPLE (Gause's Exclusion Principle). The principle stating that two species, even if having similar ecological requirements, cannot occupy similar niches in the same ecosystem, but exclude each other in such a form that each survives from different food within a different way of life, taking certain advantages over the other competitor species. (*See also* ECOLOGICAL NICHE; ECOSYSTEM.)

CONDITIONED REFLEX. Reflex action of organisms in which the response has been modified by experience; that is, it is caused by an abnormal secondary stimulus that substitutes the natural, normal, primary stimulus. (*See also* REFLEX ACT.)

CONSORT. (1) Wife or husband; spouse. (2) In animals: companion, mate, partner.

CONTEXT. The special situation, the whole environment, and surroundings where something happens.

CONVERGENCE; CONVERGENT EVOLUTION. See EVOLUTIONARY CONVERGENCE.

CONVOLUTA. Marine green and small flatworms that live in some sandy intertidal zones.

COPROPHAGY. Feeding on dung, excrement, or feces. It is a normal behavior of many animal species.

CORE TOOL. The remaining main nodule of a rock, after eliminating small superficial chips or flakes when struck with another stone or tool in order to give that nodule the desired form. (*See also* FLAKE STONE TOOL.)

COROLLARY. The proposition derived so clearly and evidently from another already demonstrated proposition that it does not require any additional proof.

CULTURE (IN ANIMALS). Bonner (1980: 10) defines: "By culture I mean the transfer of information by behavioral means, most particularly by the process of teaching and learning."

CUMULATIVE SELECTION. The process of evolution through variation and natural selection, in which the genotype, selected in the corresponding phenotype by an actuating selective pressure, is selected again in the phenotype of the descendants, but already mutated in such a form that it is now more fit to fulfill that original selective pressure that is still actuating. This process is the basis of the Darwinian evolution through variation and natural selection. (*See also* GENOTYPE; PHENOTYPE; MUTATION; SELECTIVE PRESSURE; GENETIC VARIATION; NATURAL SELECTION.)

DERIVED CHARACTER. The particular characters or structures most recently

acquired by the individuals of a group, population, or species, living or
  fossil, and not present in any of the ancestral forms. (*See also* CHARAC-
  TER; PRIMITIVE CHARACTER; POPULATION; FOSSIL.)

DEVELOPED OLDOWAN INDUSTRY. Stone tool industry and culture of the
  Paleolithic, derived from the Oldowan Industry, and developed also in
  Africa by our ancestors since the Upper Pliocene to the Lower Pleis-
  tocene epochs (from 3.5 million to 750 thousand years ago, more or less),
  characterized by more advanced scrapers and rudimentary hand axes.
  (*See also* PALEOLITHIC; OLDOWAN INDUSTRY; ACHEULIAN INDUSTRY;
  SCRAPER STONE TOOL; HAND AXE.)

DEVELOPED OLDOWAN STONE TOOLS. The stone tools of the Developed
  Oldowan Industry. (*See also* DEVELOPED OLDOWAN INDUSTRY.)

DIRECTIONAL SELECTION. Selection for a not very common phenotype within
  a population, that, due to the actuating selective pressure, becomes,
  through several generations, the most common one. (*See also*
  PHENOTYPE; SELECTIVE PRESSURE; EVOLUTION.)

DISPLACEMENT PRINCIPLE. See COMPETITIVE EXCLUSION PRINCIPLE (Gause's
  Exclusion Principle).

DIVERGENCE. (1) Splitting or branching off one original species into two or
  more descendant species. (2) The acquisition, through evolution, of
  different characters by related species. (*See also* EVOLUTIONARY DIVER-
  GENCE.)

DIVERGENT EVOLUTION. *See* EVOLUTIONARY DIVERGENCE.

DNA. Abbreviation for the deoxyribonucleic acid, which is the carrier of the
  genetic material in the chromosomes of the cell nucleus; that is, it
  transmits the information for the heredity pattern in organisms. (*See also*
  CHROMOSOMES; CELL.)

DOLLO'S LAW. Considering evolutionary change at genetic level, it is the
  "statement about the statistical improbability of following exactly the
  same evolutionary trajectory twice (or, indeed any *particular* trajectory),
  in either direction" (Dawkins, 1986: 90). The principle that states that
  the structures and their functions in organisms cannot be regained if they
  were lost during the past evolution of a lineage. (*See also* EVOLUTIONARY
  TRAJECTORY; FUNCTION; LINEAGE.)

DRYOPITHECINES. The common and informal term for *Dryopithecus*. (*See
  also* DRYOPITHECUS.)

DRYOPITHECUS (Proconsul). A genus of the subfamily Dryopithecinae, family
  Pongidae, and superfamily Hominoidea, known from their fossil
  remains. Apes who lived in the forests of Africa, Europe, and Asia during

the Miocene epoch (20 to 14 million years ago, more or less). They probably are ancestors of *Ramapithecus,* the probable common ancestor of humans and living apes. (*See also* FOSSIL; GENUS; APE; AEGYP-TOPITHECUS; RAMAPITHECUS; PONGID.)

DYNAMIC. In this book this word is used referring to social dynamic. *See* SOCIAL DYNAMIC.

EARLY DIVERGENCE HYPOTHESIS. The assumption that the lineage that gave origin to all living pongids and the lineage that gave origin to humans split from a common ancestor 25 million years ago, more or less. (*See also* LATE DIVERGENCE HYPOTHESIS, LINEAGE, PONGID.)

ECOLOGICAL NICHE. (Similar to Adaptive zone, but more limited.) The role, life-style, and position of an organism or population within its ecosystem. The "natural profession" of a species. The natural way an organism or population makes use of the environment for living, and along with which it evolves. (*See also* ADAPTIVE ZONE; POPULATION; ECOSYSTEM; ENVIRONMENT.)

ECOLOGY. The study of the interactions and relations between organisms themselves and between them and the physical environment within which they live. (*See also* ENVIRONMENT.)

ECOSYSTEM. A community of different species of organisms interacting between themselves and between them and the physical environment within which they live. (*See also* ENVIRONMENT; HABITAT.)

ELECTRA COMPLEX. Supposedly, the abnormal love a female child has for her father, antipathy for her mother, and jealousy of her mother's attentions to him. (*See also* OEDIPUS COMPLEX.)

ENCEPHALIZATION. The evolutionary trend, mainly in vertebrates, towards the formation and enlargement of the brain; mainly the formation of cerebral cortex in mammals. "Encephalization is my phenotypic 'expression' of intelligence" (Jerison, 1988a: 1). (*See also* CEREBRAL CORTEX; PHENOTYPE.)

ENVIRONMENT. All physical, chemical, and biological factors surrounding an organism, such as soil, climate, and all other factors and components of the habitat in which an organism lives. (*See also* HABITAT.)

EOLITHIC CULTURE; EOLITHIC INDUSTRY. Stone tool industry and culture developed in Europe, Asia and Africa since the Middle Miocene epoch (14 million years ago, more or less) by our early hominid ancestors; characterized by absolutely natural stones very well chosen as scrapers and flakes for graincollecting. This original industry and culture was mixed with all the stone tool industries and cultures that descend from it, such as the Oldowan, Developed Oldowan, and Acheulian Industries, because our ancestors always were able to graincollect with absolutely natural stone tools, as well as with those more advanced stone tools of the abovementioned descendant industries and cultures that they developed later. (*See also* HOMINIDS; SCRAPER STONE TOOL; OLDOWAN INDUSTRY; DEVELOPED OLDOWAN INDUSTRY, ACHEULIAN INDUSTRY.)

EOLITHS. The stone tools of the Eolithic Industry and Culture. (*See also* EOLITHIC CULTURE.)

EPIGENETIC SYSTEM. The system of interactions of all the genetic factors controlling the different stages of the development of an organism.

EPOCH. A subdivision of geological time, such as Miocene, Pliocene, Pleistocene, etc. (*See also* ERA.)

EQUIDAE. Family of mammals, including living horses, zebras, etc., and their extinct ancestors and relatives.

EQUINE. A member of the family Equidae. (*See also* EQUIDAE.)

ERA. A division of geological time, such as Paleozoic, Mesozoic, Cenozoic, etc. (*See also* EPOCH.)

ERECT POSTURE. Upright position, vertical position.

ERGOSTEROL. An alcohol; substance found in some one-celled fungus growth between the glumes, glumellas, and the grain in many grasses. When it is exposed to the sunlight (ultraviolet rays), it produces vitamin D. (*See also* GLUME; GLUMELLA.)

ESTRUS; ESTROUS. The period of sexual excitement and receptivity of female mammals of many species, during which they are able to conceive. Being in estrus or estrous: A mammal female in heat.

ETHNIC GROUP. A human group having more or less the same characters, traditions, and customs because of their racial, cultural, linguistic, etc., ties.

EVOLUTION. The process of cumulative hereditary changes in characters, through variation and natural selection, that a population undergoes in the course of successive generations. Then, if the original population divides into several different populations in the course of successive generations because each one enters a different ecological niche, different characters may result in each different population, and can originate each different descendant population be a different sibling species. Descent with modification. (*See also* GENETIC VARIATION; NATURAL SELECTION; ECOLOGICAL NICHE; POPULATION; SIBLING SPECIES.)

EVOLUTION, ADAPTIVE. *See* ADAPTIVE EVOLUTION.

EVOLUTION, PHYLETIC. *See* PHYLETIC EVOLUTION.

EVOLUTION, PUNCTUATED. *See* PUNCTUATED EVOLUTION.

EVOLUTION, STAGE OF. Any distinguishable change in any character during the process of evolution of a population. (*See also* CHARACTER; EVOLUTION; POPULATION.)

EVOLUTIONARY ADAPTATION. *See* ADAPTIVE EVOLUTION.

EVOLUTIONARY CONVERGENCE. In genetically distant related lineages, the independent evolution through which, due to the similar environmental conditions and requirements (similar selective pressures) to which they are exposed, similar morphological and physiological characters are acquired, starting from different ancestral conditions (from different genetic programs); for example: the wings of birds and the wings of moths. (*See also* LINEAGE; SELECTIVE PRESSURE; CHARACTER; EVOLUTION; EVOLUTIONARY PARALLELISM; EVOLUTIONARY DIVERGENCE; GENETIC DISTANCE; GENETIC PROGRAM.)

EVOLUTIONARY DIVERGENCE. In formerly genetically closely related lineages, the independent evolution through which, due to the different environmental conditions and requirements (different selective pressures) to which they are exposed, different morphological and physiological characters are acquired, starting from a common ancestral condition (from the same genetic program); for example: the wings of birds and the arms and hands of humans. (*See also* LINEAGE; SELECTIVE PRESSURE; CHARACTER; EVOLUTION; EVOLUTIONARY PARALLELISM; EVOLUTIONARY CONVERGENCE; GENETIC DISTANCE; GENETIC PROGRAM.)

EVOLUTIONARY HISTORY. Past events in the course of the evolution of a lineage or lineages. (*See also* EVOLUTION; LINEAGE; EVOLUTIONARY TRAJECTORY.)

EVOLUTIONARY IRREVERSIBILITY. *See* DOLLO'S LAW.

EVOLUTIONARY NOVELTY. A character newly acquired by some or all the individuals of the descendant successive generation or generations of a population, which confers fitness to them in some way so it makes it possible for them to execute a new function or functions. (*See also* CHARACTER; POPULATION; FITNESS; FUNCTION.)

EVOLUTIONARY PARALLELISM. In formerly genetically closely related lineages, the independent evolution, through which, due to the similar environmental conditions and requirements (similar selective pressures) to which they are exposed, similar morphological and physiological characters are acquired, starting from a common ancestral condition (from the same genetic program); for example: the knuckle-walking character in all living pongid species was acquired by parallel evolution; that is, acquired independently during the evolution of each one of those species, starting from a bipedal common ancestor. (*See also* LINEAGE; EVOLUTION; SELECTIVE PRESSURE; CHARACTER; GENETIC CLOSENESS; EVOLUTIONARY CONVERGENCE; EVOLUTIONARY DIVERGENCE; KNUCKLE-WALKING; PONGID; BIPEDALISM.)

EVOLUTIONARY REGRESSION. In a population, the gradual disappearance or loss of a specialization, through evolution, of a character or characters in the successive descendant generations. (*See also* POPULATION; EVOLUTION; CHARACTER; VESTIGIAL CHARACTER.)

EVOLUTIONARY REVERSAL. In a population, the reacquisition, through evolution, in the successive descendant generations, of a character or characters not completely lost during the past evolution of that lineage. Reacquisition, through evolution, of an ancestral condition. (*See also* POPULATION; EVOLUTION; CHARACTER; LINEAGE.)

EVOLUTIONARY TRAJECTORY. The events in the course of the evolution of a lineage or lineages. (*See also* EVOLUTION; LINEAGE; EVOLUTIONARY HISTORY.)

EXCLUSION PRINCIPLE. *See* COMPETITIVE EXCLUSION PRINCIPLE.

EXOGAMOUS. Pertaining to, characterized by, or practicing exogamy. (*See also* EXOGAMY).

EXOGAMY. Sexual reproduction between individuals that are not relatives. Generally the mating of males with females outside their original group. This is an instinctive and natural breeding system of most social animal species that avoids incest. (*See also* MATRILOCAL; INCEST; INSTINCT.)

EXTENDED FAMILY. Close relatives along either the father or the mother line in the nuclear family, usually not along both, living together with this family as a social group. (*See also* NUCLEAR FAMILY.)

EXTINCTION. The dying out of a species, or the termination of a lineage, leaving no descendants. (*See also* LINEAGE.)

FAT-BODY (of insects). In insects, a tissue that extends around and along the digestive tract, consisting mainly of fat stored in it. Among many other functions, it stores vitamins, as the liver of vertebrates does. (*See also* FUNCTION; VERTEBRATES.)

FAUNA. (1) Animals in general. (2) All the animal life characteristic of a specific environment, or place, or area, or of any particular past time. (*See also* FLORA.)

FAVORABLE MUTATION. A heritable mutation occurring in the genetic material of an individual organism, so that it enhances the capacity of the individual to function successfully in the same or in a new environment. (*See also* MUTATION; ADAPT; ADAPTABILITY; FUNCTION.)

FELIDS. Members of the family Felidae: cats such as lions, tigers, leopards, etc., and extinct ancestral species. (*See also* HYAENIDS; CANIDS.)

FIST-WALKING. A semierect mode of locomotion sometimes used by the orangutan, in which the arms with the hands turned inwards (supporting itself on the clenched fists) are used as forelegs when progressing. (*See also* KNUCKLE-WALKING; ORANGUTAN.)

FITNESS. The capacity of an individual or a population to survive and leave descendants when living in a particular environment, compared with the capacity of other individuals or populations. (*See also* ADAPTIVE VALUE; POPULATION.)

FLAKE STONE TOOL. A small and thin chip or flake knocked from a larger stone (core). (*See also* CORE TOOL.)

FLORA. (1) Plants in general. (2) All the plant life characteristic of a specific environment, or place, or area; or of any particular past time. (*See also* FAUNA.)

FOLIVORE; FOLIVOROUS. An animal that eats leaves as its main food for subsisting. (*See also* CARNIVORE; HERBIVORE; INSECTIVORE; OMNIVORE; SCAVENGER.)

FOSSIL. The mineralized remains of an organism or of some traces of its existence preserved petrified in the rocks in the earth's crust. (*See also* FOSSIL RECORD.)

FOSSIL RECORD. The fossils preserved in the layers of soil that, due to the action of the elements, were deposited successively in the earth's crust and preserved through long periods of time; so, they give us at present an idea of the history of life on earth. (*See also* FOSSIL.)

FUNCTION. (1) The natural normal use, action, or role of an organ, character, or structure of an organism. (2) Any natural action or activity of an organism or organisms. (*See also* CHARACTER.)

GALAXY. One of the millions of systems formed by millions of stars that exist in the universe. A giant cluster of stars.

GAUSE'S EXCLUSION PRINCIPLE. *See* COMPETITIVE EXCLUSION PRINCIPLE.

GENE. The fundamental unit of transmission of hereditary characters from parents to offspring in organisms, occupying a specific position on a chromosome. (*See also* CHARACTER; CHROMOSOMES.)

GENE COMBINATIONS. The different arrangements that the linear sequence of genes can have in a chromosome. The different actions that these different arrangements of genes, or the same original linear sequence of genes, can have on the transmission of hereditary characters in organisms. (*See also* GENE; CHROMOSOMES.)

GENE MUTATION. A sudden heritable change in a gene. (*See also* GENE.)

GENE POOL. The totality of genetic material that a population has at a given time (Mayr, 1979). (*See also* GENE; POPULATION.)

GENE REARRANGEMENT. An alternative gene combination appearing, through an evolutionary process, in the descendant generations in a population. (*See also* GENE COMBINATIONS; POPULATION; EVOLUTION.)

GENE RECOMBINATION. *See* GENE REARRANGEMENT.

GENETIC APTITUDES. The natural abilities inherited by an organism from its ancestors.

GENETIC BASIS. Based on genetically inherited characters or aptitudes. (*See also* GENE; GENETICALLY; GENETIC APTITUDES.)

GENETIC CAPABILITY. *See* GENETIC APTITUDES.

GENETIC CLOSENESS. The genetic distance between two individuals of two different but closely related species. (*See also* GENETIC DISTANCE.)

GENETIC DISTANCE. The degree of gene differences between two individuals of two different species. (*See also* GENE.)

GENETIC LEVEL, AT. "At genetic level": referring to something happening, or something that happened, in the genetic material. (*See also* GENE.)

GENETIC PROGRAM. The natural organization of the genetic material (genetic information) for the development, reproduction, etc., of an organism during all its life. (*See also* GENE.)

GENETIC RECOMBINATION. *See* GENE REARRANGEMENT.

GENETIC RELATIVES. Two individuals of two different species that have a very short genetic distance between them. (*See also* GENETIC DISTANCE; GENE.)

GENETIC REVOLUTION. The natural, rapid speciation due to a drastic reorganization (not produced by mutations) of the genotype of an isolated population, because, due to this isolation and to the new severe different selective pressures, the cohesion of the parental gene pool is disrupted (Mayr, 1979). (*See also* MUTATION; GENOTYPE; POPULATION; SELECTIVE PRESSURE; GENE POOL.)

GENETIC SEPARATION. The genetic distance between two individuals of two different and distant related species. (*See also* GENETIC DISTANCE; GENETIC CLOSENESS; GENE.)

GENETIC VARIATION. The inherited change or deviation in the genetic material of an organism from that typical of the individuals of the population or the species it belongs to; then, this organism is phenotypically different from all other individuals. (*See also* GENE; POPULATION; PHENOTYPIC VARIATION; PHENOTYPE.)

GENETICALLY. In agreement with what we know about how the genetic material operates. (*See also* GENE.)

GENETICS. The study of biological heredity and variation. (*See also* GENETIC VARIATION.)

GENOME. All the genetic material contained in all the chromosomes. One can speak of the genome of an individual, of a population, or of a species. (*See also* CHROMOSOMES; POPULATION.)

GENOTYPE. The totality of genetic material that interacts with the environment to produce the phenotype, contained in the chromosomes of an individual. One can speak of the genotype of an individual only. (*See also* GENE; CHROMOSOMES; PHENOTYPE.)

GENUS (plural: Genera). A taxonomic group classifying between the species and the family. A group in the classification of organisms comprising one or several similar species close related by descent. (*See also* TAXONOMIC; ORGANISM.)

GEOLOGICAL TIME. The time since the origin of earth until present, datable or registered by historical geology and divided arbitrarily, but such divisions coinciding with certain past geological events.

GIBBON. The smallest of the living apes. This ape is arboreal and inhabits the tropical forests of Asia; it brachiates in the trees and also uses bipedalism quite often; its arms are long. Genus: *Hylobates*; family: Hylobatidae; superfamily: Hominoidea. (*See also* APE; ARBOREAL; BRACHIATION; BIPEDALISM.)

GIGANTOPITHECUS. An extinct genus of the family Pongidae, known from their fossil remains. They lived in East Asia during the Middle Miocene, Pliocene, and Middle Pleistocene epochs (10 million to 500 thousand years ago, more or less); they are possibly descendants of *Ramapithecus*. They resembled the living gorilla. (*See also* FOSSIL; GENUS; PONGID; RAMAPITHECUS; RAMAPITHECINES; GORILLA.)

GIGANTOPITHECUS BILASPURENSIS (Giganteous). *Gigantopithecus* species who lived in India during the Middle Miocene epoch (10 to 6.5 million years ago, more or less). (*See also* GIGANTOPITHECUS.)

GIGANTOPITHECUS BLACKI. *Gigantopithecus* species who lived in China since the Pliocene to Middle Pleistocene epochs (6 million to 500 thousand years ago, more or less). (*See also* GIGANTOPITHECUS.)

GLACIATIONS. Those periods of the geological time, mainly during the Pleistocene epoch (1 million to 10 thousand years ago, more or less), when a large part of the earth was covered with snow, ice, and ice rivers (glaciers), accompanied by greater cold over the whole earth. (*See also* GEOLOGICAL TIME.)

GLUME. One of the two outer chaff bracts on the axis and at the base of the small spikes (spikelets) that make a part of the spike in grasses. (*See also* GLUMELLA.).

GLUMELLA. An inner and smaller glume on the axis and at the base of the small spikes (spikelets) that make a part of the spike in grasses. (*See also* GLUME.)

GORILLA. The largest of the living pongids. This ape inhabits the lowland and mountain rainforests in Africa; rarely uses an erect posture during locomotion: it uses its arms as forelegs, and, with the hand fingers turned inwardly, it supports itself on the knuckles when progressing in an semierect posture (knuckle-walking). It is an herbivore. Its hair is sparse. Genus: *Gorilla*; family: Pongidae; superfamily: Hominoidea. (*See also* GENUS; PONGID; APE; PAN; PONGO; HYLOBATES; CHIMPANZEE; GIBBON; ORANGUTAN.)

GRADUALISM. A mode of evolution of organisms in which the evolutionary changes occur through small cumulative changes in the course of successive generations over an extended period of geological time. (*See also* PUNCTUATED EVOLUTION; CUMULATIVE SELECTION; EVOLUTION; GEOLOGICAL TIME.)

GRAMINEOUS. Pertaining to grasses.

GRAMINIVOROUS. Animal that grazes or feeds on grasses. (*See also* GRANIVOROUS.)

GRANIVOROUS. Animal that feeds on the grains of grasses (seed eater). (*See also* GRAMINIVOROUS.)

GRAZERS' SUCCESSIONS. See MIGRANT UNGULATE SUCCESSIONS.

GROOMING. A habit common among many primate species consisting in cleaning the body of another by picking, combing, and arranging the hair and fur with the fingers and teeth. Mutual grooming is normally practiced during social interactions, mainly when forming friendships and when looking for consort partners.

HABITAT. The natural place and environment where an organism or group of organisms normally live and thrive.

HAND AXE (Acheulian hand axe). An almond or teardrop shaped and superficially flaked core stone tool of the Acheulian Industry; generally as large as the human hand. (*See also* FLAKE STONE TOOL; CORE TOOL; ACHEULIAN INDUSTRY.)

HAND GRASPING REFLEX. Also called Palmar reflex. In human infants, the reflex of inward flexion of the fingers when the palm of the hand is touched with hair. (*See also* MORO EMBRACEMENT REFLEX.)

HAREM. A small group of female animals which mate with and are under the control, care, and protection of a single male; they live together with their infants and the juveniles; they have a more or less permanent association with this male.

HERBIVORE; HERBIVOROUS. An animal that eats and depends mainly on vegetable matter for subsisting. (*See also* FOLIVORE; INSECTIVORE. OMNIVORE; CARNIVORE; SCAVENGER.)

HETEROCHRONY. A genetic change, compared with that of the ancestors, in the timing of development of a character or characters in an organism; sometimes resulting in the retention of infant or juvenile characters by the adults. (*See also* GENE; CHARACTER.)

HIPPARION. An extinct genus of Miocene and Pliocene horses, relatives of the ancestors of the living horses, known from their fossil remains. (*See also* GENUS; FOSSIL.)

HOMINIDAE. A family of the superfamily Hominoidea. The members of this family (the human family) are informally and commonly called hominids. (*See also* HOMINIDS; HOMINOIDEA; HOMINOIDS; BASAL HOMINIDS.)

HOMINIDS. Informal name for members of the family Hominidae, consisting of three genera: *Ramapithecus, Australopithecus* and *Homo*. All forms, living and fossil, ancestral or relatives of humans since they acquired characters typical of humans (consistent bipedalism, tool-using, reduced canines, reduced anterior dentition, robust jaw, virtually hairless body, etc.). (*See also* HOMINIDAE; RAMAPITHECUS; AUSTRALOPITHECUS; BASAL HOMINIDS; CHARACTER; BIPEDALISM; CANINES.)

HOMINOIDEA. Superfamily of the order Primates divided in three families: Hominidae, Hylobatidae and Pongidae; characterized by the absence of tail. Includes all fossil ancestors and relatives of living apes and humans. The members of this superfamily are informally and commonly called hominoids. (*See also* HOMINOIDS; HOMINIDAE; HYLOBATES; PONGID; APE; FOSSIL.)

HOMINOIDS. Informal name for the members of the superfamily Hominoidea of the order Primates. All forms, living and fossil, ancestral to or relatives of hominids (human family), pongids (great apes), and hylobatids (lesser apes); characterized by the absence of tail. (*See also* LIVING HOMINOIDS; HOMINOIDEA; APE; HYLOBATES; PONGID; HOMINIDS.)

HOMO (Abbreviation: *H.*). Genus of the family Hominidae. Includes modern humans and extinct ancestral species. It has a single living species: *Homo sapiens.* (*See also* GENUS; HOMO SAPIENS.)

HOMO ERECTUS. An extinct species of the genus *Homo,* ancestral to modern humans, known only from fossils. They lived in Europe, Asia, and Africa from 1.5 million to 100 thousand years ago, more or less. They probably were the creators and users of the Acheulian Industry. (*See also* GENUS; FOSSIL; ACHEULIAN INDUSTRY; ACHEULIAN STONE TOOLS.)

HOMO SAPIENS. The only living species of the genus *Homo* to which all living humans belong. It probably appeared 300 thousand years ago. (*See also* GENUS.)

HOMOLOGOUS. Those genes, structures or characters of two different species of organisms that, because similar in actual function, when compared, imply that these two species have a common ancestor (that they have the same ancestral genes), even if these structures have changed substantially during their independent evolution; example: the wings of birds and the wings of bats are homologous, while those of birds and moths are not. (*See also* CHARACTER; FUNCTION; GENE; EVOLUTION.)

HOMOPLASY. Similar characters or structures of two different species of organisms, acquired by evolutionary parallelism or evolutionary convergence. (*See also* CHARACTER; EVOLUTIONARY PARALLELISM; EVOLUTIONARY CONVERGENCE.)

HUNTING-GATHERING. A human way of life consisting in killing and consuming animals, and gleaning or collecting plants, roots, fruits, nuts, etc., from the wild for food. (*See also* SCAVENGING-GATHERING.)

HYAENIDS (Hyenas). Members of the family Hyaenidae. Doglike species of carnivore scavenger mammals that live in Africa and Asia. (*See also* CARNIVORE; SCAVENGER; CANIDS; FELIDS.)

HYLOBATES (Gibbons). Genus of the family Hylobatidae, superfamily Hominoidea, and commonly called lesser apes. They are perfectly arboreal, have long arms, and are brachiators. (*See also* GENUS; APE; HOMINOIDEA; HOMINOIDS; ARBOREAL; BRACHIATION; GIBBON.)

HYPOTHESIS (plural: Hypotheses). A scientific assumption made to explain certain facts, and tentatively accepted in order to draw conclusions that, even if unproved, can be used for further investigation. A provisional theory.

INCEST. Sexual intercourse or sexual reproduction between individual organisms that are close relatives. (*See also* EXOGAMY.)

INCISORS. Teeth adapted for chisel cutting. The front teeth of mammals. Many mammal species use these teeth also for gnawing, nipping and biting off pieces of food, as almost all primates do. (*See also* MAMMAL; PRIMATES.)

INDIGENOUS. *See* ABORIGINAL.

INFANTICIDE. The intentional killing of a recently born child.

INFUSORIA CILIATES. See CILIATES.

INFUSORIA CILIATES TROGLODYTELLA. Ciliates that live as symbionts in the intestine of wild gorillas and chimpanzees. (*See also* CILIATES; SYMBIONT; SYMBIOSIS; GORILLA; CHIMPANZEE.)

INSECTIVORE; INSECTIVOROUS. An animal that feeds on insects and that depends mainly on insects for subsisting. (*See also* CARNIVORE; HERBIVORE; FOLIVORE; OMNIVORE; SCAVENGER.)

IN SITU. In its original place or position. Said of those fossil remains or artifacts, etc., found in the place and situation in which they were originally placed and left. (*See also* FOSSIL; ARTIFACTS.)

INSTINCT. A natural unacquired behavior or response to a stimulus characteristic of a species. A natural inherited aptitude.

INSTINCTIVE ACTION. See INSTINCT.

IRREVERSIBILITY. See DOLLO'S LAW.

ISCHIAL. Pertaining to the ischium. (*See also* ISCHIUM.)

ISCHIAL CALLOSITIES. Horny epidermal thickenings that some baboons and some pongids have in the skin in the region of the posterior and inferior part of the hipbone (buttocks). (*See also* BABOONS; PONGID; PRIMATES.)

ISCHIUM (plural: Ischia). In vertebrates, the posterior and inferior part of the hipbone. In humans, the lower part of the hipbone. (*See also* VERTEBRATES.)

K-SELECTION. Selection on individuals in populations that live in generally stable environments, in which the production of few, well adapted offspring is more important than the rapid growth of that population, because the population is maintained at, or near the carrying capacity of their environment (the maximum number of individuals of this species that can live and thrive in this particular area). (*See also* r-SELECTION; SELECTION; POPULATION; ENVIRONMENT.)

KIBBUTZ (plural: Kibbutzim). Hebrew word that means "gathering." Collective settlement in Israel, cooperatively owned and managed by all members, whose physical work is very important because no hired workers are allowed. They do not form nuclear families or any similar social system; all the children live together and visit their parents a few hours a day. (*See also* NUCLEAR FAMILY.)

KINSHIP. Biological relationship by descent of a recent common ancestor.

KNUCKLE-WALKING. The semierect gait that is commonly used by the gorilla, the chimpanzee, and the orangutan: they use their arms as forelegs, and with the hand fingers turned inwardly they support themselves on the knuckles when progressing. (*See also* GORILLA; CHIMPANZEE; ORANGUTAN.)

LACTATION. The secretion of milk by mammals, and the suckling of a mammal infant from a mammary gland of its mother. (*See also* MAMMAL.)

LANGUAGE. Any mode or means animals use to communicate with each other. The human speech. (*See also* BODY LANGUAGE.)

LATE DIVERGENCE HYPOTHESIS. The assumption that the lineage that gave origin to the African pongids and the lineage that gave origin to humans, split from a common ancestor 4 million years ago, more or less. (*See also* LINEAGE; AFRICAN PONGIDS; EARLY DIVERGENCE HYPOTHESIS.)

LEGISLATE. To make tacit or explicit rules of conduct recognized, obeyed, and observed customarily by the members of a human community.

LINEAGE. Evolutionary line of descent of related organisms distinct of all other organisms.

LINGUISTICS. The study of language. (*See also* LANGUAGE.)

LIVING HOMINOIDS. The living members of the superfamily Hominoidea: humans, orangutans, gorillas, chimpanzees, gibbons and siamangs. (*See also* HOMINOIDEA; ORANGUTAN; GORILLA; CHIMPANZEE; GIBBON.)

LIVING SITE (Living floor). An ancient site in which, according to the form and position of the fossil remains and the artifacts left, archeologists infer that it was a place of intense hominid activity. (*See also* HOMINID; HOMINIDAE; ARTIFACTS; FOSSIL.)

MAMMAL. An animal member of the class Mammalia. Warm-blooded vertebrates comprising humans; generally they have the body covered with hair; the females have mammary glands for feeding their young with milk. (*See also* VERTEBRATES.)

MANDIBLE. The lower jaw of vertebrates. (*See also* VERTEBRATES.)

MANDRILLUS. Genus of Old World monkeys. Large baboons with brightly red colored cheeks and red ischial callosities. They live in Western Africa. (*See also* GENUS; BABOONS; ISCHIAL CALLOSITIES.)

MATRICENTRIC. The social system of most social animal species in which the members of a group center socially upon the females. (*See also* PATRICENTRIC.)

MATRILINEAL.   Relating descent through the mother's line. (*See also* PATRILINEAL.)

MATRILOCAL. The social system of most social animal species, in which the males originating in a group (brothers and sons) abandon that group when adults, looking for mates in other groups. Sisters and daughters remain in the mother's original group forever; they admit in that group adult males originating from other groups, and reject the adult males originating in their group. This is an instinctive and natural breeding system that avoids incest. (*See also* INCEST; INSTINCT; EXOGAMY.)

MESOLITHIC. It is considered by many authorities that this is a transitional period of the Old Stone Age, between the Paleolithic and the Neolithic, in which both periods are mixed. (*See also* PALEOLITHIC; NEOLITHIC.)

MIGRANT UNGULATE SUCCESSIONS (Grazers' successions). The "migration." This term is applied to the natural movements of the ungulate populations (wildebeest, Thompson's gazelle, zebra) in the Serengeti, Africa " . . . between their wet-season range on the open plains and their dry-season range in the woodlands . . . " (Maddock, 1979: 104), looking for good quality grasses. (*See also* MIGRATION UNGULATES; POPULA-TION.)

MIGRATION. (1) The natural, and usually seasonal, movements of groups of animals from a region to another looking for food, or for better conditions for life; mainly during summer and winter, and usually within a well defined geographical area. (2) The movement of individuals from a population to another, so, the movement of genes. (*See also* MIGRANT UNGULATE SUCCESSIONS; POPULATION; GENE.)

MIOCENE. Geologic epoch that began approximately 25 million years ago, and finished approximately 5 million years ago. (*See also* PLIOCENE; PLEISTOCENE.)

MODEL. (1) Any natural process already understood, proposed to simulate another assumed similar natural process, and designed to aid the re-searchers in comprehending this assumed similar natural process, not easily comprehensible. (2) A formulation of hypothetical processes, open to verification, that can explain an observed phenomenon not easily comprehensible.

MOLARS. In mammals, the large cheek teeth behind the incisors in both upper and lower jaws. These teeth, in the case of monkeys, apes, and humans, are used for grinding. (*See also* MAMMAL; APE; INCISORS.)

MOLECULAR CLOCK. The study of the dating of the splitting of two lineages from one ancestral lineage, by assuming that the present extent of molecular divergence in the genetic material between these two lineages is directly related with the time of their split. (*See also* SPLITTING; LINEAGE.)

MOLECULAR GENETICS. The study of genetics using biochemical characters and applying techniques of molecular chemistry. (*See also* GENETICS.)

MONOGASTRIC MAMMALS. Mammals in which the stomach is only one compartment. Generally referring to grazer mammals digesters of cellulose nonruminants, such as the equines, etc. They do not digest cellulose as efficiently as ruminants. Humans are also monogastric mammals. (*See also* MAMMAL; CELLULOSE; EQUINE; EQUIDAE; RUMINANTS.)

MORO EMBRACEMENT REFLEX. Laying a human infant in decubitus supine position (lying on the back with the face upward) on a table, by striking the surface of the table the infant responses to that stimulus trying to embrace something with its arms. (*See also* PALMAR REFLEX.)

MORPHOLOGICAL. Pertaining to morphology. Pertaining to the form and structure of organisms without considering the function. (*See also* MORPHOLOGY.)

MORPHOLOGICAL CHARACTER. The considered particular area of the body of an organism. (*See also* MORPHOLOGY.)

MORPHOLOGY. The study of the physical form and structure of organisms without considering the function. (*See also* PHYSIOLOGY.)

MULTIMALE GROUP. In some social animal species, a group of females and their offspring living together with several adult males. (*See also* UNIMALE GROUP.)

MUTATION. A sudden heritable alteration in the genetic material of an organism. (*See also* GENETIC PROGRAM; GENE; GENE MUTATION; FAVORABLE MUTATION; BACK MUTATION; GENETIC VARIATION.)

NATURAL SELECTION. All organisms show variations in their characters; they reproduce themselves so efficiently than the number of individuals in each population tend to become very large. Because the natural subsistences are limited, and because the adversities of the environment tend to eliminate those individuals having unfavorable variations, then, only those individuals who have variations which better fit them to the environment survive, permitting them to reach reproductive age and leave offspring. Then, this nonrandom and differential reproduction of the different genotypes is the leading principle that directs the course of evolution; and coupled with an environment which generally changes slowly, and sometimes suddenly, during geological time, the end result is the appearance of new species, whether, through phyletic evolution (gradual) or through divergence (splitting). (*See also* GENETIC VARIATION; TYPE; CHARACTER; POPULATION; GENOTYPE; FAVORABLE MUTATION; PHYLETIC EVOLUTION; DIVERGENCE; GEOLOGICAL TIME.)

NEOCORTEX. *See* CEREBRAL CORTEX.

NEOLITHIC. The most recent Stone Age, when human ancestors initiated hunting-gathering, herding, and later agriculture, since 50 thousand years ago, more or less, and they began to change their stone tools they used to graincollect into arms for hunting. (*See also* MESOLITHIC; PALEOLITHIC.)

NEOTENY. *See* PAEDOMORPHOSIS.

NEURAL MATERIAL. Material in some parts of the body of animals containing neurons. (*See also* NEURON.)

NEURON. The type of cells of the nervous system of animals. Nerve cell including all its processes.

NICHE (Similar to Adaptive zone). *See* ECOLOGICAL NICHE. *See* ADAPTIVE ZONE.

NOMADISM. The state of some animal species that live moving about in search for their natural subsistences, such as pasture, grains, or other vegetables, etc., usually seasonally, and also usually within a well defined geographical area. (*See also* MIGRANT UNGULATE SUCCESSIONS.)

NUCLEAR FAMILY. The small human social unit consisting of the father, the mother, and their children. (*See also* EXTENDED FAMILY.)

OEDIPUS COMPLEX. Supposedly, the abnormal love a male child has for his mother, antipathy for his father, and jealousy of his mother's attentions to his father. (*See also* ELECTRA COMPLEX.)

OLDOWAN INDUSTRY. Stone tool industry and culture of the Lower Paleolithic period, developed in Africa by some australopithecines and other hominids since the Lower Pliocene to the Lower Pleistocene epochs (5 million to 750 thousand years ago, more or less), characterized by crude choppers, scrapers, and flake stone tools. (*See also* DEVELOPED OLDOWAN INDUSTRY; ACHEULIAN INDUSTRY; PALEOLITHIC; AUSTRALOPITHECINES; HOMINIDS; SCRAPER STONE TOOL; FLAKE STONE TOOL.)

OLDOWAN STONE TOOLS. The stone tools of the Oldowan Industry. (*See also* OLDOWAN INDUSTRY.)

OMNIVORE; OMNIVOROUS. An animal that subsists eating both animal and

vegetable matter. (*See also* CARNIVORE; FOLIVORE; HERBIVORE; INSEC-
TIVORE; SCAVENGER.)

ONTOGENY. The growth and development of an individual organism from
conception to maturity. (*See also* PHYLOGENY.)

ORANGUTAN. The Asian pongid. This Asian ape inhabits the forests of
Sumatra and Borneo; rarely uses an erect posture during terrestrial
locomotion. It uses its long arms as forelegs: sometimes it uses the
knuckle-walking semierect gait and sometimes the fist-walking semierect
gait. It lives mainly in the trees and constructs nests for sleeping. Its hair
is sparse, long and reddish-brown. It is an herbivore. (*See also* PONGID;
APE; KNUCKLE-WALKING; FIST-WALKING; HERBIVORE.)

ORGANISM. Any individual living thing that effectuates all life functions.

PAEDOMORPHOSIS. The retention by adults, through evolution, of the infant
or juvenile characters of their ancestors. (*See also* EVOLUTION; CHAR-
ACTER.)

PALEOANTHROPOLOGY. The study of the human cultural and biological
evolution through several disciplines, such as ecology, archeology,
geology, etc. (*See also* EVOLUTION.)

PALEOLITHIC. The Old Stone Age. According to many authorities the
Paleolithic began when human ancestors and their relatives
australopithecines began to *manufacture* stone tools 5 million years ago,
more or less, and ended with the beginnings of agriculture 15 or 10
thousand years ago, as evidence the archeological and the fossil records.
(*See also* HOMINIDS; AUSTRALOPITHECINES; EOLITHIC CULTURE;
NEOLITHIC; MESOLITHIC; FOSSIL RECORD.)

PALEONEUROLOGY. The study of anatomy and physiology of the nervous
system of animals through their fossil remains. (*See also* ANATOMY;
PHYSIOLOGY.)

PALEONTOLOGY. The study of organisms of past geological periods, as
interpreted by studying their fossil remains. (*See also* ORGANISM;
GEOLOGICAL TIME; FOSSIL; FOSSIL RECORD.)

PALMAR. With reference to the palm of the hand.

PALMAR REFLEX. *See* HAND GRASPING REFLEX.

PALMIGRADE. Walking with the entire palm of the hand or the entire sole
and the heel of the foot in contact with the ground. (*See also* PLAN-
TIGRADE.)

PAN. Genus of the family Pongidae comprising all chimpanzees. (*See also*
GENUS, CHIMPANZEE.)

PANICLE. (1) In some plants, a cluster or arrangement of flowers on an axis (inflorescence) composed of a raceme with secondary branches that are also racemes. (2) The seeds or ears of some grasses that resemble a panicle. (*See also* RACEME.)

PARALLEL. See EVOLUTIONARY PARALLELISM.

PARALLEL EVOLUTION. See EVOLUTIONARY PARALLELISM.

PARALLELISM. See EVOLUTIONARY PARALLELISM.

PARANTHROPUS. Used sometimes referring to *Australopithecus robustus*. (*See also* AUSTRALOPITHECUS ROBUSTUS.)

PARANTHROPUS ROBUSTUS. Used sometimes referring to *Australopithecus robustus*. (*See also* AUSTRALOPITHECUS ROBUSTUS; AUSTRALOPITHECUS.)

PARSIMONY; LAW OF PARSIMONY. The principle that establishes that the theory or explanation based in the simplest but adequate hypothesis or hypotheses is to be preferred among other possible theories or explanations.

PATRICENTRIC. The social system of a few social animal species that centers upon males. (*See also* MATRICENTRIC; MATRILOCAL; PATRILOCAL.)

PATRILINEAL. Relating descent through the father's line. (*See also* MATRILINEAL.)

PATRILOCAL. Centered around the male's original group and residence. This social system has been adopted by a few social animal species due to some abnormality; sometimes due to the territorial behavior. In humans this abnormal system is sometimes adopted due to the territorial behavior of the hunter-gatherer societies and their inherited social scheme in their descendant herding, agricultural, and industrial societies; it is commonly adopted since 50 thousand years ago: bride and groom take up residence with or near the groom's parents. (*See also* MATRILOCAL.)

PEBBLE TOOL. A tool made of a pebble. A stone, generally worn and rounded by the action of water, that human ancestors used to knock other stones and manufacture tools (to produce flake or core stone tools); or they used some pebbles directly as tools, or as a nodule for core tools. (*See also* FLAKE STONE TOOL; CORE TOOL.)

PERIOD OF RECEPTIVITY. In this book I refer specially to the period in which women are sexually receptive. (*See also* ESTRUS.)

PHENOTYPE. The totality of the structural and functional observable characters of an individual organism, determined by its genetic material (genotype) interacting with the environment. (*See also* CHARACTER; GENOTYPE; ENVIRONMENT.)

PHENOTYPIC VARIATION. The observable divergence or deviation in a structural or functional character in an individual organism, from the typical individual (type) of the population or species it belongs, due to a variation in its genetic material. (*See also* PHENOTYPE; TYPE; GENETIC VARIATION.)

PHYLETIC. Concerning the course of evolution of a single line.

PHYLETIC EVOLUTION. The evolutionary changes, or even the speciation, over an extended period of time, of a single line that evolves gradually, without branching; that is, the number of species does not increase: the descendant species replaces the ancestral original species. (*See also* GRADUALISM; DIVERGENCE.)

PHYLOGENETIC RELATIONSHIPS. Relation of recent common ancestry of two or more species, according with their evolutionary history (according with phylogeny). (*See also* GENETIC DISTANCE; PHYLOGENY.)

PHYLOGENETICALLY. According with phylogeny. According with the evolutionary history. (*See also* PHYLOGENY.)

PHYLOGENETICALLY APART. Two species that are evolutionarily separated according to phylogeny. Without any recent relation of common ancestry according with the evolutionary history. (*See also* PHYLOGENY; PHYLOGENETICALLY NEAR.)

PHYLOGENETICALLY NEAR. Two species that are evolutionarily near according to phylogeny. With a recent relation of common ancestry according with the evolutionary history. (*See also* PHYLOGENY; PHYLOGENETICALLY APART.)

PHYLOGENY. The history of the evolution and relationships of a specific group of organisms, or of a line of descent.

PHYSIOLOGICAL CHARACTER. A character of an organism considered by its normal function or functions rather that by its morphological structure. (*See also* CHARACTER; FUNCTION.)

PHYSIOLOGY. The study of the function or functions of the parts and organs of living organisms, and of the whole organism. (*See also* MORPHOLOGY; FUNCTION.)

PLANTIGRADE. Walking with the entire sole and heel of the foot in contact with the ground, as humans and bears. (*See also* PALMIGRADE.)

PLAY. Recreational activities that many animals perform, individually, in pairs, or in groups, apparently for their own sake, for the pleasure which this activity yields, not for material benefits, as food, etc.; usually simulating activities necessary for surviving.

PLEIOTROPIC. Used of a gene that produces more than one effect or expression in the structures and functions of the phenotype. It is said that such effects or expressions are correlative. (*See also* GENE; PHENOTYPE.)

PLEISTOCENE. Geologic epoch that began approximately 2 million years ago, and finished approximately 10 thousand years ago; also known as Ice Age or Great Glaciations Epoch. (*See also* MIOCENE; PLIOCENE.)

PLIOCENE. Geological epoch that began approximately 5 million years ago, and finished approximately 2 million years ago; that is, it extended from the end of the Miocene epoch to the beginning of the Pleistocene epoch. (*See also* MIOCENE; PLEISTOCENE.)

POLYGYNY. In social animals, the mating of a male with several females, generally in an unimale group. In humans, the marriage of one man with more than one woman. (*See also* UNIMALE GROUP.)

POLYMORPHISM. In a population or species, the co-occurrence of individuals that present different forms (different phenotypes). (*See also* POPULATION; PHENOTYPE.)

PONGID. A member, living or fossil, of the family Pongidae. The living pongids are: the gorilla (genus *Gorilla*), the chimpanzee (genus *Pan*), and the orangutan (genus *Pongo*). (*See also* CHIMPANZEE; GORILLA; ORANGUTAN; GENUS; APE; HOMINOIDEA.)

PONGO. Genus of the family Pongidae comprising all orangutans. (*See also* GENUS; ORANGUTAN; PONGID.)

POPULATION. All the individuals of a species that live together, generally within a geographical area, forming one or several groups and interbreeding among themselves, but are able to mate with conspecific individuals of other populations.

POSTCRANIAL. Any part of a skeleton not including the skull.

PREADAPTATION. The possession, by individuals of a species, of a character useful and specialized for the way of life within the niche they are, and which, by performing a different function, this character favors the adaptation of those individuals to another niche, if the individuals of a population of that species change their way of life within that other niche. (*See also* CHARACTER; NICHE; ADAPTIVE CHARACTER; POPULATION.)

PRECISION GRIP. In humans and some other primates, the position of the opposable thumb (pollex) and index fingers when holding an object with precision and control. (*See also* PRIMATES; THEROPITHECUS GELADA; THUMB OPPOSABILITY.)

PRECOCIAL. Used of some vertebrate species that characterize by a large period of gestation, small litters, developed young at birth that are more or less independent of the mother but have a slow development. (*See also* VERTEBRATES; ALTRICIAL.)

PREDATOR. An animal that survives killing and consuming other animals. (*See also* PREY.)

PREY. An animal that is killed and consumed by other animal or animals. (*See also* PREDATOR.)

PRIMATES. An order of the class Mammalia (mammals) to which humans, apes, and monkeys belong; includes basically arboreal species. (*See also* APE; MAMMALS; ARBOREALS.)

PRIMATOLOGICAL SCALE. Considering all primates: prosimians, monkeys and anthropoid apes, the assumption that this "living scale" broadly duplicates the stages of evolution which human ancestors reached in the past. (*See also* PRIMATES; EVOLUTION, STAGE OF.)

PRIMITIVE CHARACTER. A character or structure present in the individuals of a group, population, or species, living or fossil, and already present in their remote ancestors. (*See also* CHARACTER; DERIVED CHARACTER; POPULATION; FOSSIL.)

PROCONSUL. *See* DRYOPITHECUS.

PROGNATHISM. The state of being prognathous. (*See also* PROGNATHOUS.)

PROGNATHOUS. In this book I refer to primate species that normally possess an elongated muzzle, as in baboons; or possess projecting jaws, as in apes. (*See also* BABOONS; APE.)

PRONATION-SUPINATION OF THE HANDS. In humans, turning the hand so that the palm faces downwards or faces towards the body; and faces upwards or faces away from the body. Both movements through almost 90° in either direction; that is, a total movement of almost 180°.

PROPLIOPITHECUS. A genus of fossil Hominoids members of the Pongidae family. Extinct apes known through their fossil remains from the Oligocene epoch (30 million years ago, more or less), in Egypt. They may have been relatives of *Aegyptopithecus*. (*See also* FOSSIL; GENUS; PONGID; APE; FOSSIL RECORD; AEGYPTOPITHECUS.)

PROTO-HAND AXE. A primitive and rudimentary hand axe. (*See also* HAND AXE.)

PROTO-HOMINIDS. The close ancestors of the earliest hominids. (*See also* HOMINIDS.)

PROTOZOA. Basic division of the animal kingdom consisting of unicellular animals that normally live in salt water, fresh water, or as parasites.

PUNCTUATED EVOLUTION. A mode of evolution of organisms in which the species generally remain relatively stable through long periods of geological time, and the evolutionary changes and speciation occur in very short periods of time. (*See also* EVOLUTION; GEOLOGICAL TIME; SPECIATION; GRADUALISM.)

PUNCTUATIONALISTS. Those scientists that accept and support that punctuated evolution is the main mode of speciation, and that species generally remain relatively stable through long periods of geological time. (*See also* PUNCTUATED EVOLUTION; GRADUALISM.)

QUADRUPED. Most mammals, those reptiles, and those amphibians that use four limbs in locomotion. (*See also* MAMMAL.)

r-SELECTION. Selection on individuals in populations that live generally in unstable or changing environments, in which is more important the rapid production of young and the rapid population growth, than the production of few well adapted offspring, because the environment can change suddenly, or because the resources are superabundant in short periods of time and then become exhausted. (*See also* K-SELECTION; SELECTION; POPULATION; ENVIRONMENT.)

RACEME. (1) In some plants, a cluster or arrangement of flowers on an axis (inflorescence), in which those flowers are born on small stalks of equal length arranged along that axis which elongates for a period when flowering, opening these flowers in succession from below. (2) The seeds or ears of some grasses that resemble a raceme. (*See also* PANICLE.)

RADIATION, ADAPTIVE. See ADAPTIVE RADIATION.

RAMAPITHECINAE. An extinct subfamily of the family Hominidae, known from their fossil remains. It is assumed that all members of this subfamily are related to *Ramapithecus*. (*See also* FOSSIL; RAMAPITHECUS.)

RAMAPITHECINES. Informal name for members of the subfamily Ramapithecinae. (*See also* RAMAPITHECINAE.)

RAMAPITHECUS. An extinct genus of the subfamily Ramapithecinae, family Hominidae (the human family), known from their fossil remains, and proposed by Simons (1961) to be the first hominids. They probably descend from *Dryopithecus* (Proconsul). They lived in Europe, Asia and parts of Africa during the Middle Miocene epoch (14 to 9 million years ago, more or less). They probably are ancestors of humans and the living apes. (*See also* FOSSIL; GENUS; RAMAPITHECINAE; HOMINIDS; HOMINIDAE; DRYOPITHECUS; APE.)

RATIO OF BRAIN MASS TO BODY MASS. This ratio is equal to the ratio or quotient of brain weight to body weight. It was proposed by Jerison (1973) that this ratio more or less reflects, in each vertebrate species, the degree of what he has defined as biological intelligence. (*See also* VERTEBRATES.)

RECEPTIVE; RECEPTIVITY. *See* PERIOD OF RECEPTIVITY.

RECOMBINATION. *See* GENE REARRANGEMENT.

REFLEX ACT. An unconscious, involuntary action of an organism in response to a stimulus.

REVERSAL. *See* EVOLUTIONARY REVERSAL.

RHIZOME. In vascular plants, a stem-like root more or less thick and elongated. It generally grows horizontally under or on the ground. It has roots in its lower surface, and leaves and shoots in its upper surface. Rhizomes store food and water to be used by the plant in winter or in the dry season.

RUMINANTS. Mammals that have the stomach divided in four compartments; they are cud chewers and digest cellulose more efficiently than the monogastric mammal digesters of cellulose. (*See also* MAMMAL; CELLULOSE; MONOGASTRIC MAMMALS.)

SAVANNA. Grassland with scattered trees in extensive open plains in tropical and subtropical regions with seasonal rains.

SCAVENGER. An animal that subsists consuming mainly carrion. (*See also* CARNIVORE; HERBIVORE; INSECTIVORE; OMNIVORE; FOLIVORE.)

SCAVENGING-GATHERING. A human way of life consisting in getting carcasses, consuming the carrion, and also gleaning or collecting plants, roots, fruits, nuts, etc., from the wild for food. (*See also* HUNTING-GATHERING; SCAVENGER.)

SCRAPER STONE TOOL. A small stone, usually a natural or manufactured small flake, used by the human ancestors to collect grains from grasses, by placing that small flake in the palm of the hand, and pressing, between this small stone tool and the ball of the thumb (thenar eminence), the top part of the stem they intended to scrape the seeds from, and sliding the tool over this part of the stem. (*See also* FLAKE STONE TOOL.)

SEDENTARY. In this book I use this term referring to those mammals that stay the whole year in reduced geographical areas, as the grazer ungulates buffalo, impala and topi stay in the woodlands of Serengeti, Africa. (*See also* MAMMAL; MIGRATION; MIGRANT UNGULATE SUCCESSIONS; UNGULATES.)

SELECTION. Any evolutionary process that generates that certain individuals of a species or population can reach reproductive age and can leave offspring, because the respective genotype of each one is better adapted to the environment they live than that of other individuals. (*See also* GENOTYPE; SPECIES; POPULATION; ENVIRONMENT; SELECTIVE ADVANTAGE.)

SELECTIVE ADVANTAGE. The greater fitness of the genotype of an individual relative to that of other individuals of the same population and species. (*See also* FITNESS; GENOTYPE; POPULATION; SPECIES; SELECTION.)

SELECTIVE PRESSURE; SELECTION PRESSURE. Those factors of the environment that cause organisms to be exposed to natural selection. (*See also* NATURAL SELECTION.)

SEXUAL SELECTION. The evolutionary process by which, those individuals possessing certain kind of aesthetic appeal, abilities, or strong marked secondary sexual characters, are selected as mates by individuals of the opposite sex. Some authorities consider now sexual selection as a part of natural selection. (*See also* NATURAL SELECTION.)

SIBLING SPECIES. Those species that have a recent common ancestor and are morphologically almost identical. (*See also* MORPHOLOGY.)

SITE. Place; generally referring to ancient or fossil places. (*See also* FOSSIL; LIVING SITE.)

SIVAPITHECUS. An extinct genus of the subfamily Ramapithecinae, related to *Ramapithecus,* known from their fossil remains. They probably also descend from *Dryopithecus* (Proconsul). They lived in Europe and Asia during the Miocene epoch (14 million years ago, more or less). (*See also* FOSSIL; GENUS; RAMAPITHECUS; RAMAPITHECINAE; DRYOPITHECUS.)

SOCIAL DYNAMIC. The study of the impulses (actions and reactions) that constitute the essence of the social systems of social organisms and the way individuals behave within their society. (*See also* SOCIAL SYSTEM; SOCIETY.)

SOCIAL SYSTEM. Any system of mutual dependency that allows individual animals of the same species to live together, forming a coherent group within which each individual has a role and is respected and considered, so, within it all members obtain more benefits than living individually. (*See also* SOCIETY.)

SOCIALITY. (1) In some animals, the condition and the natural tendency to pertain to a social group of conspecifics. (2) The actual formation of such social groups. (*See also* SOCIAL SYSTEM; SOCIETY.)

SOCIETY. A natural group of mutually depending conspecific organisms that live together, are exposed to the same environment, and they form an homogeneous and coherent interbreeding group, because within this natural association they obtain more benefits than living individually. (*See also* ENVIRONMENT; SOCIAL SYSTEM; SOCIALITY.)

SOCIOBIOLOGY. The study of biology and evolution of sociality and behavior in organisms. (*See also* SOCIALITY.)

SOLAR SYSTEM. The sun and all planets, moons, comets, asteroids, etc., that revolve around it.

SPECIATION. The formation, through evolution, by phyletic evolution or by splitting, of one or several new and different species from an original one species that can preserve more or less its original form, can be replaced (by phyletic evolution), or can become extinct. (*See also* EVOLUTION; PHYLETIC EVOLUTION; SPLITTING.)

SPECIES (Plural: species) A group of related fertile interbreeding individual organisms that have a close common ancestor, closely resemble each other in all characters, and are distinct of all other groups of organisms with which they are not capable of fertile interbreeding. (*See also* CHARACTER.)

SPLITTING. Said of branching off one original species into two or more descendant species. (*See also* DIVERGENCE.)

STAGE OF EVOLUTION. See EVOLUTION, STAGE OF.

STATISTICS. The study, systematic separation and classification of facts or data that pertain to any subject, matter, or group.

STATUS. In social animals, the position, role, and hierarchy an individual has within its natural group. (*See also* SOCIAL SYSTEM; SOCIALITY; SOCIETY.)

STEATOMERIA. In humans, the accumulation of large amounts of fat (adipose tissue) on the thighs and hips. (*See also* STEATOPYGIA.)

STEATOPYGIA. In humans, the accumulation of large amounts of fat (adipose tissue) on the buttocks. (*See also* STEATOMERIA.)

STRUCTURE, DERIVED. *See* CHARACTER, DERIVED.

STRUCTURE, PRIMITIVE. *See* CHARACTER, PRIMITIVE.

SUBCUTANEOUS. Located beneath the skin.

SURVIVAL PRIZE. Any potential or actual increase of the fitness of an individual obtained by an action or actions executed by that individual. (*See also* FITNESS.)

SURVIVAL VALUE. The degree of efficacy of a character or action to produce fitness to the individual who possesses that character or executes that action. The degree of efficacy of a character to adjust or adapt the individual who possesses that character to the environmental conditions. (*See also* CHARACTER; FITNESS; ENVIRONMENT.)

SWEAT GLANDS. Those glands located in the skin of mammals that secrete perspiration. (*See also* MAMMAL.)

SYMBIONT. Any organism that lives in symbiosis with another organism of different species. (*See also* SYMBIOSIS.)

SYMBIOSIS. Those types of close association, mutually beneficial, between two organisms of different species. (*See also* SYMBIONT.)

TAXONOMIC. Referring to Taxonomy; that is, to the study of the systematic classification of organisms according to established principles.

TERRESTRIALS. Animals that live or are adapted for living on the ground. (*See also* ARBOREALS.)

TERRITORIAL. Said of those animals that exhibit territoriality. (*See also* TERRITORIALITY; TERRITORY.)

TERRITORIALITY. The behavior of some animals that individually or in groups are attached to a specific geographical area or place in which they live, thrive, reproduce, etc., and defend from competitors. (*See also* TERRITORIAL; TERRITORY.)

TERRITORY. A geographical area or place pertaining to one or several territorial animals. (*See also* TERRITORIAL; TERRITORIALITY.)

TEXTURE (In rock materials used to manufacture tools). The structure, appearance, distribution, size, shape, composition, etc., of the particles constituting a rock.

THEORY. Hypothesis or hypotheses whose assumed effects are used to formulate conclusions subject to verification. (*See also* HYPOTHESIS; MODEL.)

THERMODYNAMICS. The study of the relations of heat and the physical motion of bodies.

THEROPITHECUS GELADA. The only living species of baboons pertaining to the genus *Theropithecus,* family Cercopithecidae, superfamily Cercopithecoidea, characterized by a short muzzle, canines relatively small, and relatively strong molars. They collect grains from grasses with the opposable thumb (pollex) and index fingers (precision grip), and forage mainly in sitting position; sometimes they use bipedalism for short distance movements. They develop, mainly the females, fat deposits on the buttocks. They live in open country in the Ethiopian highlands, Africa. (*See also* BABOON; GENUS; MOLARS; BIPEDALISM; THUMB OPPOSABILITY; PRECISION GRIP.)

THUMB OPPOSABILITY. The capacity that some primate species have of opposing the thumb (pollex) finger to the index finger, forming so the precision grip. (*See also* PRECISION GRIP.)

TOOL. *See* STONE TOOL.

TRAIT. Any character or quality of an organism. (*See also* CHARACTER.)

TROGLODYTELLA *See* INFUSORIA CILIATES TROGLODYTELLA.

TROOP. A collection of animals forming a social group. (*See also* SOCIETY; SOCIALITY.)

TYPE. A normal individual specimen of a species most representative of the whole species.

UNGULATES. Referring to the mammals that have hoofs. (*See also* MAMMAL.)

UNGULATE SUCCESSIONS. *See* MIGRANT UNGULATE SUCCESSIONS.

UNIMALE GROUP. In some social animal species, a group consisting of several females and their offspring living together with only one male. (*See also* MULTIMALE GROUP.)

UNIVERSE. The whole Creation. The Cosmos.

VARIATION. *See* GENETIC VARIATION.

VERTEBRATES. Animal members of the subphylum Vertebrata of the phylum Chordata. All animals with backbones.

VESTIGIAL CHARACTER. Any character of individuals of a species or population that during evolution has lost specialization and has become reduced in its functions; it has an imperfect and rudimentary development compared with the development it had when complete in its functions in the ancestral forms of that species. It is said that this character, in this species or population, is in evolutionary regression. (*See also* CHARACTER; EVOLUTIONARY REGRESSION.)

VILLAFRANCHIAN. Middle Pliocene to Lower Pleistocene (3.5 to 1.0 million years ago, more or less) period of Europe and Africa, whose representative site is in Villafranca d'Asti (N.W. Italy). (*See also* SITE.)

VILLAFRACHIAN HOMINIDS. Referring to the fossil hominids found in Europe and Africa corresponding to the Villafranchian period. (*See also* FOSSIL; HOMINIDS; VILLAFRANCHIAN.)

VOCALIZATION. The utterance of vocal sounds, as in singing or speaking.

WÜRMS GLACIATION. The Last Glaciation. (*See also* GLACIATIONS.)

CREDITS

The author wishes to acknowledge permission to reprint excerpts from the following:

Grzimek Animal Life Encyclopedia, copyright © 1975 by Kinder Verlag.

Ethological Studies of Child Behavior by N. Blurton Jones, copyright © 1972 by Cambridge University Press.

Evolution of the Brain and Intelligence by H.J. Jerison, copyright © 1973 by Academic Press, Inc.

Intelligence and Evolutionary Biology by H.J. Jerison and I. Jerison, copyright © 1988 by Springer-Verlag.

"Origins. An Age-old question: Why Did the Human Lineage Survive?" by P. Shipman in *Discover*, Vol. 8, No. 4, p. 62, April 1987.

"War Among the Chimps" by M. Ghiglieri in *Discover*, Vol. 8, No. 11, p. 70, November 1987.

"The Golden Age That Never Was" by J. Diamond in *Discover*, Vol. 9, No. 12, pp. 70–72, December 1988.

"What We Can't Learn About People From Apes" by S.L. Washburn in *Human Nature* magazine, November 1978. Copyright ©1978 by Human Nature, Inc. Reprinted by permission of the publisher.

"In Search of Adam and Eve" by Tierney et al in *Newsweek*, January 11, 1988.

"Retooled Ancestors" by B. Bower in *Science News*. Reprinted with permission from *Science News*, the weekly newsmagazine of science, copyright © 1988 by Science Service, Inc.

"At Home with the Arctic Wolf" by L.D. Mech in *National Geographic*, May 1987.

"Human Origins" by E.L. Simons in *Science*, Vol. 245, 1989, p. 1343. Copyright © 1989 by the AAAS.

"Four Legs Bad, Two Legs Good" by R. Lewin in *Science*, Vol. 235, 1987, p. 969. Copyright © 1987 by the AAAS.

"The Origin of Man" by C.O. Lovejoy in *Science*, Vol. 211, 1981, pp. 341, 344, 348, 349. Copyright © 1981 by the AAAS.

"How Did Humans Evolve Big Brains?" by R. Lewin in *Science*, Vol. 216, 1982, p. 841. Copyright © 1982 by the AAAS.

"Hand of *Paranthropus robustus* from Member 1, Swartkrans: Fossil Evidence for Tool Behavior" by R.L. Susman in *Science*, Vol. 240, 1988, p. 783. Copyright © 1988 by the AAAS.

"The Social Lives of Dolphins" by W. Booth in *Science*, Vol. 240, 1988, p. 1274. Copyright © 1988 by the AAAS.

"On 'Theoretical Framework and Tests' of Early Hominid Meat and Marrow Acquisition: A Reply to Shipman" by H.T. Bunn and R.J. Blumenschine in *American Anthropologist*, Vol. 89, 1987, pp. 444–445, 447. Reprinted by permission of the American Anthropological Association.

"Canine Teeth: Notes on Controversies in the Study of Human Evolution" by S.L. Washburn and R.L. Ciochon in *American Anthropologist*, Vol. 76, 1974, p. 778. Reprinted by permission of the American Anthropological Association.

"The Nut-Crackers—A New Theory of the Adaptations of the Ramapithecinae" by R.F. Kay in the *American Journal of Physical*

"New Perspectives on Ape and Human Evolution" by A. Kortland in *Current Anthropology*, Vol. 15, 1974, pp. 441, 445.

"Discussion and Criticism. On New Perspectives on Ape and Human Evolution" M.R. Kleindienst in *Current Anthropology*, Vol. 16, 1975, pp. 644–645.

"Comments on Wolpoff, M.H. *Ramapithecus* and Hominid Origins" by L. De Bonis in *Current Anthropology*, Vol. 23, 1982, p. 510.

"Comments on Hominid Dietary Selection Before Fire" by J.D. Paterson in *Current Anthropology*, Vol. 25, 1984, pp. 15, 161–161, 163–164.

"*Ramapithecus* and Hominid Origins" by M.H. Wolpoff in *Current Anthropology*, Vol. 23, 1982, p. 502.

"A History of Flint-Knapping Experimentation" by L.L. Johnson in *Current Anthropology*, Vol. 19, 1978, p. 347.

"Evolution of the Brain and Intelligence" by H.J. Jerison in *Current Anthropology*, Vol. 16, 1975, pp. 415, 416.

"On Gender Differences and the Origin of Language" by Jonas and Jonas in *Current Anthropology*, Vol. 17, 1976. pp. 523, 525.

"Gender Differences in Mental Function: A Clue to the Origin of Language" by Jonas and Jonas in *Current Anthropology*, Vol. 16, 1975, p. 630.

"More on Gender Differences and the Origin of Language. Reply" by Jonas and Jonas in *Current Anthropology*, Vol. 17, 1976, p. 748.

"Migration and Hominid Bipedalism" by Sinclair et al. Reprinted by permission from *Nature*, Vol. 324, pp. 307–308. Copyright © 1986 by MacMillan Magazines Ltd.